Diary of a Sapper ...

Julian Beirne

First published in Great Britain 2009 by www.lulu.com

ISBN 978-0-9561546-0-6

Designed by Julian Beirne

In memory of Andy Mount
One couldn't ask for a better friend
*****

This one is for you mate, thanks for giving me the boost when I needed it.
I could not have finished this without your enthusiasm
*****

Your book is next.
Bernie

Prologue

[Names have been changed]

At the beginning of 1983, I was in 75 Field Squadron Royal Engineers. They were part of 220 Engineer Regiment at Nunburg in Northern Germany. (West Germany as it was then). 220 were part of 1 (BR) Corps, who was the first line of defence against the Soviet hordes that were supposed to come rushing across the border and slit our throats whilst we slept. (Years later, I met an ex-soviet Kazakh soldier who told me that they thought the exact opposite).

The Falklands War had finished six months previously and the British government were spending millions of pounds rebuilding The Falklands. They sent Royal Engineers to carry out most of the rebuilding. 75 Squadron was going to go there for the first 6 months of 1983. We were to be the first BAOR (British Army on the Rhine) Sappers to go. (Wow, what an honour.)

For the first and only time in my life, I wrote a diary. Contained in the pages are the humour and emotions that we all experienced. Living in the cramped conditions of a landing craft put all of our friendships to the test. Friends became enemies and enemies were found out to be your wife's new lover. This is my story. (*God, what a cliché*) The *Italics* are straight from the diary and the normal font is what I, and the ex-army friends that I am still in contact with, remember. Now sit back and enjoy 6 months in the Falklands. Because we didn't!

Hymac 590 CT with blown off track. Taff on right

Saturday 1st January 1983 Nunburg, West Germany

In December 1982, we spent 2 weeks training with the knockers. It was like going back to training. It showed me how stupid a knocker can be without being noticed! Stayed at Joan's. (My Auntie) We spent 1982's winter acclimatising ourselves to the cold by not wearing pullovers. This all went to pot when we hit the 80oF equator. OC 1 point for entertainment 0 points for brains.

We were told in late December that a Squadron from Nunburg would be the first Squadron to go to the Falklands from Germany. In the middle of December we were paraded outside the tall five storey ex-Waffen SS barracks that was our accommodation in Nunburg/ Weser. It was a cold winter morning and snow covered the ground. Of interest to me at that time was the fact that the parade ground was covered in snow. I had the job of sweeping the parade square clear of snow. In today's modern Army, I used a Unimog truck with a snowplough, heater, radio and 36 gears. We were on parade in the morning. It was 8 o'clock and freezing, red noses dotted the 90 men that were standing in three ranks and the fog from our breath hung a foot above our heads wondering where to go. Snow covered the ground and we were jumping up and down to keep warm. No one was wearing gloves as there was a rule. If one person forgot his gloves, then no one could wear gloves. We rarely got to wear gloves. The SSM was standing at the front and was taking the parade. He braced up.

"Listen up! Squadron…! Squadrooooon… SHUN! Stand at….. EASE!" 90 pairs of boots clumped onto the path making the sound of a machine gun. Usually this meant that we would have to do it again. This time we didn't. Strange!

The Squadron Sergeant Major, (SSM O'Rouke) had our full attention. "As you all know, Squadrons of Engineers from UK are now rebuilding The Falklands." Someone farted. There were giggles in the ranks. The SSM looked around as if to dare the man to fart again. The giggles died quickly. He continued "So far, because of the commitment to BAOR, no Germany Squadron has been sent South." He stretched up to his full 5 foot 10 inches and smiled with pride "*We* have the great honour of being selected as the Squadron that will go to the Falklands" A murmur arose in the ranks. The SSM let it die down naturally, the ranks went quiet again. A voice rose out from the now quiet ranks, "I ain't fuckin' going" mumbled LCpl Hollywood. Hollywood hated going away. He wouldn't go on exercise, PT, courses, in fact anything where he had to leave his wife. He even went home for NAAFI breaks. He wasn't part of the 'team spirit' and wasn't liked.

"Can I have that in writing?" Spunky Staynes asked amidst laughter.

"We will now go through a two week intensive training period to get us ready for the Falklands. Officially, we are still at war with Argentina, they might attack again at any minute"

"Bloody Captain Mainwaring" moaned 'Top Cat' Furze, his 'Cockney' style Birkenhead accent clear to everybody.

We had mixed feelings. Pride, in that it would be us. Anticipation at the great 'Boys' Own' adventures to come, and sorrow that we have to leave our families for seven months.

"We will be leaving around the end of January and returning at the end of July, seven months gentlemen." He paused for effect and looked into people's faces. He had our total attention, "I will need a rear party of five men. Please go home to your families and talk it over. If you want to volunteer for rear par...." The SSM never finished the sentence.

"YES SIR, ME SIR" Hollywood had his hand up and was on tiptoes in order to get his hand higher. It is a well-known fact (to Holly) that the highest hand is always picked. Holly Hollywood's hand was two feet above everybody's heads. It was also the only hand.

"I was going to say LCpl Hollywood, to talk it over and give me an answer tomorrow"

"I've thought about it Sir, I'll be rear party, Sir" The SSM hesitated until a voice came from the squad.

"Hands up, who wants Holly to stay here." The sound of combat jacket sleeves brushing past the body and up into the air was deafening. The sea of arms was so thick, light couldn't penetrate it.

"OK LCpl Hollywood, you can be rear party"

Holly lowered his arm and scowled, under his breath he muttered "and *fuck you* all too."

"In order" the SSM went on "to acclimatise ourselves to the cold of the Falklands we are now going to remove our jerseys and they will not be worn for the rest of our stay in Germany" He started to undo the buttons to his combat jacket.

No one moved.

"Come on" he smiled. He was dangerous when he smiled. SSgt Simpson started to undo his buttons and one by one his movements were joined by others undoing their buttons. This became a ripple through the ranks, which then became a race to be the first Troop without jerseys, on this cold German day. 2 Troop won this dubious honour.

For the rest of December we were banned from wearing jerseys. The rest of the Regiment thought we were mad and took the piss out of us relentlessly. It was a great management decision from our Officer Commanding. It was also a warning on what was to come. If I had seen it then I would have shot myself in the foot, or joined Holly. Self-mutilation was preferable to spending seven months with him!

It was a normal cold, snowy, cold, German, cold winter and we *froze*. There were two things that the OC (Officer commanding the Squadron) had forgotten to consider.

Point one… The Falklands is on the other side of the globe and has its summer in January.

Point two… We were to fly to the Ascension Islands, which is on the Equator. From there, we were to take a slow ship to the Falklands. Both destroyed our acclimatisation. In Germany we suffered from hypothermia and in the Ascension Islands we went down with heat stroke.

Just before Christmas, we were in the Support Troop office; the offices were old tank hangers that had also belonged to the Waffen SS. We had been called in by our SSgt. A chap, that we had named Death Breath for obvious reasons. He was single, 45 years old and knew all of the hookers that lined Route Six, which was the main road to Hanover. With his breath, they probably knew him too. He had an important message for us and we waited with impatience, mainly due to the fact that it was 09:50 am. Just ten minutes to NAAFI break. (Tea break)

"I have some good news and some bad news for you, which do you want first?" he looked at us. Despite his breath he was one of the best SNCOs in the Squadron and we all had a liking for him. Orders were normally given with a smile. Now was no different, his rat like face had a large smile on it.

Pinko broke the silence "Go on Staff, give us the bad first, it will leave us the good news for the end." Pinko looked around and we all nodded to him.

"Well," Death Breath went on fully enjoying himself, those at the top want someone from this Squadron to clear the minefields that are in The Falklands. You lot have been volunteered" his smile doubled in size, he knew something else, and he loved every minute of this. No one spoke except Holly who unfortunately was in our Troop. He emitted a 'Ha' from the corner of his mouth, which was smiling. *He* wasn't going!

"Hey Pinko" I called over the room, "Just *when* did we volunteer for this mission?"

"When you signed on the dotted line, Bernie"

"Oh Staff!" I shouted.

"What is it LCpl Beirne?" he put his weight on to one foot and waited for the inevitable wise crack.

"I just remembered that I have to change my library books, please can I be excused The Falklands, please" The room laughed.

"No, but you can sweep the store room before NAAFI break" The room laughed louder and I grew a little bit wiser and shut up.

We were then told that we would get a longer leave and would have to attend a course in UK before going down South. The room cheered the roof off. This was the team spirit. Support Troop was a tightly knit group within another tightly knit group, that being 75 Squadron. They were part of 220 Engineer Regiment, who were part of 12 Brigade and at the top was 1 (BR) Corps. The British Army is tribal all the way to the top. The Brits would fight the Dutch in the bars. When there were only Brits, different regiments would fight. Only one Regiment in a town and the Squadrons would fight, you get the idea? It was them and us. The size and boundaries of 'us' could change from minute to minute.

"What is the good news, Staff?" Pinko asked when the cheering died down.

His smile got even wider if that was at all possible "I'm not going, ha ha ha. I'm off on my Senior NCOs course." He laughed.

"You can keep Holly company, Staff" Top Cat nodded towards Holly, who was smiling at our SSgt with the knowledge that he could get in six months of ass licking. Death Breath's smile died as if it had been shot with a Bazooka. He hadn't thought of that. The Troop filed out to the NAAFI canteen and I grabbed the broom.

Sunday 2nd January

Cambridge

Sandra and I visited my parents. I wallowed in the glory of going to the Falklands. So did my dad who took me to the pub and paraded me to his drinking friends. I didn't mind. The beer flowed freely.

Monday 3rd January

Cambridge
Still there

Tuesday 4th January

Waterbeach

We caught up with some of our friends who had moved to Waterbeach.

Wednesday 5th January

I went to Chattenden with Pinko today. Taff and Jock had been there since Monday. Fishing!

Pinko picked me up from my parents in Cambridge. We travelled to Chattenden in Kent with the heater blowing out cold air for the entire journey. Pinko had got used to the cold in Germany and claimed that he would fall asleep at the wheel if the temperature got too hot. I sat in the front with my winter warfare kit on, clothes that were designed for the Arctic were perfect for Pinko's car.

"Pinko, I'm bloody freezing…" I chattered as my teeth knocked together.

"Well open the window and let some warm air in"

"It's WINTER!"

"Yeah, lovely time of the year, nice and fresh"

"You know what I like about you Pinko?"

"What"

"You're totally mad"

Pinko was our Troop 'lefty'. He was into socialism in a big way. Something that is unheard of in the British Army. Most of the soldiers were right wing, if they had an opinion at all, which most didn't. Margaret Thatcher had won us all over in her first years of office by giving us a major pay rise. Pinko wanted to be a rebel, so he rebelled against our beliefs. He was a socialist. His thin frame and wire glasses made him look like a university student, he played the part well. We listened to Human League on the journey down and now they always remind me of Pinko the Socialist.

When we arrived at the gate of Chattenden barracks, we were booked in with courtesy. Courtesy never met soldiers at the gate of Chattenden, courtesy was always somewhere else, and her brothers, rudeness and fear were usually there. We were standing in the guard room being *talked* to by the Provost Sgt. He was polite and smiling. He usually scowled and shouted.

"I don't like this Pinko, they're being nice to me" I whispered.

"Me neither, lets try something" he whispered back to me, "Sergeant," he called to the Provost Sgt "My car is parked on the yellow lines by the armoury, shall I move it?" I blanched. We were about to be sent running around the square as a punishment, no one was allowed to park there, this we had forgotten.

"The Provost Sgt. looked out of the window and answered in a too-nice-voice "No, it's all-right there for a couple of minutes, lads"

I swallowed. We were doomed. 'Lads' he had said. The Provost Sgt had called us '*Lads*'. This had a 'Last Supper of a condemned man' feeling to it. Oh well, might as well make use of it. "Staff, we have some *stuff* to unload, can we park outside the block?" I emphasised the 'stuff'.

"Yeah, sure guys, but… er… not too long OK?" his conditioning was trying to break through his orders. Inside him was a bastard trying to get out.

We laughed all the way to the accommodation block.

Taff Davies and Jock Henderix, the two Cpls of Support Troop were there. They had been 'there' for the last couple of days, fishing!

Jock Henderix was not a man to upset. Although on the outside he seemed to be a soft, cuddly, jovial teddy bear, his disposition would have been better likened to a grizzly bear. Piss him off at your peril. Jock was a short stocky man and was always laughing. You could walk up to him and prod him in the ribs and he would just laugh. He wouldn't flinch away because he was ticklish or something, or even push your arm away, he would just stand there and laugh. To me he was great fun. There was a side to Jock that I wouldn't see for a few months, a side that surprised and shocked me. In a fight, he was cold, calculated, and viscous. In an instant he would work out the best way that he could incapacitate you, whilst using the least amount of energy. In addition, he would do this whilst still smiling at your face. If you can't wait to read about this man, turn to April 30th or 3rd July, but try and wait as they are the only two good bits in this book.

Jock Henderix was a Jock from a small town called Keith. He married his childhood sweetheart and then went off and joined the Paras. He first served with the Heavy Drop platoon of the RAOC. They bombed their own troops with rations and stores, (supposedly on parachutes), by throwing them out of an aircraft. He then made a wise decision and joined the Royal Engineers, and later went on to the Parachute Squadron of the Royal Engineers. That is 9 Parachute Squadron R.E.

We once had an argument whilst on exercise in Germany. We were in a Combat Engineer Tractor (CET), and were approaching a tank crossing, I was the driver and Jock was the commander. The CET has a blind spot to the right made by the cupolas and the basket for the stores and as the crew compartment is in the middle of the tank, it has a huge, three metre long bonnet.

"Get out Jock and see if there is any traffic coming" I said to him through the intercom(IC). The tank training ground mud of Soltau finished at a long line of trees, behind of which was the main road. All main roads in Germany are virtually no-speed limit zones, and the Germans like to drive fast. (The German police would refute both of these statements!) "Ah, no problems, just push the nose out into the road and if there is anything coming it will stop" Jock's voice came through the IC. I looked back at him in surprise and he waved me on, he clearly had no intentions of getting out of the commanders hatch. I slowly drove out into the road and when the camouflaged front of the CET was sticking 3 metres out into the road, I could finally see down the long straight of the German road. Simultaneously, the German driver, who had probably been dreaming about sauerkraut and listening to Strauss, saw the green and black outline of the tank against the … er…green and black outline of the trees. His reaction was instant. He stood on the brakes, and instantly proved that his car was not fitted with Anti Lock Brakes. All four tyres locked in a long and ear-piercing "SCREEEEEECH!" The car slewed to the left, hopped a couple of times on the two right tyres, and then whip lashed to the right, back to the left and then again to the right. Whilst the car was doing it's ballet on the tarmac, I calculated its trajectory and realised that it was heading straight for the side of my tank. I decided to give the driver more space in which to dance his little VW Polo and floored the throttle; the CET lurched forward out of his way.

I stopped at the same time as the German finished his road dance. The difference was that Jock and I were arguing and the Polo driver was frozen in his seat, his hands stuck on the wheel and his gaze transfixed to the side of our tank. After a couple of exchanges between Jock and me, as to whose fault it was, the driver had recovered enough to get out of his car. Jock saw this and shouted to me, "GO!", and I did, like the wind. The last I saw of the driver was of him feebly shaking his fist at us as we drove away.

Just a week earlier a whole German family had been wiped out when it hit the side of a 50 ton, Chieftain Main Battle Tank. We were close to doing the same, the bottom line was that the incident brought us closer together. I suppose it would be called male bonding today.

We walked into our room and Jock and Taff were at the end looking out of the window.

"Hey guys what's happening" I shouted across the room.

"We've been fishing, Bernie" Jock laughed.

I looked around the room, there were six beds with lockers on either side of the beds. The idea was that a soldier was given a bed space, two lockers, a bed, and a small area for himself. This was clearly not the case here. There was fishing gear everywhere. There were rods, boxes, nets, waders, wellies and duffel coats. In fact there were loads of duffel coats. "How many fucking coats do fishermen need, for Christ sakes" I asked looking at the pile on every bed.

"There're yours," Taff laughed "and the wellies" he picked up a pair of green wellies and threw them at me. I caught them. They were the type that Officers wear on social events.

"Fuckin' green wellies, man, like we're fuckin' Officers, boyo" Taff rarely said 'Boyo' except when he was excited. "Did you see the Mercedes minibus outside?"

We nodded.

"Ours" Jock dangled the keys from his fingers.

"Duffel coats" Taff pointed to the pile of new coats.

"Ours" Jock answered

"Green wellies?"

"Ours."

"Room, minus inspections?"

"Ours" Jock laughed.

"No inspections?" Pinko was amazed.

"Yep! *And* we've even got a petrol card," Taff beamed "show 'em Jock."

Jock pulled out a credit card from his pocket. "We've been all over Kent and haven't bought a single gallon of petrol. Pinko and I joined the other two in laughing. This was too good to be true.

In the movies and in fiction books, the soldiers would now go into a serious debate about why they were being treated so well and what they should do about it. The soldiers would shout and scream at each other to get their point across. That is melodramatic **bollocks**. We just accepted it and made plans to milk it for every bit we could.

We settled in amidst a scuffle between Pinko and me when Taff told us that there was only one brown duffel coat left, the rest were black. I won the scuffle. Throughout the evening the rest of the Troop came in and we had to hear the fishing stories over and over again. They had even managed to put a day's fishing on the credit card!

When Billy "Mac" McGuire came in, the stories all started again. Taff, Jock, and Mac were all keen fishermen.

That evening we went out to a pub called The Black Pig which was on the edge of the camp. It was normally reserved for the permanent staff, Taff and Jock had won the heart of Tina, the landlady.

Taff was the tallest of the Troop. He was also the second Cpl. An extrovert and a party animal; he was the life and soul of any group. When he got drunk, he got silly. Tonight was no exception.

Taff Davies came from a small mining town in south Wales called Abercarn. It, like many Welsh villages, is built on the side of a valley. It was a small town without much nightlife for the young kids, so they made their own fun, normally with the opposite sex. He had grown up with a liking for the girls and an ability to see the opportunity for fun in the most unlikely of places. He had primed the way for us and we milked the generosity of the locals and the permanent staff. Taff had primed them all with the fact that we were going to the Falklands to clear the minefields, hence the good treatment at the guardroom. We didn't buy many drinks that night. The only negative part to the night was when Tina refused to put the entire bar bill on Jock's Army petrol credit card.

Thursday 6th January

Started the course today. We're being treated like something special. Duffel coats, wellies, no parades AND a mini bus, - do they know summink we don't?

We didn't care. We ate in the Cpl's part of the mess hall. We wore our wellies and duffel coats to breakfast. The sloppies thought that we were Officers or civvies. They called us 'Sir'. That just made us laugh which pissed off the cooks, but they didn't dare say anything to the group in their Officer's coats and wellies.

During breakfast we witnessed a scene of the utmost femininity. It is something that will stick with me for the rest of my life.

The Army sent the young Second Lieutenants to Chattenden to learn the ropes before sending them to the line units. One of their duties was to be messing officer, or 'slop watch'. They had to watch over the canteen, supposedly to stop the men from killing the cooks. The young subalterns had by and large, all led very sheltered lives. To them all women were ladies, usually called Cynthia or Jennifer. This young Officer was guarding the hot plate when a large masculine bodied WRAC walked up to the hot plate. "Hey Cookie, look at these fuckers" she pulled down her pullover and shirt collar and showed her neck to the cook. It was covered with love bites. The young subaltern who was standing next to the cook was blushing bright red and looked away. "She could not keep her fukkin' hands off me, ya knaa." She laughed in her Geordie accent. The subaltern suddenly turned his head and stared at the woman. He didn't believe his ears. She looked him full in the face and picking up the serving spoon which had fallen into the beans started to spoon the beans onto her plane "I like me beans Sir, they make me fart like fuck." The Officer went even redder, if that was possible, and looked around the room for somewhere to hide his eyes. There was nowhere, the girl blew him a quick kiss and walked off. Whether the girl was a lesbian, was open to debate, whether the subaltern had altered his view on women was not.

After breakfast we ambled down to our white Mercedes mini bus, and drove down the hill to the Training Centre. We entered through the main doors and ambled around the displays that were littered around the entrance. The displays were in glass cabinets and were made out of Airfix models and train set stuff, someone had spent a lot of time on the displays. We had been in the Sappers for a total of a hundred years and yet no one had ever seen the displays. A man in civilian clothes came out of a lecture hall and beckoned us in. "Come in boys, come in" the voice came from a thin man with too many pointy things on his body, his chin, nose, and fingers were all pointy. If ever a man was a role model for professors, this was he. He was balding, dressed in corduroy and shaking. His voice had a nervous wobble to it and his mouth was clearly very dry. When he opened his mouth one could hear his tongue detach itself from the top of his dry mouth. "Er…erm… sit down wherever you want." We trooped in and sat at the front. "Right… er … have you been told what you are doing?"

"No Sir" Taff called out.

"Oh" disappointment in his voice "er… well you've been brought here to er… to well… to carry out a task in the Falklands. We…er… the Argentineans that is… laid a lot of mines in and around the Falkland Islands. We have no maps of the minefields and cannot clear them by hand. We lost a few of you chaps just after the war by clearing the minefields and the British government doesn't want to lose any more. So we at… oh! Sorry" surprise in his voice "I haven't introduced my self, I am Trevor Hardcastle, from the research and development department at Porton Down, and does anybody here know about Porton Down?" Spunky shouted out that he did. He had gone there as a detachment from his last Squadron. The idea was that the soldier got extra pay and the government got human guinea pigs to test their new chemical agents on. Only soldiers that were mad or skint volunteered for this duty. Spunky was usually both!

"Oh, good" this pleased the Boffin, someone knew where he worked, "We are… er… have …erm… developed a mechanical mine train. We want you to test it." Pause "if you don't mind" he added.

"Before we send you chaps to the Falklands we want you to get to know the machinery. Today, we have arranged for you to drive them and tomorrow you will need to be in Porton Down to er… see… us blow up the … er… tractors and things, OK?"

"What time do we need to be in Porton Down tomorrow then, Sir?"

"Oh, er… I hadn't thought of that, er.., is 10 o'clock OK"

It was and we were.

We were introduced to a Sgt from the training school. He was bemused about what we were to do and had been ordered to escort us around. He had a class to run and didn't have the time to act as a chaperone. We all knew the camp and so he left us to our own devices.

We drove up to the bomb disposal training school to see our mounts. As we drove through the walls of the yard it was clear where we were. Apart from the usual Royal Engineer notice board there were hundreds of bombs sticking out of the ground. Bombs, rockets and missiles, it was a bomb disposal Aladdin's cave. Over in a corner of the EOD camp was what we were looking for. We ambled over. We were about to be made as welcome as a hole in a water bottle in the middle of the Gobi Desert.

We saw two brand new County tractors that had wooden slatted wheels. They were fitted with servos on all of the controls and video cameras projected a picture back to a TV in the back of a Landrover. We walked over to the Landrover. Taff walked up to the WO who was the senior most SNCO there. He was controlling the tractor with the hand control unit.

"How's it going Q, we're from 75 Sqn. We've been sent here by the Porton Down Boffins to get used to this equipment" Taff said with a smile.

"Well whoopee fucking do, corporal, do you really think that we are going to let some *field Oggies* fuck up this equipment?" he looked towards the bomb disposal corporal in the back of the Landrover with a knowing look, he emphasised 'field Oggies' as one would say 'Dog Shit' when one trod in it. The corporal smiled at the in-house joke but when the Q looked away he looked towards Taff and raised his eyebrows in an apology for the stupid remark. Recognition registered in his eyes, "Taff Davies?" he questioned.

Taff leaned into the back of the Landrover, "BOGY BURNS! fuck me! What are you doing with this crowd of fucking wankers then?" The Warrant Officer stiffened at the insult, "He is conducting tests on this highly expensive equipment, *Corporal*," he emphasised the *Corporal* "now if you and your crowd of Knockers would like to get out of the way we will continue."

"Play with it as much as you want Q, we'll get our turn in the Falklands. Com'on Bogy, get out here and tell me where you went after Munsterlager"

"You can use it in half an hour corporal, I have to go to London then, now piss off"

Bogy jumped out of the Rover "ten minutes Q" and walked off with Taff.

We watched the Q for a couple of minutes and when it was clear that we were not going to get a go we all wandered off to see if we could find anyone that *we* knew.

It was a waste of an opportunity, especially as we were the ones who had to operate the equipment down South. Unfortunately, the Q had more rank on his arm and therefore RHIP. (Rank Has Its Privileges)

Friday 7th January

We went to Porton Down today and blew up a Hymac and a County tractor! The Army hired a (crash test) dummy to sit in the cab of the Hymac and to see if it was safe. For £90,000 !

I would have done it for £1,000!

Taking into account what they want us to do and what the tests show I made a name for us. "SASS" "South Atlantic Suicide Squad"

We reached Porton Down at sunrise. The Wiltshire hills rolled off into the distance. It was early morning and Wiltshire was just waking up. The cold winter sun was reflecting off the dew on the grass. It looked like a white translucent carpet. The area looked like a picture postcard. It was an unusual setting for the only establishment in the UK that produces germ warfare weapons. [Allegedly]

We were directed by the security to an office. More Boffins were introduced to us. They all looked the same, I suppose we did to them. They showed us films of when they had set fire to different mines. To our surprise they all exploded after a couple of minutes. We in the Sappers always thought that PE4 plastic explosive could be burnt in place of the Hexamine cook blocks. I was glad that I had never tried it! It may have been the detonators exploding.

The idea behind the mine train was to rotavate up the peat and thus chop up the mines and then using a Dutch stubble burner, set fire to them. Hmmm, seemed like a good idea to us. We told them so and that pleased them. To us it was funny that Boffins would want the opinion of a few lowly Sappers. The closest that we had ever got to mines were ones made out of cardboard and sand.

After lunch we went out to their private test range. I saw sheep and cattle in the grounds of Porton Down. I looked closely at them. Did they have two heads? Had the Boffins been testing biological warfare bombs on them? This was the place if they wanted to do so.

The sun had begrudgingly scrabbled up to somewhere near the top of the sky, it's cool light lit up a village in the base of a valley some two to three miles from our test range. It had one of those churches that had both a tower and a spire. Thirty or so houses clutched to the church for sanctuary. Their peace and quiet was about to be disturbed. In the Porton Down range was a brand new Hymac 590CT excavator. It had an armoured cab and wide swamp tracks. The tracks were made out of small one-metre pontoons which gave it the ground bearing pressure of a mosquito.

Alongside it was also an old County tractor with those wooden wheels that we had seen yesterday. The wheels were called "Elk" wheels after the inventor. A Mr Elk I presume.

Both of these beautiful, expensive pieces of equipment we were about to blow to pieces. *WHAT FUN!* This was the Secret Squirrel type of stuff that one reads about in Picture War books, and we loved it.

The Boffins showed us the explosive charges that they had placed around the equipment. They were supposed to simulate digging up mines, we tried to look cool and unimpressed. They showed us the damage to the Elk wheels that they had done previously with smaller charges. We still tried to look cool and unimpressed. They then introduced us to PX2312b. PX2312b was a crash test dummy that they had hired for the day. It cost them £90,000. I offered to do the job for £1,000 and was turned down with a laugh. I *was* joking but who'd have known that ten years later I would be in an identical excavator in Kuwait clearing minefields for £1,000 for every four days. Life has a funny way of being stranger than fiction.

After setting the charges we retired in our mini bus to behind a blast wall. A Sapper SSgt was turning the handle to initiate the explosion. We stood by him as he was one of us. All of the Boffins stood together in another corner. "You do this all the time, Staff?" Jock asked

"No Sir, they just called me over from Tidworth, I'm with the Engineer Regiment there, 8 Squadron." He explained without looking.

We looked at each other in surprise. Taff was the first to recover and answer. "Er… why did you call us Sir, Staff?" The Staff Sergeant stood up from his crouched position and took a long slow look at us. "I presumed by your dress that you were either Officers or Special Forces." Top Cat (TC) Furze burst out laughing, his laughter made him bend backwards at the waist, "Haaaaaaa ha ha ha that's a good one, me an Officer, oh fucking hell, stoppit, *ME* a Rupert" he flipped over to bend forwards and continued laughing. "Hoooo ho ho ho Spunky! fucking Spunky, *Special Forces,* get away, get away." His laughter was infectious, and it started us laughing at him.

"Who the hell are you then to get that stuff?" the Staff pointed towards our duffel coats, green wellies and the Mercedes mini bus that we had come in.

"We're all from Support Troop, 75 Squadron, Staff" Taff answered with a large friendly smile.

I stepped forward "Oh we *are* Special Forces all right, Staff. We are the S.A.S.S. That's the South Atlantic Suicide Squad. They want us to operate this stuff in the mine fields." I thumbed towards the diggers that were over the hill and about to re-modelled.

The SSgt took a long look at our clothes and us and commented, "I bet they take those duffel coats off you before you go in the minefields." We laughed. He could have been an absolute bastard once he realised that we didn't out rank him, but he was emitting friendly waves and we were relieved. Jock stuck his hand into his duffel coat pocket "If they take these coats back, then they can have these as well, we used them to go fishing in" he pulled out his hand and in it was a handful of colourful maggots.

"Oh, you grot, you've got maggots in your pocket?" I shouted.

"What's wrong with that?" Taff asked and he pulled out handful of red maggots from *his* pocket.

The SSgt was chuckling and was still trying to figure out who we were, when Mac entered the circle. He had just finished smoking a rollup. Mac was a small wiry man of about twenty five years. He seemed to always be on uppers or speed; he did everything in top gear. No time to think, no time to consider the consequences, just do it, and do it quick. "What you got here?" he looked in Jock's hand, he was also a keen fisherman, "these fuckers are cold, you gotta warm them up to get them to wiggle" and he grabbed a small handful and shoved them into his mouth.

Everybody in the circle dropped away from Mac, like Muslims from pork, "EEAAHHH" we all shouted, out of the corner of my eye I saw a Boffin put his hand over his mouth as his body bucked and tried to persuade his stomach not to vomit.

"Mhat?" Mac smiled "Mhat mis ma mroblem, mit keeps mem marm" as he pronounced the 'K' in 'keeps' three warm and happy maggots were catapulted over Spunky. Neither Spunky nor the maggots were happy, the maggots because suddenly they were cold again and Spunky because he had been out 'grotted' by Mac. There was no way he was going to put a maggot in his mouth, and Spunky was supposed to be the head grot, the biggest minger. In English he was an untidy, dirty, and unhygienic, he was a do anything man and he had a reputation to keep.

"Mhat? MHAT??" Mac shouted with clenched teeth, he grabbed another small handful from Taff's hand, and shoved them into his mouth as well. A small jet of sick shot out from between the Boffin's fingers, his body was complaining as to what he had just witnessed. The Boffin tried to keep the vomit in but failed miserably.

Taff laughed "Hey don't you mix my maggots up with Fatso's there. Mine are nice and fat, his are thin and bony"

"Bony? Maggots don't have bones you Welsh tit" Jock retaliated.

And so it went on, and on, and on. It was very very rare for soldiers in the Royal Engineers to argue with each other. Happy banter was the order of the day. These films, that one sees, where the sections of soldiers are always at each others throats, is something that I never witnessed in the Sappers. Even if you didn't like a guy, you would both make an effort to get on. (Like Holly) When a Troop of Sappers build a bridge, it is all hands together. Nobody wants a slacker. We worked as a team and played as a team.

The SSgt twisted the plunger and blew the machines up. A muffled 'crump' floated over the hill, it was nothing impressive. We drove back over the hill and could only see a pall of smoke when we approached the area. There is a 1000 metre safe distance that one must give explosives when used to cut metal. In Kuwait ten years later, we would hide behind an APC not ten yards away. 'Great fun'. (Hint: - Always look up to see what is coming down, it might be bigger than you and not want to be your friend!).

"This was to simulate a 7kg mine," a Boffin told us when we arrived at the equipment, we are going to use 9kg charges but can't today because of the humidity"

"What has that got to do with it?" I asked.

"When it is too humid there is a maximum amount of charge that we can use. That is 6kg. Any more than that when the humidity is greater than 87% and windows get broken in that little village down there" he pointed to the village that I had seen in the valley of the low rolling hill.

"Wow" I was amazed "You worked all of that out"

"Er… no," he smiled an embarrassed smile "trial and error, actually. We broke a lot of windows and got barred from the local pub until we got it right"

"So even you Boffins get it wrong sometimes"

The Boffin grew a couple of inches with pride; apparently they liked to be called 'Boffin' by ordinary people. We considered it a mild insult.

Later we saw the high-speed film of the explosion. It lifted up the 590 excavator by one metre, threw out the track, and dumped it back down.

And what was the result from PX2312b?

It wasn't safe for humans.

Monday 12th January

Went back to Germany. Seeing as I took 2 seasick pills I wasn't surprised at not feeling seasick.

Sunday 16th January

We got our winter warfare kit today, talk about getting the blunt needle at the end of the queue. We got nowt. Pinko got gloves inner but no (gloves) outer.

What a farce! We queued up for ages for the equipment but as we were last in the queue, (1, 2, and 3 Troops were called forward first) we got the remnants. The theory of winter kit is that one has many layers. All of that theory goes out of the window when we are only issued with parts of the kit. Pinko only got the outer parts of the gloves. No inner gloves, it is the inners that kept the heat on the hand. The parka's were great, thick and warm and in two layers instead of the old one layer. Some had the waterproof outer part of the parka others had the warm inner lining. Some even had both. (Mainly the stores personnel) Outside the stores we all got together and compared what we had. I swapped my over boots for a pair of gloves inner. I exchanged a thermal vest that was too small for Spunky's hat and I managed to get a parka liner for two pairs of thermal socks. The last two were swaps that I would later regret.

Monday 17th January

We got a talk off the OC today about the Falklands, stupid sod has still got his head in the clouds. SSM gave us a talk also, "get your hair cut" would've sufficed.

0755 hrs and all 100 of the Squadron were stood at ease by SSM O'Rouke. An Officer in an NCOs uniform, SSM O'Rouke was the politest SSM that I have ever met, and I would have followed him into battle anywhere. "Listen in 75 Sqn, the OC will be coming out in a few minutes"

"Is he gay then?" a voice from the ranks.

"No Parker he is *not* gay," a smile rose on the SSMs face, "he will be coming out here to give us a pep talk on the Falklands. You will all listen carefully, he knows what is going on and we all should be able to gain some useful information." Pause, a smile "There will be no *farting*!" he looked at a few lads in particular and emphasised the word. Light laughter tittered up the ranks, "No giggling, girls," he looked at TC Furze, "and no wise cracks boys. Be on your best behaviour, or else."

The OC. walked out of the office block. "Here he comes. Squadron! Squadrooooooon… Shun!" He marched two paces to meet the OC, stopped and saluted. The OC saluted back and then stood us at ease. It is a well known fact that Officers in the British Army cannot give correct drill commands. Any Officer that looks like he might have the ability to give good commands has it beaten out of him at Sandhurst. No one ever had to lay a finger on our OC. "Squadron, squadron…stand at …." a couple of Sappers moved their feet in anticipation, "ease" the word 'ease' dropped out of his mouth as if by accident. Men moved their feet in the same manner that the order was delivered, slowly. The SSM twitched but kept quiet. "Listen in chaps," the OC mumbled "We will be travelling out to the Falklands on Tuesday 25th January. Now we have a date."

"But I don't love you Sir" a voice from the ranks.

"Shuttup Furze" the SSM hissed.

The OC continued oblivious to the muffled laughter in the ranks, "It is a truly glorious moment for 75 Field Squadron. We…," he paused at the use of the word 'we' and wallowed in the momentous occasion that he was creating "…will be the first Squadron to go from Germany"

"OOOH" said a voice in the ranks

"Furze!" SSM hissed.

"Can I go and tell my mum, Sir" Ray Parker shouted out loud.

"In a minute Parker, in a minute" the OC thought that he was serious; tittering broke out through the ranks. "We will be going down there in a construction mode but we must be prepared to repel the Argentineans if they attack again" the SSM rolled his eyes towards the sky "Oh no, please, not the war speech" he whispered a short prayer to his god. It wasn't answered. The OC launched into a long rambling talk about fighting the Argentinean hordes. Sappers started to shift their weight from one foot to another, others were whispering to each other and two had their eyes staring off into space, their minds elsewhere. I was one of them. Then the crunch came that brought us all back to the ground. "In order to ensure that we are up to the same standards as the glorious men that 'tabbed' from Goose Green to Port Stanley we will carry out the same march in The Falklands."

No voice came from the ranks.

I couldn't believe what my ears had just told my brain. I strained to hear what he said next in the hope that I had misheard.

"To make sure that we are up to this march we shall have a practise tomorrow." Pause for effect "Tomorrow we (Royal we) shall march eighty miles! In the Falklands, we shall do the same route that they did during the conflict."

Still no voice came from the ranks.

"You can now go home and tell your families and I will see you all here tomorrow at 0700 sharp. Carry on Sergeant Major" and with that, the devils messenger was gone.

"FUUUUUUUK" came a strained, disbelieving voice from the ranks. It perfectly summed it up for all of us. In that one word was the disbelief and horror of what the OC had just told us. We have to march eighty miles in the Falklands and eighty tomorrow. FUUUUUUUUK!

"Squadron, squadron shun" the SSM saluted the OC even though he had already gone and then he turned to us. His talk backed the OC's. He was a company man, he also told us that it was not going to be a holiday in the Falklands. We would maintain the BAOR standards in hair length, dress, and how shiny our boots were. No one spoke. He fell us out and we went home in a daze.

Tuesday 18th January

The OC had an idea to walk 80 miles, Thank Christ we only had to walk 40. We started out at 0945, and started walking at 1230. Sod walking, we (Support Troop) got a taxi; it was the best nine mark I have ever spent!! We stopped in 2 guest houses for a beer and had an hour's sleep. 18 hours later we got back in. There were no Bedfords there so we had to sleep in the open until the wagons came. They then squeezed 150 men in the back of 3 Bedfords. Fantastic 75 squadron organisation! Oh, they gave us Wednesday off, thank God.

(Authors Note: This is a long chapter, so I recommend that you go and get a cup of tea and a fag. It kinda reflects the length of the march to follow! Got one? Well if you don't smoke, go through the motions.)

We paraded at 0650hrs and the roll was called at 0655hrs. The field Troops (Knockers) had been there for thirty minutes. The Troops used to parade at the same time as us in Support Troop. But the Troop SSgt would look out of his window, see all of his Troops parading five minutes before the parade, and go out and call the roll. So the men would parade ten minutes before the parade in order to get lined up before the SSgt came out. No good. The SSgt would look out of his window and see them out there and then call the roll. Etc, etc. So, a man would turn up for the 0800 hrs parade at 0755 hrs and he would get extra's (Extra work) because he wasn't there before the SSgt. Still with me? Good. This went on until the Troops would line up at 0725 hrs for the 0800 hrs parade!

We drove out to an area somewhere in Germany and de-bussed in a wooded area. The countryside was covered in snow and our breath condensed as it hovered in the air above our heads. Under the tree canopy it was warmer and the snow was patchy but it was still cold enough to make us stamp our feet to keep them warm. After standing around in a squad for twenty minutes the SSM told us of the check points that we had to find, put us into groups and set us off, in different directions, I might add. It was 1230 hrs and we had forty miles of misery in front of us. Just outside the start Taff stopped us and got out the map.

"This is the route that they have given us lads, it passes no towns or villages, the crafty bastards," he ran the route with his finger to show us, "We'll head for this one first and then go this way round, any questions? No? Good! Let's get this fucking thing over with" and picking up the map he strode off. He was *not* a happy Sapper.

Fifteen miles and three check points later Mr Sun had disappeared around to the other side of the globe in order to cheer them up on that side. He had tried to no avail to cheer us up so in the end he gave up. We now had Mr Moon. A Miserable bastard is Mr Moon. He's cold, and on this night, wet. We picked the next check point and then had a serious Troop talk, like they do in the movies.

"Fuck this for a game of soldiers, I'm knackered" I gasped as I fell down onto a seemingly dry patch under a tree. It wasn't dry but I was beyond caring.

"Me too," voiced Taff, somewhere out there in the darkness. His voice was also around six inches off the ground indicating that he too was lying on his back "Let's go to a bar."

"Don't be stupid Taff, we're in the middle of nowhere, there's no fucking bar out here" TC this time, also on the ground. I could tell by the voice that he was looking at the stars and was also knackered.

"Nope, you're wrong there, boyo, according to my map there is one on the other side of this hill" Taff had an 'I know something you don't' tone to his voice, I could also tell that he was smiling when he talked. Interested, I pushed myself up onto my elbow. Before I could voice my question Pinko beat me too it. "Taff, the OC made sure that the route didn't go near *any* villages, he said that before we left." Pinko's voice was strained, a sort of pleading, 'Please prove me wrong' type of moan.

"Ah yes," he took a drag on his cigarette and blew out the smoke, "but that was before I led you the wrong way for the last two miles, Schneeren village is over this hill and the map shows that there is a guest house there"

"Jezus"

"Fuck "

"Where?"

"Zzzzzzzz"

Everybody jumped up and ran to the fence that was cresting the hill, down in the valley were the lights of a large village.

"Yeah, good on you Taff"

"Let's go"

"Wake Spunky someone"

"Bernie, get Spunky!" Jock shouted as he clambered over the fence.

"Bugger!" I ran back to the tree that we had sheltered under, and left so much in a hurry, and found Spunky fast asleep.

"Spunky, wake up," I shook him violently so that he would wake up quickly. "Wake up you fat fuck!"

"Piss off, let me sleep"

"There's a village over the hill with a gueste in. all of the lads have gone for a beer, get….." suddenly I was talking to myself; Spunky was running down the hill.

"HEY!" I shouted, "You forgot your gat (gun)"

"Let the OC get it, it belongs to him anyway" he shouted back.

One of the disadvantages of being a LCpl is that I was supposed to be a little bit more responsible, so letting out a deep sigh I picked up Spunky's gun and started off down the hill after the rest of them.

I caught up with them at the bottom. They were all on the pavement of a main road, which went under a bridge. We were bathed in the yellow of the streetlights, and it made our combats look a funny colour. The road, and the path were deserted, any vehicle that we saw or heard was to be considered one of our Squadron Rovers. The rear party had been set the task to catch people that were cheating. They were driving the routes.

"Down this way" Taff pointed to under the bridge, his nose was buried in the map and he and Jock were following the route to the gueste. Most of the Troop started to follow. Pinko was cold and pissed off. When he was pissed off, he complained. "What the hell are we doing here? We should be trying to finish. This is just going to make the bloody trip longer, I don't want to go to no fucking gueste, I just want to go home, fucking OC is a wanker for making us….." etc. etc.

"Shuttup Pinko, you can wait outside if you want" Mac laughed.

"Yeah, wait outside and listen to us drinking" TC carried on the wind-up.

"They won't let us in with the guns" Pinko moaned.

Silence…. He had a point. Taff walked through the little group. "Com'on then I am thirsty."

We walked after him, "Pinko don't reckon that we'll get in with the guns" I bleated after Taff. (Bleating after a Welshman is not recommended; in fact doing anything related to sheep is liable to get a funny response from one)

"Well if we don't ask we will never know will we? I'll go in and ask, don't worry boys" Taff was our colloquial German speaker.

We continued to bimble down the path. As we walked under the bridge, I noticed that there was no graffiti. If it were in England there would be all sorts of suggestions on what we should do with our bodies, most being either physically impossible or spelt incorrectly.

On the other side of the bridge there was a town signpost and a sign that welcomed us to Schneeren. If the town's folk had seen us, maybe the welcome would have been extremely short. Like "GO Away."

We resembled Dad's Army; we were strung out in a motley line, with Taff at the front striding forward towards the promise of a warm guesthouse and some beer. He was using his 6 foot 4 inch frame to his best advantage. He was two inches taller than I was and his long gangly legs were used to walking up the Welsh valleys. Being a Fenlander, I stood no chance of keeping up with him. His head was round and thin with a vast expanse of forehead above his eye brows. If he hired out his forehead to bill boarders, he would have been rich. His beret was covering what little hair he had on the back of his head and his hands were in his pockets. In the middle was 'Top Cat' Furze. His beret was on backwards, it resembled a flat cap that way. Pulling up the rear a good 50 metres behind Taff were Paddy Quinn and Pinko. Paddy because he was the fattest of the Troop and Pinko because with Paddy he had someone to complain to who couldn't out run him. Hence a captive audience, when it came to listening to Pinko's complaining, comradeship went out of the window. If Pinko was moaning to Paddy, then he wasn't moaning to us, therefore Paddy could suffer for the benefit of the Troop.

I was in the middle laughing with TC (Top Cat) He was also the life and soul of the Troop. Short and thug-like, he had the Scouse sense of humour with a cockney accent. When he walked, (as he did frequently) he rolled his shoulders like a bodybuilder or a bouncer. He could always see the funny side of a situation and was normally the one with the wise cracks in the squad. He was currently laughing at me. I had tried twice to give Spunky back his SMG but he had refused to take it.

Readers, forget the image of the LCpl ordering the Sapper to take his gun. I tried that and Spunky just told me to fuck myself. TC found this hilarious. So did I, but I had to pretend to be serious. It was all part of the game. It passed the time. Every step was a step closer to the finish.

Jock was with Mac. They were telling each other lies about fish that they had never caught. All in all there were eleven in the Troop. Hollywood was on the party organising the checkpoints. Good old Holly, he was sitting in a Bedford or a Rover, brown nosing with any senior that couldn't avoid him. There was a few senior staff patrolling in vehicles to try to spot us. If we saw, (we usually heard the Landrover's distinctive whine first) we would hide in the bushes.

We started to enter the town and after a couple of hundred metres, Taff stopped by a guesthouse.

By the time we had caught up with him, it had been agreed that Taff would go in and ask if we could come in with our guns. Taff gave his SMG to Jock, and went in. Paddy ambled up with Pinko. Pinko was still in complaining mode. "What the hell are we doing here? Lets keep on walking, I don't want a drink, I just want to go home… etc."

"Jezus, fukkin' Christ, save me someone" Paddy cried in his broad Belfast accent, and went to walk in the gueste.

"Wait there Paddy, Taff has gone in to find out if we can bring in our guns" Jock put his arm on Paddy's shoulder.

"What if we can't?" Mac asked.

"Then Pinko can sit out here and look after them. You did say that you didn't want to go in didn't you Pinko?" Paddy teased Pinko.

There came a loud rumpus from inside the bar. Many voices were talking at the same time.

"Shit, he's getting an earful from the locals" I voiced.

"We should go now before the police come" whined Pinko. Taff came out of the door at that moment with a smile on his face. "OK boys, they don't mind but you have to put your guns over your shoulder with the barrel pointing towards the ground.

We complied immediately. Including Pinko, I noticed. When everybody had their guns slung, Taff walked back through the door, "Com'on then" he said over his shoulder.

We walked in; I was in the middle of the group. The bar was empty but hot. Cigarette smoke mingled with the smell of beer. There was a real fire in one corner that lit the room with its flickering light. Small lights with tobacco stained red shades stuck out of the wall, each light was over a small alcove with church-like benches and a large wooden table in the middle. One alcove had its table turned onto its side so that all we could see was the top. This in itself was interesting as the table looked very heavy.

The landlord was a typical German. He was blond with shoulder-length curly hair. A giant shaggy moustache hid his mouth, which was smiling; he was cleaning out a large glass in preparation for filling it. English soldiers don't drink the normal small glasses of beer that is served in Germany. 'Eine Grosse Beer' is the first phrase that the English soldier learns in German. It means one large beer.

When Pinko, the last man, had entered, (it was a bar, and therefore Paddy was second-in behind Taff) Taff said in a too loud voice. "Are you all in then"?

Before Pinko could open his mouth the room erupted into a scene from a kids war-game. Ten soldiers jumped up from behind the table and started shooting us. Or rather, they started shouting "AAAAAAAAAAAHA."

"PIEOW, PIEOW."

"RATATAT RATATAT RATATAT."

"AAAAAAAAAAAHA AAAAAAHA."

The barman's face had disappeared behind a huge laugh. All that was visible were his tonsils and his teeth.

When the childish machine gunning had petered out to a few 'bang bang's' (I do remember someone shouting 'bang bang misfire jam!') we realised that 2 Section of 3 Troop had ambushed us good and proper. To make matters worse Taff was in on it, as was the barman.

"Guten arbend Soldaten, sie sind tot" (good evening solders you are dead) he laughed tears running down his face.

"ZweiundZwanzig grosse beer bitte" Taff shouted. (Twenty two large beers please, two each)

The barman clicked his heels in mock Prussian fashion and shouted "Jahowl" in reply.

"And another ten here, bitte" Ray from 3 Troop shouted utilising his only German word that he knew.

"JAHOWL" he clicked even louder. This was going to be a good night for him tonight.

We had been in the guest house bar for around an hour, or to be more precise, the time it took to swallow two large German Pils, one schnapps and one bockwurst. The table was packed with empty half litre beer glasses and food plates. Smoke filled the room like a low rain cloud. It was layered depending on its origin. I had a large German cigar stuck in my mouth that caused the lower layer of smog, Mac had a rollup dancing between his lips and TC had a condom on his head. It was blown up to the size of a large beach ball and covered TC's nose, eyes and hair. Every time he breathed out of his nose, it got a little bit bigger. Taff was holding his sides with pain, the tears rolling down his cheeks, Spunky was laughing a constrained "ha ha" and Mac was showing teeth but no sound came out. His laugh was refusing to embarrass his body. I was like Taff and was howling with laughter, even Pinko was giggling in between muttering "Childish TC, very childish."

The layers of smoke started an angry dance around the main light, the cause of which was that the door had just been opened. A blast of cold air swirled inside and upset not only the smoke, which had been enjoying itself but also everyone else in the bar.

"Shut the fucking door" Jock shouted.

"Fut der futting toor" TC muffled through the condom, which brought on fresh laughter.

Just then the condom burst.

The cold air was followed by the appearance of two heads peeking around the door. One belonged to Stu Stines and the other was Stevie Byrd's, both of 1 Section, 3 Troop.

"Hey come in and shut the bloody door." I said picking pieces of condom out of my beer.

"JA, kommen sie in, soldier, we are beer drinking." The barman shouted through the smoky haze. We had been carrying out the English custom of buying the bar staff drinks every time we bought a round. Unfortunately, there was only one of him and we had split into little three man groups for rounds. He was plastered, but not before he had introduced us to Schnapps, Apfelschnapps and Pamplemouse mit Wodka straight out of the freezer. The two heads disappeared for a second and then the door burst open again and in walked the whole Section. Jokes and insults were made on how long it had taken them to reach the gueste. Their guns were thrown into a Section heap like ours and new smoke was made to join the stuff that was lost to the night.

Two hours later we fell out of the guesthouse promising the landlord to return one day and marry his ugly daughter. The final rounds of toasts were to Germans and our Queen. Those toasts made two bottles of schnapps disappear. We had exchanged checkpoints with the other Sections. Some of the checkpoints had orienteering hole punches others just a letter that we had to copy.

We still had a couple of points that we had to punch on our card. These we couldn't get with cheating. Or could we? We staggered a mile down the road, the whole Troop was on a high, and we were laughing and joking. Something was trying to push through my mind's drunken haze. I was joking with Steven Wooster. He was a tall bulky lad from the West Country, simple but as honest as the day is long and because of his surname he was nicknamed Jeeves. Suddenly it hit me like a truck. "THE GUNS! TAFF, THE FUCKING GUNS!" it needed no further explanation. We all stopped dead in our tracks. We all looked at each other. No one had a gun.

Taff's eyes grew wider and wider, his mouth managed to splutter a "B...but...FUCK!" he was in DEEP, DEEP shit. To lose a gun is a career death sentence. To lose the whole Troops' in a German boozer would mean an immediate transfer to a *Military correction centre*.

"RUN LADS, LIKE THE FUCKING WIND, RUUUUUUUUUN!" and run we did. Ten sprinting soldiers ran the mile back to the guesthouse and nine burst through the door. Fortunately, the guns were still by the table. Unfortunately, 3 Troop were still there to see our monumental screw up. It would be all round the Squadron by the next day.

We walked outside the gueste with our guns and saw Paddy, panting and bright red in the face, wobble up to the wall and fall against it. He was so out of breath that he couldn't talk. "Di… oh… jez… di… did … you." pant pant "get… oh oh… fuc… jez me … art… guns?" he looked at me and I burst out laughing, he was done in, totalled, he couldn't keep up with us walking let alone running, and he had arrived two minutes after us, *BUT* he had given it everything he had. If he had walked we would have understood, but he didn't. We ran so he ran. Some people are good at maths, some good at painting and some good at running, Paddy was hopeless at running, he was an excellent swimmer, spoke three languages, was the Troop mathematician and the best Backhoe Operator that I have ever met, but running, no way. He was later hounded out of the Army because of this. What a waste. Right now, he was part of our team. He had no chance of getting to the gueste before us, but that hadn't stopped him running. That made him part of us, he had tried as hard as the rest of us. That is what the comradeship of the Forces is all about.

Mac had his gun and he told him but refused to let him carry it. "You get your breath back Paddy, I'll carry it." Just to help him get his breath back, he gave Paddy a rollup and lit it for him.

"Fuck this for a game of soldiers, I've got a plan, wait here" Taff went back into the gueste.

We sat down by the wall, smoked and talked. Two minutes later Taff walked out with that cheeky pixie look on his face. He was up to mischief.

"What's happening Taff?" Jock asked.

"Just wait boys, just wait" Taff answered with a wry smile.

Something was going to happen. After a couple of minutes, it did. Two large Mercedes taxis turned up. "Our transport awaits us guys,"

YEEEAHHH!! We all jumped into the taxis, the guns on our laps. Taff and Jock, being the Corporals, got a front seat each, the rest of us squeezed into the back.

Our taxi driver was a small thin family type man with round rimmed glasses. He saw the guns and went white. "Kein sheissen."

Taff lifted up his gun and showed him the empty magazine slot, "No bullets Boyo." he seemed to relax a little, "Englander Soldaten?"

"Yes mate, English soldiers, World Cup 1966, remember?"

This made the driver laugh, "Where to football hero?"

Taff opened the map and showed him the next checkpoint. The driver studied the map for a few minutes then let out a long "Aahhh! OK we go" and shot off. He grabbed his microphone and spoke German into it. The other taxi started to follow.

"What'd he say Taff?" Spunky asked.

"He told the other driver where we are going and said something about Americans."

"Ah, you speak German eh?" the driver asked Taff.

We struck up a conversation with the driver through Taff. The heater was turned up and a local music station turned on. Even through my own drunken haze I could smell the booze that was in the air of that taxi. The heat, the music and the rumbling of the taxi eventually got the better of us and the conversation died out and snoring could be heard in the rear of the taxi. After fifteen minutes, we started to go up a large hill. "Your place up here, I stop before top OK" he turned around and smiled at us. We had no idea why. Another five minutes and what must have been 10,000 feet up, he turned out the lights and stopped the car, in that order.

"Ok Englander, we are here" he whispered and pointed to a light that came from around the corner. We got out and the other taxi pulled up behind us. We all fell out of the taxi, laughing, we had to fall out as the four of us in the back were intertwined with each other. Taff walked up to the front window of the other taxi as I stretched my legs, the cold night air having a sobering effect on me. The window of the taxi came down electrically, as it did a thick hot cloud of cigarette smoke wafted out along with soft music, snoring and a lot of heat. "You stay in the car and we'll look for the punch," turning back to us he (for some reason that remains unknown) whispered "spread out and look for the punch. The punch was an orienteering hole punch with which we had to mark our card.

TC, Spunky, Mac, Taff and I walked up the hill to the slow left-hand corner from where the mysterious light was shining. As we rounded the corner dressed in combats with the guns in our hands, we must have been an utterly frightening sight. At least that's what the American serviceman thought that was on gate duty at the top secret American radar base on the top of the hill. When we rounded the corner, he was twenty five metres from us, leaning up against the barrier and in daydream land. His daydream must have turned to a nightmare, because he took a sharp intake of breath that we could hear twenty five metres away, screamed, "EEEEEEEEEK Jezus, Jezus, goddamn… oh no… muther…" and he ran into his hut whilst trying to undo his holster. A holster that contained (we later presumed) a pistol with *real* bullets. A screeching alarm split the crisp night air and powerful spotlights illuminated the whole base. No one said anything, we all ran. As we rounded the corner our taxi had already turned around and was waiting for us with its lights out and engine running. We dived into the back of the taxi as Taff leaped into the front and the taxi shot off at a breakneck speed, the hill adding to the powerful Mercedes' engine.

We travelled for a good two minutes at around 160 kph before anyone spoke. "What the hell was that?" Taff asked no one in particular.

"That American radar base, taxi not go there, not allowed, you attack base?" the driver answered the question.

"No, we must find stamp for paper" Taff showed the taxi driver the check paper. He started to roar with laughter and grabbing the mike spent two minutes telling all of the other taxis our screw up.

"Ain't that just fucking typical of our OC," TC chuntered, "puts a checkpoint next to a top secret radar base where the guards have real bullets, and then tells us that we have to creep up in the middle of the night and find it. Creep up and get shot more like it, the stupid big nosed bastard."

"He does have a big nose doesn't he" Spunky laughed.

"Like a Bloodhound" I put in.

"More like a Bulldog" TC howled with laughter as we all did.

"Bignose" I pondered the name and pictured the OC. "Bignose… I like that name, it suits him," I put on a royal voice "forevermore, shall, the OC be called, BIGNOSE."

"BIGNOSE!" the taxi roared.

The taxi took us to another gueste very near to our next checkpoint and we paid the drivers 9 DM each. We offered a large tip. They enjoyed the excitement so much that they refused the tip, shook our hands and still laughing, got back into their cabs, and shot off.

We entered the gueste with our guns this time and encountered lads from 1 Troop and 2 Troop. The scene of drinking and telling tales repeated itself. I'm afraid that the drink got the better of me and I have very little recollection of this gueste. I can remember us telling the other groups of our encounter with the American base and them telling us that we were miles off course. It has probably gone down as a terrorist attack on the base's records. We swapped the last of our checkpoints and after a few more drinks stumbled out into the freezing night air.

We were in the cold, dark night, miles from home and on the edge of a forest. In all of the houses, lights could be seen in the windows. Families were watching telly, eating food, and enjoying their life. We had to spend the rest of the night walking. It was a very unhappy prospect.

"We've got to go into the centre of the wood, follow me lads" Taff set of at a pace that could only be described as a 'bimble'. No one wanted to be there, no one wanted to walk another inch but it was the only way to make it end. *"One foot in front of the other."* Very soon the banter ended and the pain set in, legs that were stiff just went numb, as did the mind. *"One foot in front of the other."* The alcoholic daze helped us switch off and walk and walk and walk. *"One foot in front of the other."* That is how you are trained to walk a long distance, get behind a person, put your head down and look at the backs of his feet, then put one foot in front of the other. When a stop was called, we would fall down on the ground and close our eyes. It was the small hours of the morning and sleep would come instantly. Sometimes Taff or Jock would wake us; sometimes they would be asleep as well. We were Sappers not Special Forces. We spent the days greasing up our weird and wonderful equipment not carrying out forty mile route marches. My memory of this part is a lot of dark German forests, dirty forest tracks and a lack of talking. There was no conversation, no humour and no enjoyment. We had run out of cheats, our endurance was reaching its end and worst of all we all had sobered up. Somehow, we arrived at the last checkpoint. When we checked it against the answer that the last group had given us we found that they had given us a wrong answer. All we had to do was walk back to the beginning. The thought of that even made Pinko stop whinging. We set out towards the finish, which was another seven miles away. As we went through a village, we smelt fresh bread being baked. What a beautiful smell! Our stomachs were rumbling and we had the munchies after the boozing that we had done hours earlier. The local bakery had its door open a crack and the smell wafted down the German street and assaulted our nostrils. We gathered round the shop entrance and sat down. The heat from the ovens was being blown out the door. Heaven was sitting down and breathing in this mouth-watering smell. We carried out small talk and Mac made a rollup out of the last of his tobacco. It was pencil thin as it contained around four strands of tobacco and a few grains of dust. This object d'art, this precious possession, this last cigarette was shared by all of the smokers as they had all run out of fags miles ago.

One of the bakers came out and seeing soldiers sitting around his entrance, half asleep, half dead and sharing what was either a thin cigarette or a small reefer, took pity on us and offered us some freshly cooked bread. This we took gratefully and devoured it like Piranhas devour their prey. He smiled when he saw how we liked his bread but he didn't offer us any more. He went back in and we just sat trying to build up the strength to stand up and walk the remaining seven miles. It might as well have been a hundred miles to us. Dawn was starting to break and the birds woke up and started to sing. What were they so fucking happy about? Obviously, they didn't have a Big nosed bastard for a boss who has delusions of being a General of a crack Special Forces unit. Even if the birds did suffer the same type of boss as us, they could fly!

The bird's songs echoed through the morning mist that was hugging the snow-covered ground and the sky to the east started to brighten with the coming of the winter sun. It could have been a beautiful scene had we not been so knackered. What *was* a beautiful scene was the bus that was approaching us. Just to the front of us was a bus stop. No one had noticed it before, but now we all did at the same time. The bus had its headlights on as it was still very dark, and the cabin was lit with internal lights. Good, the seats were empty. In a second we were up and running for the bus stop with an energy that came from god knows where. Ten pairs of arms were waving at the bus to stop, and stop it did. Taff stood on the footplate and spoke to the driver. He had a huge smile on his face like the barman but I was too tired to notice, all I wanted to hear was the driver say "Ja."

"Gehern sie nach Schneeren?" Taff asked in his best German.

The driver said the magic "Ja" but from the back of the bus came a strange "Not for you, you fucking wankers." It certainly didn't come from the driver as he was roaring with laughter.

We all looked into the empty bus and heads popped up from behind the seats. 2 Troop and Head Quarters Troop had got to the bus first and were hiding from view.

We got on and swapped insults and stories with our friends. The driver shut the door and still laughing, set off. Every time that we saw another set of car lights we all dived under the seats as we did at every village. This, the driver thought was hilarious. He was on the graveyard shift and was having the time of his life. Wait until he told his friends, what a story he had.

At another village we all ducked behind the seats and heard the bus driver shout, "Soldaten hier." The bus stopped, the door opened and an English voice asked "Are ya gannin t'Schneeren, man?"

"NOT FOR YOU YA GEORDIE TWAT" Taff shouted.

The same scene was repeated with the jokes and stories and the bus set off again. Twenty minutes later we stopped the bus half a mile from the finish. We offered the driver all the money that we had but he refused it. I guess to him this story was priceless.

After the bus had gone, we sorted out the order that we had set out and walked back with five-minute intervals between groups.

We came up behind a Section from 1 Troop. This Section contained Lieutenant Jeremy Montgomery (Monty). He was the son of a Brigadier or General. Like us, he was also on his last legs. We dragged ourselves over the finish line where the SSM was standing. He was congratulating everybody on completing. He was also washed, shaved awake and full of beans. We on the other hand looked like a bunch of refugees. He directed Taff to the OC's tent to book in. I followed to see what lies Taff told the Major. Jeremy was still in front of us and he seemed to be perking himself up for something. Before he went into the tent he straightened his beret, dusted himself down, straightened his uniform, and stretched to his full 5 foot 10 inches. Taff followed him in. Monty came out first two minutes later his face a bright red, Taff followed thirty seconds later, laughing; he related to me what went on in the tent;

Taff had followed the Lieutenant in. Monty had marched the two paces up to the OC's table and stomped to a halt, his right arm supposedly snapping down to his side in a 'smart soldier-like fashion'. To exaggerate this movement he had swung his arm up, to be level with his shoulder, but either because he was too tired or because he was an idiot he lost control of his right arm and it shot up and hit the Hurricane lamp above his head. On the way up the arm was on its own. On the way down however, it had company. The glass that his hand had just broken was twinkling in the light as it raced his arm to be the first one down. The glass never made it to the ground as it sprinkled itself all over Monty's uniform. He stood there stock-still getting redder and redder. His eyes were transfixed on a part of the tent at his own height.

"You stupid pillock!" the OC growled. 2Lt. J. Montgomery went even redder and he started to stutter as was his way when dealing with the OC. "Er… er, ss...ss…ss…sorry sir, er… 1 Section, 1 Troop reporting in, Sir"

"I can see that you idiot, how was it?"

"Er… fine Sir, great in fact, I er… I feel as if I could do it again" he tried to smile but as he looked down to the OC, pieces of glass fell off his beret, sprinkling the OC's coffee and biscuits with glass.

"Look what you have done now, that is all Montgomery", he looked towards Taff and ignored Monty. Monty's head reached critical mass as far as redness was concerned, and executing a wobbly right turn he marched out of the tent.

"And how are you and your men Cpl Davies?" the OC asked in a friendly tone.

"Fucking knackered, Sir."

The OC burst out laughing, "Good, good, that's the idea, tell them well done from me, that's all, Cpl Davies." and brushing the glass off his biscuits he stuck one into his mouth.

After Taff had told me what had happened, we went over to the cook's table where they had set up hot soup. We were harboured up in a clearing in yet another German wood. There were many guys there and more were drifting in all the time. We grabbed a pint of hot oxtail soup, sat up against a tree, and watched the people coming in. The smell of soup and the smell of the pine forest intermingled and tried to interest my smell sensors. My smell sensors just told the smells to 'FUCK OFF, We're shut for the night' and switched off. The soup was one of the best that I have ever tasted. My legs were like lead. They felt like they were glued to the ground, and were too heavy to lift. My body was cold and I had trouble keeping my eyes open. The soup sent a warm glow cascading down my throat. From there, it spread around my body. Very soon, I lost the battle to stay awake and drifted off into a deep sleep.

*****

The sun was directly above my head and was so strong that it prevented me opening my eyes. Not that I needed to, I could feel the hot sand burning my toes and the sound of the waves crashing on the shore just in front of me. I was sunbathing on a Desert Island, two bronze skinned natives were stroking my brow, and one of their hands gently dropped down my chest, across my stomach and onto my crotch. I looked up into her beautiful large brown eyes and I noticed that her breasts were naked, the other girl started to shake me violently by the shoulder, "Hey stoppit, not so hard" I complained.

"Com'on Boyo, time to go," she said with a Welsh accent,

"Eh… What? I didn't know that you were Welsh" she shook harder and my head bounced off a tree that had somehow appeared behind me. I opened my eyes and the Desert Island and the girls disappeared. "SHIT!" I swore I was still in some grotty German wood. I looked up into the smiling face of Taff. "Piss off Taff; I was having a good dream."

"The transport's here but there's only three Bedfords" he said with an urgency that I couldn't comprehend for about two seconds. In that time I visualised the room that there was in the back of a Bedford 4 ton truck, I pictured the whole Squadron, on parade, all hundred of us and then I pictured the whole Squadron trying to get into three trucks. My legs got the message before my head did. My head wanted to get back to the Desert Island, but my legs didn't want to spend the whole of the return journey standing, so they got up and ran like the wind, my head having no choice in the matter, followed. I reached the back of the truck at about the same time as did ninety-nine others. There was a mass scramble into the back of the truck, and luckily I managed to get onto a tarpaulin at the rear. I was lying down and someone was lying on my leg, it was making my leg numb so I asked him to move but he couldn't move as someone was lying on *him*. We must have looked like a human game of 'Pick up sticks.'

We bounced our way back to camp, I quickly fell asleep but the dream of the Desert Island would not return. Instead, I got into a dream of being trapped under a collapsed building. I was only rescued when we arrived in camp and I was awoken. We fell out of the back of the truck, *I mean we literally fell*, my leg refused to work as it hadn't had its full supply of blood for the last twenty minutes, and when the blood started to flow the pain was terrible. Everybody was complaining about their legs. No one had escaped the 'pins and needles', except the OC and the SSM. We stood around at the bottom of the accommodation block and cried at our own pain and laughed at everybody else's. A sort of "Aaarg... Me fukkin legs... ha ha ha... arrg...ow. Jock you wimp! Ha ha ow ow!"

The OC paraded and congratulated us. I didn't hear a thing that he said, my brain had switched off hours ago and was asleep. The body was on autopilot. We were dismissed and I limped to my beautiful black Golf GTI with the extremely heavy clutch spring, Pinko said "See you on Thursday then" and that gave me the only clue that I needed that we had been given Wednesday off. I didn't even bother to question him about it, I just took it off.

Wednesday 19th January

Slept, ate and did nothing. I walk with a limp. Taff Davies can't walk. 3 went down with exposure. 2 went down with exhaustion. 1 with a bugged knee and finally they lost Stig. The whole squadron walks with a limp, if they can walk. Not bad for a 75 Sqn. fuck up.

My legs were tight but not as bad as I thought they would be. I lay in bed and enjoyed doing nothing. Sandra and I lay in bed and cuddled. It was great just to lay there in her arms. In the back of our minds was the thought that the days that we could do this were numbered. I tried to store up the comfort that one feels in the arms of one that you love. I tried to remember it so that I could enjoy it in the Falklands. The day passed far too quickly. We went down Nunburg town and looked around the shops. I bought a mouth organ and a small switchblade to take to the Falklands. We tried to stay up for as long as possible in order to make the day last longer.

Far too soon, night came and we admitted defeat and went to bed.

Thursday 20th January

We thought we were being so clever getting a taxi. The only group that didn't, (cheat) won. (You believe that? I don't) 1 group got a bus, taxi and a train! Another group split up and one went round one way, the other went round the other way. When they met they got a train, slept on the platform and walked 2 km in. REME got a taxi back from the first check point and slept in the hedgerow until dawn. Up yours Major Smythe!!

I tried to get out of bed and couldn't move. It felt like someone had strapped two scaffold planks to my legs, they were so unbelievably stiff. It wasn't only the legs, all of my lower back and shoulders were stiff. I had to walk to the toilet stiff legged. I couldn't even sit on the toilet as my legs refused to bend and there was not enough room to sit with my legs outstretched. The muscles were now complaining about the long march. It was a crazy idea, we had had no build up training, and we were just thrown straight on the march. I got dressed amidst much "ooh" and "ahs," waddled out towards the car and drove into camp. The Golf now seemed to have a clutch pedal spring worthy of a Centurion tank. Every time that I had to press it, a pain shot up my thigh. I now regretted buying a five-gear model instead of the four.

On parade, everybody was the same. We spent the day drinking tea and telling stories to the other Sections about how much we had cheated. We were the *amateurs*. MT Troop caught a train and REME slept under the hedgerow in their maggots. Come morning they ambled in and told the OC that they couldn't find ANY checkpoints. What it did prove was the Sapper's ability to improvise, (and also REME's ability to do nothing and get away with it).

Friday 21st January

Our day off started with a parade. Cheers OC! I then spent the rest of the day trying to fit 6 months clothes into a kit bag.

Result:

Kit bag - 1

Bernie: - 0

I lost.

The Sqn. had a farewell do tonight. I didn't go. Just as well as I heard later.

The piss-up was a morbid affair. The only people that enjoyed themselves were the rear party and their families. Everybody else's mind was on the long separation that was to come. Not a good party.

Saturday 22nd January

On Duty

Need I say more!!

Jeeves also brought a gob organ.

The last Saturday before I leave and I was on duty. What a bummer!

Sunday 23rd January

Trying to fit the rest of the kit into the suitcase. Finally I did it, don't know how. Pinko and Spunky put their kit into my cellar.

Gretel came round and slept on Friday. God knows why

I can't remember anything about this day.

Monday 24th January

Practised the stupid parade! Weighed all the kit and sent it packing. The sun is out but I don't feel like smiling. I really want to go to the Falklands but I don't want to leave.

How do you say goodbye for six months? "Back in a tick" doesn't seem appropriate. I bet I've forgotten something. I don't think I'd feel all that better if everybody else was going and I wasn't, at least I've got someone to come back to!!

I went about my daily duties in a trance. In autopilot, hanging over me all the time is the black cloud of me leaving the next day. I tried not to think about it but whenever I did it plunged me into a dark chasm of unhappiness. I wanted to go but I didn't want to leave. I certainly didn't want to go through the next day. That will be a very tearful day, both Sandra and I knew it but tried to go about our business as if it was the same as any other day. We failed. In camp, all of the singlies were happy. They were off on an adventure, no one to leave behind. We finalised all of the preparations for leaving and were knocked off. I went home to a very subdued house. Why was I doing this? Why didn't I become a bank clerk or something? Sandra was very 'touchy'. I am sure that I was as well, always holding and squeezing each other. Night came and we reluctantly went to bed and made love, it wasn't the best ever and it certainly didn't make up for the next seven months. We did it but were too sad to enjoy it.

Fuck this for a game of soldiers.

Tuesday 25th January

Said goodbye to San amid much tears and went into camp by Spunky's car. We had a stupid parade in the dark then we got on a bus and waited. When we got on the VC10 only a problem with the engine stopped us. Refuelled in Dakar, NW Africa, then plain sailing via VC10 and Wessex to USS Uganda and it is bleeding hot in here. Got to sleep at 2 o'clock.

We didn't start to cry until the final hug. We both knew that it was coming and went about our morning abolitions and breakfast like a pair of robots, not daring to think about what was coming. But come it did like an approaching thunderstorm. Spunky rang the doorbell and that was our signal. I opened the door and shouted down the five steps that I'd be along in a minute. Turning back I held onto Sandra as she started to sob in my arms. I felt the tears well up in my eyes and crawl down my face. We kissed lightly on the lips, and then returned to the hug. Neither wanted to let go but we both knew that we must. We held each other for another second, and then another and another, the seconds turned into a minute, the minute was followed by another minute. Sandra's body was racked by sobs and my tears rolled off my cheeks onto her hair. I couldn't let her go because I knew that when I did it would be the last that I would touch her for seven months. This was the girl that I loved above all other humans on the planet and I wanted to spend the rest of my life with her and then I then go and leave her. Why? For what purpose? Will it affect the world if I stay here with her? I couldn't be the first to let go, I just couldn't. Neither could she.

"Come on Bernie, you don't have time for a shag! The sooner we go, the sooner you can write her a letter." Spunky shouted up the apartment stairs. We both laughed through the sobs, it was just the cue that we needed. We broke apart and I looked into her eyes, they said it all.

"Love you" I whispered.

"Love you too," she replied "now go." The 'go' barely came out. I realised that there was another flood of tears that she was trying to hold back until I left. She opened the door and I left without looking back. That was a hard thing to do, but I couldn't look at her again. I just walked down the stairs with the tears still flowing down my cheeks.

Spunky didn't speak. It was just as well because I didn't trust my voice to speak without blubbering. We got into his car and drove to camp without a word. Spunky respected my sorrow and waited until I broke the silence. When I did, I found that my voice had regained some of its confidence, I only squeaked on the last word, because of this squeak I didn't talk for the rest of the journey. We drove through the gates past the guardroom, "Well, here we are" I muttered only to test my voice, it didn't blubber, great. The Squadron was outside the block in a gaggle. We parked up and joined the crowd. I was amongst friends and shut off all thoughts of Sandra. Unfortunately, she didn't have the same distraction, she was alone. Soon I was eager to start the adventure, but first we had to have a parade for the OC. He wanted a 'Hero's going off to war' parade. We paraded in the dark. No one was there to watch us. No one cared.

We marched off the square and onto the bus; I took a photo of the guys in the back of the bus. The first photo of many I would take, The 'Boys Own' adventure had BEGUN!

We waited…

And waited…

And waited…

Spunky leaned over the seat and whispered to me "Looks like you could've had that shag after all."

"The whole fucking Squadron could've gone to Hamburg for a shag" I replied angrily. I wanted the adventure to start. I'd paid my dues with the goodbyes and now I wanted fun. Eventually it came, we set off and jerked and bounced our way down the autobahn to the airport, but Mr Waiting hadn't finished with us yet.

*****

"Sergeant Major, how are the men?"

"Happy Sir"

"Well don't just stand there man, piss them off"

We stood around Gutersloh airport and found that we had no nosebags. (packed lunches).

We raided a food machine and stood around.

We smoked and stood around.

We watched the aeroplanes and stood around.

I took more photos of our exciting adventure. So far, the pictures were of bored soldiers, waiting. After someone had come to the decision that we had stood around for long enough, we were called onto the VC10, known as a Vicky10. Flown by the RAF they have the seats facing backwards. As we boarded Scouse Barley was the first to notice this, "Hey Corporal," he shouted to a RAF Steward "You've put the seats in backwards"

"Shuddup and sit down."

"Charming," Scouse laughs "they don't treat you like that on British Airways."

"You don't fly with your Sergeant Major on British Airways!" the steward hissed in a veiled threat. We took the threat seriously and sat down.

I had just been told to fasten my seatbelt when the plane started to roll. They don't waste any time on RAF flights. The difference between civilian and military passengers is that we shut up and strap up when told, if we didn't the Sergeant Major would soon hear about it. The VC10 taxied up to the end of the runway. I looked across to Spunky and our eyes met. We smiled at each other, we were obviously both thinking the same thing, this was it, the end of the waiting and I felt like cheering.

There was a roar and we were pushed into our seatbelts as the pilot opened the throttles. No one was afraid like in the movies. No one was clutching the seats with white knuckles because we were all glad that at last we were flying off on our great adventure.

No such luck.

The runway was rushing past my window at such a rapid rate the white lines were a blur, 'in a few seconds we will leave the ground' I pondered, but we never made it off the ground.

Suddenly the engines were slammed into emergency reverse and we were thrown back into our seats. Now we were glad of the backward facing seats. We were braking sharply but it seemed to take too long. The brakes and tyres squealed and reverberated throughout the cabin. How much runway was there left? Was there an aircraft on the runway? Will we hit it? What was happening? Why were we braking? All these questions were going through my mind. The wings were bouncing outside my window and the nose of the VC10 dipped and jumped up and down like a dog playing with a ball. After an agonising few seconds we were finally stationary, it must have taken only twenty seconds, but I counted every one. Whatever was on the runway, we must have missed it. I looked around and realised that the tension in the passenger compartment could be cut with a knife. Scouse Barley broke it by declaring in a very loud voice "Anybody got any toilet roll? I just shat myself."

Everyone laughed. We had all just experienced the same fear and that was just what the doctor ordered. The cabin erupted with talk and laughter,

"Jezuz, I thought we were dead"

"That's never happened to me before."

"What was the problem?"

"Let go of my hand now, please."

I looked to see that my hands were still gripping the arms. I slowly let go and looked down the aisle and saw the Steward Cpl slowly get out of his seat. He was blanched white with fear. He had probably run over a plane crash many times in his mind, seen all of the films, and done the training, he knew better than us what could have happened and it had spooked him. He walked down the aisle and talked to everyone reassuring us and when he got to our seat I noticed that his hand was shaking.

The tannoy burst into life. "Er... Ladies and gentlemen, we have had a small problem with the engine oil pressure in number three engine so we aborted and are going to taxi to the hangar and get the mechanics to investigate. I hope that the emergency stop didn't frighten you, but it is better that we sort out the problem on the ground than in the air"

"I'm with you on that one!" Scouse shouted.

We taxied our way to the hangar and were told to stay on the aeroplane whilst the mechanics fixed the engine.

"More bloody waiting!"

"Change the rubber band you wankers."

"Did the pilot forget his sandwiches?"

These and other helpful hints were shouted down the aisle.

Eventually the mechanics found what was wrong and fixed it, with bubble gum and blu tack presumably, and we had another go at this flying thing. This time I noticed that everybody was quiet and tense during the takeoff. There were no more problems and we got airborne and headed for Dakar, the capital of Senegal. Dakar is on the West Coast of Africa. The Ascension Islands is halfway from Africa to America so Dakar was a fuel stop.

We landed and were allowed off the plane but were not allowed to stray from the immediate vicinity. We were also told to stay away from the ditches. Being obedient soldiers, we walked straight to the ditch. It stunk to high heaven, shit, urine and dead cats is the best description of the stench. To add to the smell we all pissed in the ditch. We weren't allowed to smoke as they were refuelling. Dammed unfair we thought, but seeing as the plane was surrounded by black militia guards with guns we obeyed. A couple of the guys tried to talk to the militia but they refused to answer. We didn't realise that they only spoke French. After half an hour in the stench of Africa we embarked and took off again. This time we were headed for a barren volcanic rock that is called The Ascension Islands.

*****

FOR RENT One grade 2 listed Island in down-town Atlantic. Close to the Equator and mid way between the continents of America and Africa. Within easy bombing distance of either continent. Ideal as a refueling stop, atomic test area or nature reserve for dung beetles. Offers are accepted from the under-represented areas of the community.

PRICE: - £12,000,000 pa or provide a home for Princess Ferguson and it's yours.

*****

The first thing that I noticed as we walked out the door of the Vicky 10 was the heat. We were now on the Equator; from the cold of Germany to the Equator was a large jump in temperature. The effect of the temperature rise wasn't helped by the fact that we were wearing combat jackets, and we instantly wished that we weren't. Obviously, we couldn't take them off that would've been too sensible. The second thing that I noticed was the smell. Volcanic rock has a burnt metal smell. An island made out of it smells of nothing else except burnt rock. The smell was overpowering.

We were herded into an American USAF bus and taken to a holding area. Large B52 bombers and American aircraft were all around us. The British were renting out the island to the Yanks as a refuelling base.

We did some rapid waiting and in only a few minutes were herded onto a Wessex helicopter. The Wessex wound up its engine until we were suitably deaf and took off. It was pitch black outside the chopper, all we could see were the lights from the airfield. We touched down on the back of a group of lights that were bobbing around in the sea and were herded below decks. We had no idea of what the ship looked like, I was lucky as I was put into a cabin that was just above the waterline. Others weren't. At least I could open the porthole for fresh air. When I did, I noticed that the air outside was hotter than the air inside. There were twenty in our 'room'. At around 0200 hrs we finally got into bed. However, could we sleep? Not in that temperature, it was stifling. There was one sink in the cabin and all through the night, I heard people getting up and having a drink. I was too knackered to even move and finally dropped off to sleep at around three o'clock.

Wednesday 26th January

Unloaded choppers this morning then we went swimming, it's a great way to fight a war. Jock stood on a fish to kill it and splatted it.

2 Tp have been named Jo-ho Tp. everybody went fishing at teatime. Jock caught an eel, he was very careful taking out the hook so that it didn't bite off his finger. When he had done that he took his foot of its head and turned around where upon it bit his heel (laugh) I nearly wet myself!!

There are arguments about the queuing for food.

I had just dropped off to sleep, or so it seemed when the tannoy burst into life. "Get out of your cots, its eight bells" or something stupid like that. It was Navy talk and I just ignored it, as did everybody else. No one moved.

"ALL OF YOU GET YOUR FEET ON THE FLOOR, NOW!" this was the voice of Lumpy Phillips, 1 Troop SSgt, we all recognised his Glaswegian accent and in a second everybody was standing on the deck.

"Good morning HQ," he smiled "Breakfast has started, it is along this deck, I suggest that you move yourself, parade is at 0700 hrs."

The 'breakfast' bit made everybody move. There was a mad panic, people were fighting for the one sink, trying to splash water on their faces, TC's electric razor was being used by everyone, and socks that were taken off four hours ago were put back on.

We made a dash along the corridor in the direction that Lumpy told us and went smack into the back of a hundred metre long queue.

"What is the queue for?" I asked the man at the end.

"Breakfast" he answered gloomily.

"Ohhh… shit." In front of us were all of the field Troops. Lumpy had woken them first. It was 0640 hrs and we were not going to have enough time to eat. The smell of cooking bacon was teasing us down the hall. I still had to shave and clean my boots so I dropped out of the queue and went back to the room. (Sorry, '*cabin*', must use Navy talk). I shaved and cleaned my boots had a dump in an apparatus and with five minutes to spare calmly but still hungrily walked up towards the helideck. As I walked past the canteen it was empty, there was no queue so I nipped in, walked up to the hot plate and shoved two sausages and three rashers of bacon into my mouth. I was still trying to chew them when the Sassman called us to attention on the helideck. The rind on the bacon refused to be bitten through, I had to chew when I wasn't been looked at. If anyone had asked me to speak they would have been covered in bits of chewed up pig.

It was 0700 and the sun was beating down into our eyes. We were all doing our impressions of the Japanese Army. The SSM had thoughtfully stood so that his back was to the sun. That meant that our eyes were directly in the path of the sun's rays. The rays refused to divert their path after their long journey from the sun to the earth so they tried to burn straight through our eyes. I heard rather than saw the OC come to the front of the squad, he called us to attention, and then stood us at ease. Maybe he believed that we needed more practice at this complicated manoeuvre.

"Welcome to the SS Uganda" I immediately had visions of the Captain being a fat black General who ate passengers in his cabin. The OC carried on, "You will be forming a working party that will unload helicopters this morning, then, after that, you can relax in one of the ships' two swimming pools. Enjoy it while you can because we shall use the voyage as a time to sharpen up our combat skills, we are still officially at war with Argentina. Keep an eye on the notice board and enjoy the voyage. Take over Sergeant Major." In order to test if we had forgotten how to come to attention the SSM made us do it again. The OC left and the SSM split us up into working parties to unload the choppers. "When the choppers come in you will be called over the tannoy so stay alert."

"Stay alert, Britain needs Lerts" TC piped in.

"Shuttup Furze."

"Yes Sir."

"Any questions?" the SSM foolishly asked.

I tried to open my eyes to see if the SSM was smiling or not. If he was, then it was permitted to ask questions. If there was no smile on his face then woe betide any soldier who dared to actually *ask* him something. I couldn't see anything because of the sun so I took a chance, "Sir, room service forgot to clean my boots this morning."

I heard a chuckle and knew that I was in the clear, "They only do that on the top deck, Beirne"

"Who do I have to sleep with to get a bunk on the top deck Sir?" Spunky asked.

"I suggest one of the cooks, Staynes," everybody laughed. We had all seen how effeminate some of the cooks were. "Listen in. Squadron… squadron shun… Faall out!" We did and ran down the stairs to the galley. We had only been on parade for around ten minutes and the breakfast food was still on the hot plate. We enjoyed a full breakfast and ambled down to the cabin.

The helicopter came in and we unloaded it in double quick time. We went back to the cabin only to be called forward again to unload another chopper. This went on for all of the morning. There was a long queue for lunch, which cheered us up no end, and after lunch, we went swimming in the forward swimming pool. The SS Uganda was being used as a hospital ship; previously it was a cruise liner of some sorts. It had beautiful wooden banisters and quiet writing and reading rooms. It had one swimming pool in the front and one in the back. The shipyard had stuck a huge helicopter pad on the rear end, ('Stern' I am reliably informed is the naval word). This became the sunbathing deck. It overlooked the swimming pool and became the area were everybody met. We went out on the deck after lunch and met lots of guys from 15 Squadron, Royal Engineers. They were also going down to the Falklands but were having a better time of it than we were. The Royal Engineers move their soldiers in ones and twos rather than moving the whole Regiment and because of this you get to know many people in different Regiments. The helicopter deck at the back of the Uganda was a meeting place for old friends. We sat, smoked, and told stories (or lies) about things that we had done since we had last-met. The friendship that is built up through this kind of bonding lasts the years. I didn't know anybody so I put on my shorts and went swimming in the pool. Swimming in a pool on the back of a ship that is rocking in the sea is fun. The water in the pool was sea water; after I had drunk enough sea water I got out and walked back down the deck. All along the sides of the deck were people fishing. I met up with Jock and Mac who were fishing side by side. Jock had just caught a Moray eel and he was trying to get the hook out of its mouth without the eel biting him. A wise decision as the eel had a row of sharp teeth. Jock put his foot on the head of the eel and gently pulled out the hook, he now had a circle of onlookers around him, and most I noticed were cheering on the eel. Jock was laughing because we wanted the eel to bite him, it appealed to his sense of humour. He extracted the hook and jeered the laughing crowd. Unfortunately, he also took his foot off the head of the eel. It saw its chance and with the last of its dying energy bit onto Jock's heel and refused to let go. The crowd erupted with laughter as Jock tried to open the eel's mouth. He was hopping on one foot and trying to open the mouth whilst failing miserably to keep his balance. Eventually Mac spoiled the fun by cutting the head off from the body and thus releasing the grip on Jock's foot. True to form, Jock continued to laugh. He seemed to be a ball of fun, always finding the funny side of a situation. At this point in time, I didn't know about the other side of Jock. He could carry out extremely viscous calculated acts of violence a second after laughing and then go back to the laughing a couple of seconds later. This is the difference between the British Special Forces and the American. The Yanks are all muscle and testosterone. They ooze violence. The Brit. Commando or Para is a fun loving, small but lithe time bomb. Totally professional in his job, if you piss him off you'll regret it. You don't need muscles like Arnie Schwarzenegger to cut a man's throat, just the right nerves of steel. Jock had these, as I was to find out later in the tour. Jock and his tiny wife were from Keith in Scotland, she was the sweetest woman you could ever hope to meet, but blind as a bat. She had glasses but refused to wear them outside and consequently could not make out people whom she met in the street. Jock's favourite joke was not to speak to her when they passed in camp. She would walk straight past him until he started laughing and then she would stop and ask "Jock? Is that you? Why didn't you say something? Och man, you're so cruel."

I stood and watched them fish for a while longer, "What are you using for bait, Mac?"

"Trigger fish" he pointed down the side of the ship with his rolled up cigarette. Mac smoked rollups or OP's. (That translates to rollup cigarettes or other people's cigarettes) "See those black fish on the surface?" I said that I did, "Well watch this" and he threw his stub into the water, the Trigger fish attacked the stub like Piranhas.

"Jezus, what did you use to catch the Trigger fish" I asked.

" A fag butt, I hooked a fag butt on to a small hook dropped it down onto the water and one swallowed it whole, I pulled it up, cut it up and used it for bait to catch more. They are dangerous little buggers, look one tried to take a bite out of my finger" he showed me a scratch on his finger. It was hard to see as his fingers were covered with fish scales and fish blood. Being a hater of anything that swims in its own faeces and urine it revolted me. Mac saw my reaction to his hands and acted on it. "What's the matter, it's only fish blood," he laughed. He took out another rollup from his tobacco tin and putting it in his mouth dug into his pocket for his Zippo lighter. I saw that the rollup paper was now saturated with fish scales and guts. "Mac, you're a grot"

Mac enjoyed the revulsion that he caused in me, and lighting the end of his micro thin, knobbly, fish smelling cigarette, he continued blessing the fish hater with his endless knowledge.

"The knack now is to get the bait past the Trigger fish before they eat it, all of the good fish are on the bottom"

"What… where the fish poo is?" I asked

Mac looked at me and smiled, "Yeah, look, this is what you have to do" he bent down to a pile of broken fish at his feet and picked up a piece of a Trigger fish and threw it away from the boat. As he did so a fish scale 'popped' off the burning end of his rollup, it was obviously too hot for it and was making its break for the water. I watched it float down to the water fifteen metres below and saw the Trigger fish go into a feeding frenzy on the remains of their friend that Mac had thrown in. Mac dropped in his hook and let it sink to the bottom. "Made it, if you don't do that, the little bastards eat the bait off the hook." Another fish scale 'popped' off Mac's fag but went the wrong way and hit Mac on the forehead, he took the fag out of his mouth and looked at it totally perplexed at what might have come off the end. The fish scales on it were invisible to him.

Mac looked at me, his brow deeply creased in a question, his fag still in his hand. Before I could tell him what it was, his eyes moved to see something behind me and he started to quickly reel in his line. I turned around and saw that Jock was pulling on his rod; the rod was bent double and was pointing down towards the sea. I went over and joined the crowd, as I was in his Troop I was able to get next to him. He fought the fish for up to five minutes; I got a picture of him with sweat pouring off his brow and the muscles on his arm straining to pull up the rod. He lowered the rod whilst reeling in and then hauled the rod up with all his strength and then repeated it again, and again and again. His reward was a beautiful Angel fish, the size of a large dinner plate. I photographed it and he threw it back in, much to Mac's disgust, who was ready with his knife to disembowel it. Jock's kind action to the fish didn't go un-rewarded, as the fish hit the water it was stunned, the Trigger fish weren't and devoured it in less than thirty seconds, some even jumping out of the water in order to get to the Angel fish. We watched the bubbling water and the free nature show and when the fish had been devoured I turned to Jock and stated "Nice humane action there Jock, I'm sure that the Angel fish thanked you with all it's heart before it was eaten." As usual, Jock roared with laughter. I stood and leaned on the polished wooded banister of the Uganda and watched the sun drop below the sea and melt on the surface of the water. No painting could ever reproduce the colour of the sun on the sea; it is something that we rarely see in the UK. In England, Mr Sun spends most of its time behind Mr Cloud. We walked down to the galley and joined the queue. Or should I say we joined ONE of the queues. The queue went in both directions from the door. Both claimed that theirs was the proper queue. The argument got quite heated between a Signals guy and an Ordnance man. Both were at the front of their respective queues and neither wanted to give up going through the door first.

The queue in front of these guys disappeared, Jock and I were watching them argue, we were ten people behind them, nobody wanted to tell them to move forward as they were still arguing about who should go through the door first. Suddenly Jock said "I've had enough of this" and stormed to the front of the queue. He positioned himself in the middle of the two combatants, put his hands behind their heads and before they could say anything, smashed their heads together, then gripping their hair he pulled them both out of the way and turning and smiling to me said "tea is served" and walked in through the door. No one stopped to give the two men a second glance, both queues 'zippered' in one after the other. Food was far more important.

After the evening meal, everybody gathered on the decks, some to fish, some to drink and some to think about home. I was standing next to Jock and Mac, who were fishing. It was dark and the water was lit up by the lamps that shone over the edge of the ship. People were milling around all around us, and as we were on the lowest deck that one could fish off, there were people above us. I was leaning on the wooden handrail looking over the side. The Trigger fish were still there feeding on anything that entered the water. It was a beautiful evening; the sky was awash with blood as the sun bled over the clouds on its dying ascent to the other side of the world. "Hey Jock, fancy it raining on a night like tonight."

Jock looked at me over his rod and said "It ain't raining Bernie"

"Yes it is."

Jock's reply was to look at me and then to look up. I followed his gaze and immediately regretted the decision to look up as I got a face-full of piss. Jocks concern was apparent by his huge laugh. I ran to the left five paces and looked up again. "HEY! You just pissed on me you bastard!" I shouted.

"You lucky fucker," Andy Scott shouted down "that is Airborne piss, you crap hat. You are honoured." Another pair of legs that belonged to Gus Devlin joined Andy's and out popped his worm. I jumped away from the edge as the stream cascaded past our deck. Even Jock moved this time. Most of the ex-9 Para Sqn guys were up there. When they wanted to pee, they peed. I went to my bunk and washed and when I returned I positioned myself well away from the Airborne guys.

Thursday 27th January

We were rudely awoken in the morning and had to join a 300 m queue for breakfast. They got some of us to do a bean lift, we managed to lift 2 crates, which we cooled and hid.

The staff gave us a 'don't do this, don't do that' lecture. We were told to keep the portholes shut when we were at sea. Portholes shut? In this heat? No fucking chance. I will let the ship sink before I shut our porthole. We set sail today at 1700 hrs. This is where the fun begins. No one has been sick yet, sea is very calm.

There are lots of 'Red' people running around. They don't know the strength of the sun.

Again we were woken by Lumpy Phillips and again he had woken his troops first, when we got to breakfast the queue went down half the ship, we all made a vow to get up earlier the next morning. On parade, we were detailed off to do a 'Bean lift'. What that meant was that when the helicopter came in with the stores under slung, we had to carry them down to the store. Part of that lift were crates of soft drinks, we managed to hide two crates of Coke Cola which we broke open and put in the sink with cold water to keep it cold, or more realistically, we covered it with warm water in order to keep it slightly cooler than boiling. This was the Equator and it was hot, hot, and hot.

After the last helicopter had dropped its load, I went exploring the ship. It had many decks. The further down you went the hotter and louder it got, the further up you went the more luxurious and air-conditioned it was. Right at the bottom was where my friend Andy was. Andy was a Plant Operator but was attached to the Troops, he was in the middle bunk of three, and like us, and there were twenty-four in the room. His porthole didn't open it was welded shut, which was just as well as he was below the waterline. The heat below the waterline was tremendous; there was no air conditioning and no ventilation. It was then that I realised how lucky I was in my cabin and from then on I never complained about being called last for breakfast. Those below the waterline not only had it worse but had further to go for breakfast, nearly all of the Troops were below the waterline. A lot higher up on the infrastructure, the cabins were more luxurious. Amongst these cabins I found a beautiful writing parlour, it had mahogany desks with green leather inlays on which to write. Hovering above the green leather was a beautiful green and brass reading lamp. Old books stood in the wooden book cases that surrounded the room. Velvet curtains and plush green carpet drowned out any sound apart from the air-conditioner which slowly whispered its spicy cold breath into the room. I went back to my room, got a writing pad, and on the returning, wrote a letter to Sandra. It was the perfect environment for getting ones feeling together.

After an hour I walked back down to my cabin, Top Cat had got his Animal out. Animal was a glove puppet of the Muppet fame. He took it everywhere with him, right now he had his hand up its bum and brought it alive.

"Ooh look, here comes Bernie, where've ya been" the glove puppet screeched.

"I found a little writing room, somewhere where we can write with out being attacked by a stupid puppet" I replied talking to the puppet and tapping it on the nose. Animal was part of Support Troop and deserved the same courtesy as the rest of the Troop. The tannoy interrupted any reply that Animal might have had, "All 75 Squadron to report to the training room in fifteen minutes." We made our way up to the training room and sat around talking until the SSM came in.

He told us that we will be setting sail at 1700hrs, and the Captain would be coming down to tell us some do's and don'ts on the ship, we were to treat him as if he was an Army Officer and when talking to him call him 'Sir'. A couple of minutes later the OC and Captain Birds Eye walked into the room, we were called to attention (sitting) and then told to sit at ease. The Captain then ran through a list of do's and don'ts. Don't open the portholes, don't come into the infrastructure cabins, don't use the writing room, don't use the front swimming pool, do clean all rooms, do clean the wash rooms, etc. I warmed to this guy immediately. We were then given the rest of the day off to sunbathe and enjoy ourselves, this we did in the rear swimming pool, the front being for Officers only. They didn't want the 'Dirty Unwashed' contaminating their water. At five o'clock we "weighed anchor and set sail" apparently. I saw no evidence of either sails or a weighing machine, thereby highlighting how stupid naval talk is. What I did notice was a *very* loud rumbling, a vibration throughout the ship and a gentle rocking. Slowly we started moving in the water, a white wake appeared behind the ship and would stay there until we reached Port Stanley. Another dumb point about the Royal Navy, why not just put a sign on the sea saying, "➔ Ship this way, please sink.➔" In the Army we wear clothes that blend in with the vegetation and if we need to we can hide in holes. Not so the RN, they have a huge trail behind them for anybody to see. As the boat started to rock I started to laugh, I don't normally suffer from seasickness, but just in case I did on this journey, I had brought boxes of seasick pills. I had been popping them since I got on board, my body could adjust to the motion slowly. Meanwhile I would be able to take the piss out of all of the others that were suffering. That was the *main* reason for taking them. The sea was very calm and that was not good. I needed huge swells to make everybody sick. There was another form of entertainment on the ship at the moment and that was 'Sunburn Rubbing'. The ship was saturated with red faces and bodies. Englishmen who had just come from a winter in Germany were lying out in the Equatorial sun and getting very, very burnt. There were loads of men walking around with bright red beacons sticking out of the top of their uniforms. The idea was to rub their sunburn and make it seem like an accident. "Oops! Sorry mate, I tripped," I would apologise as I dragged my hand down a bright red arm. My fingerprints would show up as white marks on their skin. I told Spunky and TC of this form of entertainment and they were delighted. We determined that that would be the evening's entertainment. "Pissing off Redskins" we set up a competition to see who could get the most. By the end of the night TC had won, mainly by his "accidental standing" on the foot of a Signalman whose feet were glowing pillar box red. We gave him ten points for that!

Friday 28th January

He he... lots of people feeling sick this morning. Not me, sea, very calm. We did naff all except get sunburnt. I didn't. We passed the Cunard Countess @ 12° clock this night. Everybody was laughing and cheering on the Cunard. Sounded like hell of a party. I heard one person cheer from this old tub, which was probably the Captain. He knows that he's going back. We did a beer lift today and nicked 14 crates of beer. The Major said it was worth it. He had to 'cos he couldn't find the beer.

The queue at breakfast wasn't as long as it had been up to now. It didn't register why until later. I walked into the galley with Spunky, and after getting a square metal plate of the best breakfast in the world, (a British Army breakfast) sat next to Jock who was stuffing the food into his mouth as if it was his last meal. He started talking whilst eating, "Woto Bernie, Spunky, what ya do last night?"

"Fuck all," Spunky replied "swam, watched the movie and had a shit."

"What, all at the same time?" Jock asked with a smile and egg yoke running down his chin.

"Might as well as done, fucking film was crap, some shit about a Yank cop getting shot"

"Have you heard what Bignose has got lined up for us tomorrow?" Jock was talking to his plate as he was trying to scoop up baked beans into his mouth with the knife. Most kept falling off which would only make him scoop faster.

"Nooo…" I said slowly, I was fascinated by his eating method "why don't you use your fork Jock?"

"Takes too long to pick it up" he picked up his plate and sucked the baked bean, plum tomato and egg juice of the plate "Aaah that's good!"

"KEEP YOUR HANDS AWAY FROM HIS MOUTH AND YOU WILL BE OK" Spunky shouted to Pinko who was approaching the table, Spunky had his arms between Jock and Pinko in a 'Hold-back-the-Animal' position.

"Is the pig feeding again?" Pinko laughed and put his plate on the table.

"Yeah, wiv your sausage mmmbgh" Jock grabbed Pinko's sausage and jammed it into his mouth.

"Shit," Pinko moaned, which was not a lot considering that it came from the most vocal Sapper of the troop.

"Well? <u>What</u> has Bignose got lined up for us then Jock?" Spunky quickly shoved his sausage into his mouth as I did mine. It was the only place that Jock couldn't get it.

"A fucking Superstars competition!"

"Ohh NO!" we all said in unison. Superstars was a program on the TV, sports stars competed to find out who was the fittest by doing loads of push-ups, sit-ups and other stupid things like the dreaded squat thrusts.

"He wants to challenge 15 Squadron."

"How embarrassing" Pinko said it for us all.

"How do you know Jock?" I dragged my bread around the plate to soak up the juice.

"Give's a bit, and I'll tell you" he was looking at my juice soaked bread which was the best bit of the breakfast.

"Jezus, are you legs hollow?" I handed over the bread and it disappeared into his cavernous mouth, "Mwell ma margent major, manted to know…." he tried to swallow but the bread got the better him, his hand shot out to my mug of tea but I got there first, he looked around the table for a drink but only saw other hands grabbing their mugs, there was none. "com'on moo marstards, givvus a drink"

We were laughing at his discomfort. He was laughing but his mouth was full, his eyes desperately looked around the galley for another target, he found one. Jeeves and Taff Davies were on the next table, Jock got up and mumbling a "You don't mind if I have a drink of your tea do you?" which came out as "Moo mont mind mif mimmemmm mmmm?" he grabbed Jeeves's mug and drained it, finishing it with a loud "AAAAHHH, yeuck, no sugar"

"JOCK! I don't talk breadspeak, what the hell did you say" I put my mug back on the table.

"The SSM asked me if I was a PTI (A bastard in a white vest that took us for Physical Training) he needs some to set the course, sit-ups, squat thrusts and all of that crap."

"Well, that has just ruined my day" Spunky voiced it for all of us.

"OW! WATCH OUT FOR MY SUNBURN" a shout went out over the galley.

"OH SORRY Stevie, I slipped" TC's Cockney, Scouse, Birkenhead, accent wafted out in a mock apology. We looked round and laughed as TC winked at us. My spirits had just been lifted again; rubbing a few Redskins should cheer us up.

On parade we were detailed off for another bean lift, but this one was different. It was beer, beer for us. We went back to our bunks and waited to be called over the tannoy.

We were trying to play Lilly the Pink on our harmonicas when the call came. "Helicopter coming in, FOD alert. FOD alert" FOD was the name for the rubbish that can be sucked into the intakes of the choppers. We weren't allowed to throw any rubbish out of the portholes during a FOD alert.

We ambled up to the flight deck. Even though we, (Support Troop) were on the highest deck for the great unwashed, (Sappers and Jnco's) we arrived at the flight deck last. Such was the magnificence of our amble, we were expert amblers. If the OC had ambling on the Superstars contest, we would have won hands down, or more accurately, hands down pockets. The Knockers were up and around the helicopter, they were considered 'Gung ho'. We were supposed to be REMFish. (Rear Echelon Muther fuckers. A term that the Yanks used in Vietnam and therefore also on every Yank War film) we were made to form a chain from the helipad to the store that was under the bar at the stern. Because the Knockers were first, we found ourselves down in the bowels of the ship. Soon crates of beer were flying down the line. From man to man the crates flew, no one had time to look to see if the next person was ready for the crate, and it was just thrown. Jeeves and Spunky were next to me. Spunky threw it to me and I threw it to Jeeves. My back was to a corridor, suddenly an idea struck me. A crate landed in my arms and instead of throwing it on to Jeeves I shouted, "Take my place Jeeves" and I disappeared at a run down the corridor with the crate in my arms. I ran and heard an "Eh, wha… ooof" and a crash as a crate hit the floor behind me. I ran to our bunk, hid the crate under my bed, and ran back and took my place in the line. Spunky and Jeeves were laughing. A couple of crates were passed on and then Spunky shouted "Take my place" and giggling hysterically like a girl, ran down the corridor. This was immediately copied by Jeeves. The bastards had worked this out whilst I was away. I now had to catch the crates, run two paces and throw them with all my might to Pinko. Within thirty seconds, both were back. Then Pinko disappeared with a crate, and so it went on.

When the last crate was passed we went back up to the helideck where the Major, who was in charge of stores, gathered us round him in a gaggle and spoke to us with a smile on his face, "That was excellent chaps, three hundred and fifty crates of beer off loaded in 9 minutes 25 seconds. I thought it was going to take all morning. I have never seen stores offloaded so quickly, again thank you. It seems that fourteen crates have gone missing somewhere along the way but let me tell you, it was worth it. Great, that's all I have for you now" and laughing he walked off.

"Mummy, mummy, I've found a decent Major, can I keep him?" TC asked no one in particular.

"No, put him down, you don't know where he's been" Tiny Westminister squeaked. Tiny was around five foot nothing, in HQ Troop, a driver and always wore a smile. Everybody knew him and liked him.

"Hey, Tiny" Stevie Byrd called over "What happened to the beer?"

"We dropped them into the sea, Stevie."

"Oh" Stevie smiled knowing full well that he wasn't going to find out where the beer was. Served him right for being at the front of the line where he couldn't steal a crate.

"Tiny" I held up my hand like the Victorian gentry might have done when asking a lady to dance "Would you care for a dwink" I put on an affected Officers voice.

"Oh, Super" he replied and holding my hand we walked into the stairwell "How awful, those nasty chaps stealing all that beer, eh what"

"Yes. Tewible. Tewible."

We went to our bunk and emptied a crate into two sinks and filled them with coldish water. We all opened a can and got out our gob irons. Spunky was the best, he was the only one who could play a tune. Animal played TC's gob iron and was actually better at it than him. Spunky was part Aussie. He had spent a lot of his youth on the beaches of Australia. He was a confirmed beach bum and was proud of it. He was also a pervert and a grot. I don't think that he intended to be unclean; there were just more important things to do than wash one's clothes. When we used to watch porno videos that we hired from the German supermarket video shop, we would all be drooling over the action and Spunky would be rolling with laughter. Over what I never found out, but his laugh was 'dirty' and infectious. We would all end up laughing. Porno movies have never been the same without Spunky's laugh. The Troop all went to Hanover one weekend. We found the red light area and went into a peep show. Being young Englishmen we were shy and had certainly never been in one before. We stood around outside building up the courage when Spunky said "Com'on ya poofs" and strode in. we got the lay of the place and changed our DM notes into coins and all went into a booth to see the dancers behind the screen. The coins were to put into a machine that allowed a screen to come up which let us see a young, naked, disinterested girl writhe around inside the booth. We all could see each other's eyes. There was one pair that was missing. Spunky!

When my money ran out I walked out of my booth and found Spunky on a Space Invaders machine. He had spent all of his change on Space Invaders. Now in a Peep Show, for a soldier, *THAT* is what I call perverted!

I was lying in my bed, trying to get to sleep. It was hot; the sheets were at the bottom of the bed. All I could hear was snoring coming from around the room, the air conditioning blowing out warm air, and the sound of the sea coming through the open porthole. It was soporific, the sound of the sea was a lullaby to my ears. It was singing me to sleep. In my dreams I was miles away, then slowly a sound filtered through my light sleep, the sound of singing and cheering, as usual in times like this the mind takes over and created a dream whereby I was at a party. I enjoyed it the party for a short time until through the sleepy haze it dawned on me that the sound was coming from outside my head. I opened my eyes and listened. There was Jeeves' snoring, there was the air-conditioner and washing over all the sound was the sea coming through the porthole. But, in between the sounds, barely discernible, was definitely the sound of a party. Music, singing, shouting, cheering, and the sounds were getting louder. I jumped out of bed and took the two steps to the porthole, I stuck my head out of the porthole and looked behind the ship and saw nothing except the wake disappearing into the distance, I looked forward and my eyes were presented with an apparition coming out of the darkness. A cluster of lights was slowly coming towards us; the sounds were coming from cluster of lights. As it got closer I was able to discern that it was a ship, the sounds of the party were drowning out every other sound, as it got level I could make out that it was a large white ocean going liner, the entire side facing us, on every deck, was full of people. They were waving their arms whilst cheering shouting and singing. They were clearly a lot happier than what we were. I managed to pick out words from the bedlam. Words like "Stag on you turkeys," "Days to do," "Going home, going home, going home" and lots and lots of laughter. I never realised before how much meaning you could get from laughter. They weren't laughing at a joke, they were laughing because they were enjoying themselves, they were laughing because we were going the other way, *towards* the Falklands, and it was a mocking laughter. The two ships started to pass each other, the other ship, which I later learned was the Cunard Countess, blew its horn, then from a few yards above my head came a solitary, sad cheer. It had no happiness to it and it lacked emotion and gusto unlike the cacophony coming from the other ship five hundred yards across the sea. That must be the Captain, I thought, he knows that he is going straight back. I watched the "love boat" disappear into the distance and listened until I could hear the cheering no more. Slowly I pulled my head back into the cabin and looked around; I was the only person awake so no one else had noticed this momentous occasion. I felt cheated that nobody had shared this with me and so with no one with which to discuss it, I got back into bed and dreaming of the party that was going on in the Cunard Countess, eventually dropped off to sleep.

Saturday 29th January

Saw "Mick the Naff' today, and then we did that great English sport of gentlemen, "Sit-ups." We played 15 Squadron Plant Troop. They didn't turn up. Now who is stupid? Sea still bloody calm. Lots of Redskins about. We sat and watched the stars come out,

Jeeves, Spunky and me. I then had a blow out in both flip flops. So we carried them out on a pillow amidst "Here comes the bride" on Jeeves' gob iron and said a short prayer then ceremoniously dumped them over the side with cries of "The flip flops are dead, Long live the flip flops."

After the parade on the helideck I bumped into Mick the NAAFI manager. He was the NAAFI manager of the families shop. He volunteered for a tour in the Falklands with the NAAFI. I hope that they paid him good money. At ten o 'clock we paraded in sports kit for that great English sport. 'Superstars'. This consists of press-ups, sit-ups, squat-thrusts and sprint races. Normally it is pure physical exertion. The person that can do the most wins. All scores go towards the team score. Now, when that is tried on a ship, Mr Physics wants a larger part in it. When the ship goes down the wave, the body gets lighter, when it rises up on a wave the body get very heavy. Now imagine doing press ups on this rolling ship, press up and you fly up so that your elbows lock and your hands leave the deck, and when you go down your body weight doubles and your nose smashes off the wooden deck.

Sit-ups are no better, except that you either fly up or you burst a stomach muscle when the weight piles onto your body in mid sit-up. Alternatively, your head, assisted by the now amused Mr Physics, bounces off the deck on the way down when the ship rises up to meet it mid way. Imagine the force of a huge ship being driven upwards by the waves and now imagine trying to head butt it! (This should only be tried by a Glaswegian!).

Another disservice that this 'super' sport gave us was not immediately apparent. The deck of the SS Uganda is polished wood. The idea behind Superstars is that you get one minute to do as many repetitions of the exercise as you can manage. You are going flat out, giving it your everything, you don't notice the other competitors, you don't notice your personal umpire who is checking that each sit-up is done to a certain standard and you don't notice the wooden deck ripping strips out of the skin just above your arse! (more about that later.) We waited, and waited, and waited for 15 Sqn to turn up, the

OC had challenged them but that didn't bother them one iota. How I wished that I was in 15 Sqn. I asked the SSM for an instant transfer but he just made me go first with the squat thrusts for opening my mouth. Support Troop came very close to the bottom. Only HQ and MT got lower scores. All we got for our troubles were sore limbs.

We queued up for lunch again, the sea was like a millpond and no one was feeling the effects, I was still taking the pills. We dossed around after lunch and watched people get sunburnt. Some more fun for the Redskin rubbing team!

As it got dark Jeeves, Spunky and I sat on the top deck and watched the stars pop out of the darkness. The Big Dipper was very low in the sky, soon it would disappear altogether. We sat and drunk our two rationed cans of beer, and tried to play a whole tune on our harmonicas.

"Hey guys, that star is moving." Spunky had stopped playing his gob iron.

I stopped playing and looked up, the sky was full of stars as there were no city lights to dull the sky, and they were showing up like dandruff on black velvet, "Which one?"

"That one" Spunky pointed up to the sky. Where he was pointing were two million stars, a large one seemed to move, or was it the boat.

"Probably a plane" Jeeves observed.

"Too high and too fast" Spunky finished his beer and crushed the can in true 'Jaws' fashion, "They don't make beer cans like they used to do they"

"Maybe a satellite" I tried to crush my can and it nipped my finger between the folds.

"Hey cool" Spunky said it for all of us. We sat in silence and watched the satellite as it sailed across the heavens. "What time is it?" I asked, we noted the time and made a vow to be out here the next day to look for it again.

I stood up out of my deck chair and took a step, "SHIT! I've had a blow-out in my flip-flop" the piece that went through the big toe had pulled out through the sole. Spunky and Jeeves laughed at my predicament, I took another step forward, and the other one broke in sympathy. "Two, broke! I don't believe it, I've had these flip-flops since Cyprus, and they're my favourites."

"They'll need a full military funeral then" Jeeves remarked. He was correct. There are some things in a Sappers' life that has to be taken seriously. The burial of a favourite pair of flip-flops is one.

"It'll have to be a burial at sea," Spunky stood up with a serious look on his face; "I'll get a cushion" he set off down the stairs.

"If it is alright with you Bernie, I'd like to play a moving piece on the gob iron to accompany the burial."

"Hmm, yes, that would be nice, Jeeves" I was loosing the battle to keep a straight face, "What piece did you have in mind."

"Here comes the Bride." Jeeves answered "That's the only tune I can play."

I burst out laughing, I had lost the battle. "Sounds nice Jeeves" I tried to say between laughs "Should create a few tears."

"Of laughter, perhaps, let's go and tell the others" we made our way down to the accommodation deck, on the way down we told everybody that there was to be a flip-flop burial at sea, unexpectedly this created a lot of interest. Obviously, they were as bored as we were. We met Spunky coming out of our cabin; he had a pillow on which to put the flip-flops. With as much solemnity as I could muster, I placed the flip-flops on to the pillow. "Take care of them" I sobbed.

"We are experts at this kind of thing madam" Spunky reassured me.

He started to slow march down the corridor, I walked behind him with my gravest face and Jeeves came up behind with the mouth organ. Behind Jeeves there was TC with his hand stuck up Animal's bum, Tiny Westminister, Pinko who was laughing but mumbling "this is childish," and two or three others from different cabins.

The procession slow-marched down the corridor to the tune of "Here comes the Bride" played very badly by Jeeves, he was trying valiantly not to laugh and was failing. When playing a mouth organ it is imperative that laughing is not done, laughing and playing do not like each other as was clear by the 'music' coming from behind me. Every time he laughed the harmonica emitted a high pitch squeak. "THE FLIP FLOPS ARE DEAD! LONG LIVE THE FLIP FLOPS!" Spunky shouted. Heads popped out of doors all along the corridor, the astonishment that was on their faces soon turned to laughter as the flip-flops on the pillow slowly went past. "They were a lovely pair, I'll miss them" I said to Jock as we walked past. I heard his roar of laughter as I carried on; I looked behind me and saw that the corridor was full of people. We went up the stairs and along the deck, it was quite a procession. From behind me came more cries of "The flip-flops are dead, long live the flip-flops!" and occasionally Jock's booming voice came through with a "Fucking Muppets" which was his favourite derogatory expression. Jeeves' playing had deteriorated to the point where he was blowing through his harmonica and laughing at the same time, it was so bad that Spunky and I were laughing, "Jeeves! That is crap" Spunky laughed.

"I can't help it" ha ha "PAAARP" ha ha.

"You just can't get the staff these days Spunky" I moaned. We reached the middle of the ship and went up to the handrail, "Almighty Sea! Take these flip-flops to your Holy Sanctuary for they have served our slave Bernie well, and now deserve a rest in your watery bosom" Spunky called out to the sea. I noticed that the crowd had gone very quiet except for a few chuckles and a quietly laughed "Muppets!"

"Would sir like to say a few words before the official dumping?" Spunky asked me, and then added "Fucking Hell!" as he looked towards me. I noticed that he was looking past me, I turned my head to see what had caught his attention, and my eyes were greeted with a deck *FULL* of faces. It seemed that everybody was there, the word had gone round and the Troops had come rushing up from the lower decks. We had a huge audience. I spoke in a loud haughty voice "I met the deceased in Cyprus, they served me well in the whore houses of Limmasol and followed me to the whore houses in Germany, never has a foot been more honourably clad in a whore house than when clad in these flip-flops, I shall not forget them"

"We shall not forget them!" Spunky shouted in true Remembrance Day fashion.

"DUMP THE BASTARDS!" I shouted. Spunky upended the pillow and a deafening cheer went up from the crowd. It came from the left, the right, above and surprisingly from below. I looked around, the deck was crowded with laughing, cheering faces, some were not even in the Engineers, on the deck above me were more faces and below, hanging out of the portholes were cheering faces watching the flip-flops' last dive to their watery grave. Spunky turned to me and said between laughs "What'll you do now for flip flops?"

"I've got another pair in my bag; Sandra made me buy them before I left." That was a moving night.

We were banned from using the front swimming pool and certain other areas. They were deemed too good for the likes of us and were only for the use of the Officers. Areas like the beautiful writing room were 'Out of Bounds.' I now had to write in the cabin whilst balancing the writing pad on my leg. My writing was bad enough on a table, with this imbalance it made it totally illegible. The difference in rank really shows up on a ship. On an Army camp, one never ventures near the Officers' mess. It is a taboo area, but on the ship, we were banned from entering certain stairs and doors. I knew that the segregation had always been in the Army but it had never been shown to me in such an obvious way.

Sunday 30th January

Found out today that 3 REME went sick with heat stroke, and today Sandy Shore collapsed from exhaustion. Too much PT in the sun! We did much damage to our botties whilst doing sit-ups. Smudge Smith went sick hoping that the nurse would look at it. No such luck. He had a Matlot Doctor.

Dicey!

Spunky, TC, Jeeves -n- me sat star watching last night and played our gob organs whilst discovering the ' Horns of Amadeus' nick nick club. Very childish but highly amusing

I woke up on this morning with a pain just above my arse; I jumped out of bed and saw that there was a blood stain on the sheets. "Hey Jeeves" I turned my back towards Jeeves, who was still in lying in bed, "have I got a scab above my arse?"

"Look out Jeeves;" Tiny shouted from his bed, "he's after yer bum."

"If I was after anybody's arse, Tiny it would be yours. I'm sure yours is far nicer than Jeeves' hairy thing."

"Er... I'd be far happier if you leave my bum out of this conversation, thank you, and yes you have got a scab above your arse, what the hell have you being doing during the night." Jeeves remonstrated.

"I can assure you Jeeves," I spluttered " that if I was going to jump into bed with anybody it wouldn't be you, and for your information I got this scab from doing them fucking stupid sit-ups on the deck yesterday. Why don't you have one? How many sit ups did you do?"

Jeeves pulled back his sheets and rolled onto his side, on his sheet was the telltale blood stain and like me, a scab had formed above the top of his arse. "Oh shit, I have one as well."

"Eraagh... so do I" came a voice from the other side of the cabin.

"And me." Everybody who had tried their hardest on the Superstars had a large pusy scab on their arse. These wounds would be with us for many, many weeks.

At breakfast, Smudge Smith from MT was complaining bitterly about his scab. He told us that he was going to go sick with it. We all preferred to suffer with the scab rather than go and see a Matlot doctor.

We spent the day on training and in the evening Spunky, TC, Jeeves and I went on to the top deck and drank our two cans of beer. We spotted many satellites and formed a small club that derived from the Monty Python's programmes.

Monday 31st January

My bleeding bum is getting worse, I'm sure. It is all pusy now; I can't get a scab to form. I ain't going to a porthole bender doctor so that he can look at my arse. The Star Gazers club had a good piss about in the pool and in the evening spotted 5 satellites and numerous shooting stars on the sun deck. I'm really missing Sandra now and it's only been 5 days. How I wish she was here.

Not much that I can add to that, so I won't.

Notes for January

Nothing happened today as it doesn't exist.

At the end of every month was a section in the diary for notes. This is all I put for January, at the end of the other months I made a summary of the month on the notes page.

SS Uganda and Ascension Island in background

Tuesday 1st February 1983 South of the Ascension Islands

Sea still boring. At tea time we had Goulash, well, when I got to the hot plate they ran out of -lash. Plenty of gou- but no -lash, so along came this cook and grabbed a GALVANISED BUCKET full of this shit from under the counter and poured it into the Goulash dish. I bet they think Gourmet is a type of washer. Wobbly and Glynn Bryan pissed about in the empty pool so I turned the water on and nearly soaked them. Wrote my Valentine poem.

*****

'My Love'
The words that I write though small and forlorn
Describe the way I feel
But when I left that Tuesday morning
The tears I could not conceal.
So surely now it is quite plain to see
It's breaking my little heart
Not having you besides me
For the time that we're apart.
My love for you is deeper than the sea
And higher than the sky, but without your love to comfort me
I would surely die.

*****

[If I was to earn my living as a poet, I wouldn't earn enough to power up this computer, not with lines like that, but it does display my mindset at the time]

I was on guard, guard duty on a ship! Who the hell was going to creep up on us? I was duty JNCO. It was the best time to spot the dolphins and porpoises. They tended to swim alongside the ship in the early morning. When do dolphins wake up? Are they floating around in the sea and when the sun arises do they stretch their flippers and think 'oh, let's go and race a ship.' Imagine being a dolphin, there is no work, no tax, no road rage and hardly any predators except man. Cool! During the late evening I was given a message to take up to the OC. He was on the top deck, the very top deck, right below the flag. You couldn't get any higher on the ship unless you wanted to climb the flagpole, or radar mast or whatever the tall pointy thing was that stuck up from the top of the ship. So I leave the lower ranks area which is sweaty hot, on bare metal floors and with small portholes which should be, but aren't, closed and enter the WO and Sgt's area. Nice! Polished wooden floors, big portholes which are all open and the area is nice and breezy from the hot wind that blows through the upper decks. I walk up the stairs to the Officers area (I had to be shown the way by Lumpy Phillips) and walk onto carpets. There are no portholes open but the area is cool indicating air conditioning. It is nice and plush, wooden walls make the corridor resemble a sauna. I ask Lt Sugar where I can find the OC and he points up "Up?" I ask, "There is another up?"

"OH, yes, haven't you been there yet?"

"No Sir"

"It is where the Captain and the OC live, prepare for a shock" he pointed towards a stair. I walked up the stair. It was lined with paintings of dead sailors and sea battles that were only 'Great' for the people who read about it in a paper. For those that were there, it was hell! There is nothing 'Great' about a six inch shell or cannon ball smashing through the steel or wood that you relied on to keep you safe. There is nothing 'Great' about a psychologically scarred battle surgeon sawing off your arm with a hacksaw and throwing it out of the porthole without first checking if you have your wedding ring on that hand.

"I say Sir, could I be an awful bore and ask you to take my wedding ring off that hand that you have just cut off?"

"What? Oh, sorry old boy, just thrown it to the fishes"

"Ha ha, never mind Sir, I never liked my wife anyway"

"Ha ha"

"Ha ha"

"Great sea battle wasn't it?"

"Oh yes! Truly great."

"Excuse me now; I have to remove your legs."

I approached a closed door at the top of the stairs; it was frosted like a toilet window. I went to open the door and saw that it wasn't frosted but covered in condensation on the outside. I wrote 'YOU TIT UOY' in the condensation, and opened the door intending to read it on the inside. I was hit by a huge lump of cold. Mr Cold is a fat bastard and is heavier than Mr Hot, when I opened the door a large square block of Mr Cold fell out of the corridor and down the stairs. As it went past my body it made the hairs on my arms stand up. I walked into the rest of Mr Cold and shut the door. The little bit of Mr Hot that had entered the corridor to replace Mr Cold instantly regretted his move as the rest of Mr Cold, who had been too slow to get out of the door, fucked Mr Hot good and proper. Goose bumps so large, that my skin area increased by two football pitches rose on my skin and I started to shiver. An RAF Cpl walked around the corner and laughed at me. I was in shirt sleeved order, which was overdressed down in the bowels of the ship, he was wearing a pullover and peaking out the top of his collar was a tie, he was probably wearing it to stop Mr Heat from escaping out the top of his collar. "Nice here, innit?" he laughed.

"It's bloody freezing, have I walked into the freezer by mistake?" I looked around, if it was a freezer then it was the first freezer that I had ever seen that had shag pile carpet and paintings of even 'Greater' sea battles. "You need a jumper on to work up here." he laughed.

"What do you do then?" I was curious.

"I'm a steward for these" he nodded towards the cabin doors. The doors would not have out of place in the Savoy Hotel. "Who are you after?"

"Bign…Major Smythe, I have a message for him" I corrected myself."

"Hey, give it to me, I'll make sure that he gets it" it was a friendly request not an order. I gave him the message and made small talk about the décor of the place and then left.

As I left the freezer box it was Mr Cold's turn to get rogered by Mr Hot. I walked into an even bigger lump of hot. As I walked down the stairs it got hotter and hotter and sparser. It was like the movie; 'The Time Machine' where it all changes before your eyes, only for me all I had to do was walk down some stairs. I decided to walk right to the bottom of the ship on the excuse of seeing my mate Andy Scott. As I descended I noticed that the ambient noise rose. At the top of the ship in the freezer box was silence. All I heard was the whisper of the air conditioner. As I got lower and lower, sounds that were always there returned, the sea bashing against side of the ship, the throb of the engines, and at the bottom the rumble of the prop shaft. The lower I got the hotter and more humid it got until at the bottom the only difference between being in the sea and the air, was the smell, I was just as wet. A couple of hundred men sweat a lot. Without air conditioners to remove the humidity the air blowers just share the sweat with everyone. I'm sorry dear reader but I could not then and still cannot understand now, why two men live in absolute luxury when there are a hundred men living in hot, humid and noisy conditions just thirty feet below. What makes them any different? Are they sons of God? Were they born divine? Would it upset some great godly plan if everyone on that ship had adequate conditions? I guess that this is a communist idea. Having lived and worked in the former Soviet Republic I know that it was no different for the Communists. There were those at the top with decadent luxury and then the rest in poverty. At least in our system we could work hard and get a decent standard of living. The only people who complain at that are the idle bastards who don't want to work and make their living causing trouble and selling the Socialist Worker on street corners. Send the fuckers to Kazakhstan and let the Kazakhs tell them how the Soviets raped their country and left them with nothing except some radioactive ground, that's what I say.

Wednesday 2nd February

The sea is really rough; lots of people are feeling sick now. Walking is a completely new skill, one second you're heavy, the next you're light. Burrages' feet are forcing me out of my bed space. It was a very boring day. Started limbering up. On a moving ship it is nigh impossible. They want us to 'spring clean' the ship, obviously to save money hiring the staff to do it.

'At last,' I thought as I woke up 'a rough sea.' The horizon in the porthole was rolling from one extreme to the other. When I got out of bed it was all I could do to stand on my feet. "Hey hey hey hey hey, it's fun fun fun time, get out of bed you wankers and try and stand up" I shouted across the cabin. People started to get out of bed and were thrown across the cabin; life had taken on a new meaning. The fun had started. When I bounced my way along the corridor to go to breakfast there was no queue. Bounced being the word, I was bounced from one side to the other and that is how I made my way down the corridor. When I had selected my breakfast and put it on the plate, I had to get from the hot plate to the table, this took three attempts. I would walk forward five paces and stagger back three, forward five, back three. That seemed to be the way to go. When I sat down the plate skidded from one side of the table to the other. I took two seasick pills out of my pocket and swallowed them with some hot tea, no point in relying on nature to keep the vomit down. On the next table to me, Scouse Barley was pushing his sausage around his plate. His face was a yellowy- white. "What's the matter Scouse, gone off sausages?"

"I know that I can eat it, but I don't know how long it will stay down for" he pushed the sausage to the edge of the plate and looked up through the porthole, "Who keeps moving the fucking sea?" He asked. I had cut the white off from the egg and now scooped up the runny yoke and put it, whole, into my mouth. "Well at least it doesn't look like this, Scouse" my ploy worked and he looked at me as I spoke. And as he turned his head, I burst the yoke with my tongue and let it run out of the corners of my mouth. I finished this little performance with a small cough which succeeded in splattering yellow yoke over my breakfast plate. "Oh my God" was all Scouse said as he stood up and ran out of the door. "You forgot to clear up your plate Scouse" I laughed after him. Just then Jock came in, filled up his plate as full as normal with food, and then in only two attempts managed to sit next to me. "How are you feeling Jock?" I asked him.

"Fine," he answered as if everything was the same "why do you ask?"

"I thought the sea might have put you off your food, Jock"

"No fucking chance mate" and with that his head went down and his fork turned into a blur as it shovelled food into his mouth.

"It don't look like many people want breakfast this morning, Jock" the canteen was empty, Jock and myself were the only ones there. Jock looked up from spooning the beans into his mouth to look round, he took a long slow look around the canteen, then his eyes landed on me, he scrutinised me carefully and asked " Don't you get sea sick?" .

"Not with the amount of seasick pills that I have in me"

"Good for you" and he went back to his beans.

The Captain of the ship wanted the soldiers to spring clean the ship. We had our orders of what had to be done, things like, the portholes had to be scrubbed clean, the pipes had to be dusted and wiped, the floors scrubbed, and other sailor type things. "Bugger that" Pinko moaned "I didn't make the ship dirty; why the hell should I clean it."

"For once I agree with you Pinko, who does he think that we are? We are on this ship in order to get to the Falklands, not to clean his ship for him!" Everybody thought the same way as Pinko. There was no way that we were going to clean his ship for him, in fact we were going to do the opposite, and we were *not* going to clean his ship for him. The Captain was coming round to inspect the cabins the next day; it was called Captain's rounds. We all agreed not to clean any thing that we had been told to do. We would take the punishment rather than clean his ship.

Thursday 3rd February

Nobody bothered to 'spring clean', yet the inspection went very well. Two Bum Boys were caught in the act during the early hours of the morning. They were crew. I'm not surprised. Watched Agatha Christy's 'Evil under the sun'. 'Twas good!

The Captain came round and inspected his newly 'cleaned' ship. We were told that he was 'suitably impressed'. It just showed us how often he visited the lower decks, or how easy it was to impress him.

Friday 4th February

We had a talk today on winter clothing. The best piece of kit we have been given, the hat, we are not allowed to wear in Port Stanley AND the SSM won't allow us to wear our Parkas unless it is about -10 and we are on guard. Only 600 miles to go. We get in on Sunday but we won't leave until Monday. Probably a freight party. We got drunk tonight on Malibu and played our gob irons.

The SSM walked to and fro on the plush carpet in the bar that was the WO's and Sgt's mess. The Squadron had been squashed into the bar area because it was the largest room on the ship. The helideck was being used by 15 Sqn for training, so we were in the bar.

Lumpy Phillips walked in. No he didn't, he strode in. Lumpy never walked anywhere; he always strode to places as if in a half march. It wasn't a swagger, Lumpy was not that type, it would never have been called an amble, well, not to his face anyway, no... He strode in to the hall and half shouted to the SSM "All present Sir, none left in the bunks." Good old Lumpy, he refused to adapt the Navy speak like the SSM had.

"Ok, Squadron, listen in, first, I wasn't happy with the room inspection yesterday, just because the Captain was, it doesn't mean that I have to be. Next time you WILL clean your rooms for the Captains rounds" he let it sink in with a moments silence as he looked around the room challenging someone to say something. No one was that stupid. The SSM was always very good with his silences.

"Now, for the good news, your Extra Cold Warfare (ECW) clothes. I will now tell you what you can," pause for effect "and can not wear in Port Stanley." We all looked at one another in amazement, what was he talking about? He continued "Your" another one of his pauses, this one said 'distaste' "Deerstalker hats will not be worn when around Port Stanley," He smiled at the chorus of moans that went up "Neither will the parkas or the gloves. They will only be authorised if the temperature drops to below –10 and you are on a guard where you cannot walk around. You will NOT look like a shower of shit; you will wear the same uniform that you wear in Germany, berets, combat jackets and lightweights. Is that clear?" Heads nodded everywhere, including mine. I had packed all of the above and now had to carry it four thousand miles there and four thousand miles back.

Saturday 5th February

The brass got a signal that people on the Cunard Countess that passed us on the 28th were so pissed that they couldn't get off the ship. We got the bollocking and were told that it won't happen to us on the way back.

We came 7th on the section tests. If they marked it a different way we would have come a lot higher. I'll be glad when we get to the F.I.

Posted San a 9 page letter today. We get into Stanley at 0500 tomorrow, but we don't leave until Monday.

Sunday 6th February

We got a 2 hr talk from the G1 + G4. Then the mail came round. "LCpl Beirne... No Mail"

We are finally in THE FALKLANDS. Not much to look at really, weather is nice. Most of the passengers have left. Stripes and Blues Brothers are on the video. We're going on the LSL Durraint.

Watched people leaving ship in a LCT.

:-(No mail symbol. [Julian: There is no LSL Durraint, it is in fact the RFA Geraint but that is what I believed the name to be at the time so I kept it.]

I stood on the front of the ship, and watched the Falklands come over the horizon. It resembled a Scottish Island; it was all heather with a dull looking grass. The soil looked black, probably peat. We slowly sailed past the outer harbour where many of the ships were harboured and as we passed into the inner harbour I had my first impression of Port Stanley.

"It looks just like a disrupted Rubik cube, TC" we were both leaning on the rail looking over the front.

"We came all the way down here to protect that?" He grumbled.

We dropped anchor in the middle of the inner harbour. Across from us was the LSL Sir Tristram. It was all bombed and burnt out. Dangling on the side were three sheets, in large letters painted on these sheets were the words "STAG ON YOU TURKEYS."

"Funny Greeting" I turned to TC, he had stopped laughing, and he was scowling "Wasthematter?" I asked.

"What the FUCK is that smell?" he twisted his face as he looked round. I turned my face into the wind and it hit me, raw sewage. We walked to the other side of the ship and looked out across the water; there was a large green ship with a white funnel. The smell originated from that ship, of that there was no doubt. "I hope we don't get that ship."

"Well one thing you can bet on" TC said in his best authoritative tone "It ain't for the Officers."

The "HMS Rangatira" as we were later to find out, was mainly filled with the RAF from RAF Port Stanley. Being an ocean going cruiser the sewage was pumped out the back to be distributed by the propeller. It had no treatment facilities. When it was in harbour it…yep you guessed it…. It pumped the sewage out the back to be distributed by the tide. We were later to find out that in the morning when everybody got up and in the evening the stink escalated quite considerably. The Blue Jobs always maintained that they couldn't smell it inside the ship. They would, wouldn't they?

Monday 7th February

We left Uganda and went to the RFA Geraint. It is very packed. We've got 16 in our room and it's a small room. Pinko is in a 42 man room. He and Mark are going to work with 1 Tp. I went sight seeing down Port Stanley. Took a few pics. It is like a shanty town. There is a NAAFI shop that sells everything. Stanley is so peaceful, who'd guess that there has been a war here

We gathered our belongings together, boarded helicopters and flew across Port Stanley to land next to a hospital. After we were all unloaded, we were driven from the hospital to the main jetty. From there we waited and waited and eventually boarded a LCT or Landing Craft Tank. We chugged our way up to the back of a large silver grey landing craft. The rear ramp of the ship was down and we embarked the craft onto this ramp. It led into the middle of the ship which was a large hollow area like a sports centre. We entered corridors at the side of this large garage and found the cabins. I was put into a cabin with some of the Support Troop. Well, to call it a cabin would have brought the wrath of the Trades Description Act against the owners of the ship. It was a thin long room full of beds with small lockers at both ends. The lockers were one foot wide and three deep. That was where we had to store all of our kit. It was impossible, of course. When we entered the cabin we conducted the time-honoured method in the corps of the Royal Engineers of selecting bunks. By elbowing Mac out of the way and by kneeing TC in the leg I managed to acquire the top bunk on the left-hand side. Unfortunately this was one of the worst to get. Mac got one of the converted sofas which were stacked only two high. My bunk was the top bunk of three. I had eighteen inches between the top of the mattress and the roof. I could nearly, but not quite sit up. Still, no one could swamp me in the middle of the night. There were twelve lockers and eleven Sappers trying to get their kit in at the same time. This clearly didn't work so we had to do it in shifts. Taff 'Bagged' the spare locker. In my cabin were, Taff Davies, Mac McGuire, Jock Henderix, Top Cat Furze, Spunky Staynes, and some others.

I walked around the ship and found where all the other guys were berthed. Some were with HQ Troop in a very large room down the corridor. Over the tannoy came an announcement that there would be a boat arriving at the rear ramp of the ship that would take people down to Port Stanley. We had nothing else to do for the rest of the day so I got my coat, my camera, and went to the back of the ship and waited for the boat. After a short while a small chug-a-lug boat burbled its way up to the back of the ramp. It was a RNAR boat, or a Royal Navy Auxiliary Reserve boat. We would come to hate these people; they were the bane of our lives, brought to the Falklands only to make our life a misery. Over the next six months they would treat us like cattle, refusing to let us on their boats, refusing to let us inside when it was bad weather, and even refusing to give us a lift when they drove past us in their trucks. On this occasion the trip passed uneventfully and I disembarked on the main jetty in Port Stanley. I spent the rest of the day walking through Port Stanley and taking pictures. It was destroyed by the war, or so I thought.

The roads were potholed and there was rubbish everywhere. Some of the buildings were burnt out. I located all of the shops in the town, if you could call it the town. It was a blazing hot day and the sun was beating down and making the colours of the houses vibrant. I got some excellent photographs of the green and orange or pink and blue houses. In the centre of the town was The Kelper Store, this was kept supplied by the NAAFI. I took a whole reel, thirty six pictures, of the town. When the picture counter on the camera went to thirty seven I was happy, and when it went to thirty eight I was ecstatic, when it went to thirty nine I was worried. Eventually I opened the back and found that I hadn't loaded the film. David Bailey, watch out!

It was getting late, and I didn't have time to take all the pictures again, so I made my way back to the jetty and got on one of the small boats that took me back to the Geraint.

I was back in time for tea, it was cooked by Chinese cooks, and in fact all the staff that cooked on the Sir Geraint was Chinese. It was excellent, like eating in a Chinese restaurant. We all sat around and talked about our first day in Port Stanley. We were detailed off to different Troops. Pinko went to 1 Troop; I was to work on a new road to a floating hotel.

Tuesday 8th February

"My heart soars like a dove." I got a letter off San today. We went to Stanley Airfield to work. The road side is littered with the

debris of war, bullets, mess tins, dead horses and a plant graveyard. TC was unhappy; he hasn't got a letter yet so Chief Clerk sent him one. San's letter was like finding out that you have won the pools. I was on a high all day. Spunky got Argie goggles and a tin of roast beef, it smelt like Kennomeat! Started teaching Wes Hardy karate. Saw McGus and Shawn Ruddige. ☺

We all got up at the same time and tried to get washed and dressed. It was chaos. After a lot of "pass me this and pass me that" we made our way up to the 'cookhouse' and had our first surprise. The Chinese cooks did not eat breakfast, so neither did we! We made a cup of tea, ate a couple of slices of bread with tomato ketchup, and made our way to the rear ramp.

Port Stanley was covered in a mist; the sun was trying to burn its way through and made the mist glow with its radiance. The Sir Geraint was tied to a harbour buoy and swung with the tide. Right now, we were facing towards the west end of the inner harbour. We could see all of the ships in the harbour; the smelly one, a destroyer, a few small transporters and a large tug. Around these, like angry wasps, buzzed a flotilla of small boats. They would go to a ship, stay for a few minutes and then leave. A helicopter took off somewhere to our right and flew across our heads. A Landing Craft Tank (LCT) turned towards the ship and started to lower its ramp as it approached. Water lapped up the ramp as it made its approach. It made contact with the RFA Sir Geraint's ramp and the LCT's propeller churned up the water as it pushed against the large ship. We all walked onto the ramp and stood in the base of the LCT. It waited for a minute as a couple of men dashed out of the bowels of the Geraint and ran on to the LCT. The ramp was lifted as the LCT reversed and the gap widened between the two ships. As we turned the front pointed towards Port Stanley, a couple of men from 3 Troop ran out onto the ramp and waved their arms. The SSM raised his hand with three fingers and shouted "Three extra's each" over the gap. This raised a chorus of laughs and taunts to the hapless men, who could only watch us disappear towards the jetty.

I was standing at the front of the craft. As we sailed forward, I learned a very important lesson with regards to LCT's. The waves were hitting the front of the landing craft and were being splashed up through the gap between the ramp and the bed of the boat. I and the soldiers around me were getting wet. We pushed back as far as we could but the people behind us weren't having any of it, they pushed us forward. There was nothing to do except grin and bear it. The crisp air was replaced by the salt of the sea, my clothes were speckled with sea water and I could smell the saltiness of the air. A hundred thousand sailors over five thousand years had smelt the same smells. It was all part of the adventure and it was great. "Hey, Bernie," Jock shouted across the boat, he could see the smile on my face, "fish piss in that water!" Suddenly the atmosphere lost its romance. I was getting covered in fish piss!

On berthing at the jetty we jumped across the small gap to the wooden jetty. Yesterday I had to climb up a ladder to get out of the small boat. Trying to grab a slime-covered ladder when the boat that you are standing on is rising up and down is no fun, this was much more civilised. The SSM paraded us on the jetty and we were marched through Stanley towards what would become our Squadron office. WE MARCHED! Like Troops that had just liberated The Falklands from the enemy, we marched. We weren't the first Troops in Stanley, we weren't even the first Engineers in Stanley, and we were just the first Troops who had a pseudo-Rommel as an OC. Locals and servicemen watched us alike, with amazement and scorn probably. We were winning no popularity contests with our victorious march. I suppose with no transport there was no other way of getting there. Eventually we reached our future office. It was called 'The Secretariat'.

The office was next to the hospital, and the helicopter DZ or Drop Zone. Known to the locals as the football field, (they had no idea about military matters). A Wessex helicopter flew in with an under slung load and dropped it on the field. This was the inside bits to the Squadron office. We were detailed off to collect it, carry it to the office, and then under the guidance of the chief clerk, unpack it. This went on all morning. On our third run to the football field (Sorry, Helicopter DZ) we diverted to the hospital and persuaded the nurses to make us a cup of tea. This started a good relationship between our Troop and the hospital. It later blossomed into darts matches and getting so plastered that we had to sleep in the ward beds.

The first item that we set up was the cook's shelter. As soon as we did, the sloppies started cooking. We had lunch and then were trucked up to Port Stanley airfield where we had to take over the construction plant from the out going Squadron. The road from Port Stanley to the airfield was littered with the debris of war. We passed dead horses, piles of bullets, and hundreds upon hundreds of piles of Army kit that the Argies had left. This was the area where the war had finished; the Argentineans sat around in little groups and dumped their mess tins, boots, goggles, gloves and anything else that they didn't want to take back to Argentina. Most of the kit had been burnt, it was so cold when the war had finished that they'd burnt their personal kit in order to keep warm. It was a sorry sight, an Army in defeat. Nobody talked, we just looked.

Just before the entrance to RAF Stanley, was a minefield. It was a barrier minefield, designed to stop us from getting to them on the airfield. It was marked out, to a fashion, with a strand of barbed wire, and one could see that in a corner of the minefield, one of the mines had exploded and had left a large hole. We found out later that the Argentinean soldiers were so bored that they had started to throw stones at the mines. Their mines! A mine doesn't care who it kills, friend or foe makes no difference, it has done its job, and this mine had apparently killed one of the Argentineans and wounded two others.

The airfield was a bustle of activity. Unlike RAF camps in England or Germany, which are normally quite peaceful, this RAF camp was alive. Like the difference between a sleepy country village on a Sunday morning and Piccadilly in London on a Saturday night. There were Blue-Jobs everywhere, they were striding instead of walking, everybody had a purpose and they had to do it now, nobody was taking their time and nobody was standing around talking. Large tents had been erected all over the airfield; personnel were bustling around the tents like ants. Fuel trucks were driving up and down the road and a Hercules C. 130 was winding up its engines. The road took us round the bottom of the runway. As we rounded the bottom a Phantom F4 took off over our heads, its afterburner throwing two large spikes of flame out of the back of the engines. The truck that we were in had no canopy, and we watched it rocket over the top of our heads whilst it rumbled our bones to the very marrow. This was 'Picture War Library' stuff and we loved it. The road doubled back on itself and went back up the other side of the runway. Opposite the control tower was where REME had its workshops. Behind the workshops was a construction plant graveyard, it was all British Army equipment, and for months it was the only place that REME got their spare parts from. Unfortunately some of our plant was in there, the rest of it should also have been in there! We met up with our opposite numbers from 50 Squadron, and started the long haggle over what we would and would not except from them. In the end we were on a losing wicket because in a few days they were getting on to the SS Uganda and were going home, and that was all they cared about. We were going to get the plant whether we liked it or not.

In 50 Squadron Plant Troop I met a few friends of mine, Eddie McGus and Shawn Ruddige. Everybody knew somebody, so we sat around and talked, and talked and talked. A typical conversation would be something like this;

"EDDIE! You old bugger, what are you doing here? Last time I saw you was in Andover in the Queens Head" (I know it is a stupid question, but it gives the soldier time to think of a better question. If the conversation starts with "Hello mate", then your friend has forgotten your name.)

"Same as you Bernie, are you in 75 Squadron now?"

"Yeah"

"Hey, how many days you got to do?"

"xxx" (the number is irrelevant because the person asking knows that he has less than you)

"Ha, Ha, NOBODY has that many! Stag on you turkeys"

Mild friendly laughter "Ha, ha, yes, very good Eddie, are you handing the plant over to us?"

"Can't. We've run out"

"Run out of what?"

"Thursdays! Ha, Ha, Ha"

"Er… Yeah, very good mate"

"Ha, Ha, Ha,"

"Shuddup will ya?"

"Days to do, Days to do, Days to do," (Sung to Souza)

"Fuck off Eddie" Walk off in disgust with the taunting following you in the wind. This we endured until another RE Squadron came to the Falklands and they became the sprog Squadron. We then taunted them.

*****

In the Officers mess the conversation would follow slightly different lines;

"Rodney, I say, what a surprise, haven't seen you since Sandhurst"

"Rupert old boy, are you the OC for 75 Squadron?"

"Absolutely, what?"

"How many days have you got to do?"

"I've no idea, old chap; I've only just got here"

"Ha, Ha, nobody has got that long to do"

"Sorry?"

"Stag on you chickens"

"Are you mad?"

"Days to do are getting few, Rupert old boy, Ha Ha"

"Fuck off, Rodney", Walk off in disgust with the taunting following you in the wind.

*****

But in the Sgt and WO's mess would be heard;

"Hello Lumpy just got here have you? Ha ha ha"

"Call me Lumpy again and I'll smash your teeth down your throat!"

"Er... oh yeah...er... sorry Pete...er... would you like a beer?"

*****

We found an area on the edge of 50 Squadron's territory and started to make a tea hut. Whilst looking for wood for the hut we found a cache of Argie equipment that had been left behind. Spunky found a few cans of meat. We opened the cans and it smelt like dog food. We ate it anyway.

Wednesday 9th February

We left the Geraint @ 0730 and didn't get to RAF Stanley 'till 1100. We fixed an Allis Chalmers. The Sqn lay on a barbecue at the Sqn office. No one wanted to go but we had to. What a night, TC got a letter, Jock got pissed and I laughed so much I hurt. TC took the piss out of the SSM for smoking dope (A cigar) the OC told Taff to quieten us down as the CO was there. That, just made us sing louder. Jock annoyed a Matlot and spilled beer on the floor whilst fighting Andy Scott.

Thursday 10th February

We did fuck all at work today. Getting pissed off going into Stanley to do nowt. Spunky broke his leg. Suspected broken fibula TC found a staff but left it at work. Getting pissed off with the bleeding so called 'air conditioning'. When it was hot it wasn't on now it is cold we can't turn it off.

TC had his first ever wet dream tonight. He puts it down to the fact that he hasn't had a wank yet and his balls are too full. We volunteered for fire / gd duties. God knows why.

The work day consists of sitting and waiting and waiting and sitting. 50 Sqn are supposed to be handing the plant over to us, but they aren't getting it up to our standards. All that they care about is going home.

We were detailed off at 50 Sqn to flatten an area. They gave us a beat up D6c bulldozer with which to do it. I took the first go, worked for a couple of hours, and then handed over to Spunky. At lunchtime I walked over to the D6 and waved to Spunky. "Hey Spunky! its lunch time." I made an eating motion with my hands. He smashed the throttle lever forward, which killed the engine, stepped onto the tracks and did a slow long stretch. "God I'm starving and this machine is knackered" he pushed out his arse and let rip with a long, loud fart, "Parrrrptt" "Aahhh, I needed that" he smiled at me. He was keeping up his reputation.

I laughed at his fart and replied with an appropriate remark for his position, "Spunky, you're a grot" we both laughed and I turned away to walk back to the Rover that would take us to the Secretariat. I heard Spunky land on the ground and shout out in pain, I turned round and saw him roll on the ground holding his leg. I walked the few paces back to him. "Wassup mate?" I asked.

"Landed wrong, I think I've twisted me bloody ankle" his face was twisted in pain.

I crouched down and felt over his leg, there were no bones breaking the skin. "Can you get up?"

"I'll have to, wont I" I helped him to his feet but he was in too much pain to walk so he used me as his crutch and I walked him over to the Rover. Jock and TC came out and helped him into the front seat of the Rover. Not, I might add, with out them taking the piss out of him. It didn't mean that we didn't care for him, in fact the very opposite was the case. If he was a stranger we would have been very business-like, but this was Spunky, one of us. The last thing that he wanted was our pity, so we gave him none. We made him laugh instead.

"Don't get used to that seat, Staynes, it's the Cpl's seat, don't want your arse ruining it" Jock commented with a chuckle.

"It's not his arse that you want to be concerned with, it's what comes out of it that might ruin your seat, Jock" I said loud enough for Spunky to hear. Spunky's reply was to let out another long low rippling fart that made us all laugh. "Oh God, open the window for fucks sake" I shouted.

"Nope" Spunky said with a mock hurt look on his face "Wont!" and that's what the banter was like all the way to the hospital.

It might seem to the non-serviceman that we are callous, that is not the case. Years later I stood over my friend as he slowly died from horrific burns after he was dragged out of his burning house. He was coherent and was bursting for a pee. We persuaded him to have one lying on the ground, he did. We cracked jokes with him. That was on a Friday. He died on the Sunday. On Monday, in the office we were all cracking jokes about him dying. Writing it now seems all very callous and cold hearted but I can remember thinking then that it broke the tension. Our friend was dead and we were in the Army and had to get on with things. We did! Years later as a civilian, I spent a year clearing the minefields with two hundred and fifty other British ex-servicemen. Every time one of us was killed, the atmosphere in the canteen was subdued, but the next morning it was back to the jokes and normal work. The last six months of that year was spent with the same number of American ex-servicemen. When the first Yank was killed we were given three days off and all had to attend 'Workshops' to help us get over the grief. What a load of psychological crap. We, the Brits wanted to say "Pull up your socks, grit your teeth, and get on with the fucking job", but were aware that we were getting full pay for NOT being in the minefields. We weren't stupid, so we went along with it, but we didn't enjoy it. Maybe it is a British trait, forget all that wailing and beating of chests. A stiff upper lip and all that jazz, that's the British squaddie.

We arrived at the hospital and carried in Spunky. He was immediately attended by a group of bored nurses, bored female nurses with skirts and lumpy jumpers. Suddenly Spunky's lot seemed to be better than ours. We were ushered out by the Sister, who was also a bit of a doll and we ambled across to the Squadron office and had lunch.

After lunch we went back to the airfield and dossed around. TC found a stick that resembles a Bo Staff. I persuaded him to take it back to the ship. I had been practising karate for a few years and the Bo Staff was one of my favourite weapons. For the uninitiated, a Bo Staff is basically a broom handle.

At 1800 hours we drove back to the jetty. We parked the Rover up near the jetty and waited on the wooden jetty for a boat to take us to our ship. There were always two Royal Military Police on the jetty, affectionately known as Redcaps or Monkeys. They were always shouting orders at us. They had a little hut on the edge of the jetty. It was called The Cage, as that is where monkeys are normally kept. After being told to keep our hands out of our pockets and to put out our fags for the tenth time, a small boat chugged up and the boat driver shouted "GERAINT, NAVY POINT AND THE SHIT SHIP" which meant the Rangatira. We pushed our way on and rocked our way to the Geraint. We off loaded on to the rear ramp and walked past the stern guard, which was someone from the ship in a little hut. (And not a serious looking man) Into the room, go for a cold shower, up to the galley eat some compo food and then the rest of the night is yours.

TC was dozing in his bunk after tea and woke up with a moan. I was writing a letter to San, we numbered our letters. There was a two to three week turn round on mail.

"Whass the matter Top Cat?" I looked up from my letter.

He looked up at me and laughed "I've just had a wet dream!" I heard Jock laugh from his bunk.

"Aw! That ain't fair, I've never had one, what's it like?" I asked

"It's great, just like the real thing, even down to the wet patch"

"Awww, you grot, what you gonna do, sleep on the wet patch?" Jock laughed

"Just rub it in, it's good for your skin" Mac's smiling face peered out from his bunk.

When the laughter had died down Jock asked "Who were you dreaming about, Ami?"

Top Cat couldn't resist the cue. "No Jock, it was your wife."

Jock joined in, it was all part of the game, "Fuck, that's where she was, I wondered why I couldn't find her in my dream."

"She wanted a REAL man for once, she's had enough of that little bratwurst of yours" TC laughed.

Jock looked up at TC his face deadly serious, he pointed his finger at TC. I thought that TC had gone too far and Jock was angry, until Jock spoke "Just make sure that you leave 50 DM on the side before you leave."

"Hey I got a letter of my wife today, she went down Route Six (A road where the unregistered hookers and soldiers went) and sold her body, she got 300 DM and 50 Pfennings"

"Who gave her 50 Pfennings?" said a voice from the other side of the room.

"THEY ALL DID!" everybody shouted the standard reply and burst out laughing.

"TC" I shouted down, my bunk was at the top "When was the last time that you had a wank?"

"I haven't had one since I left Germany" he was serious.

"Jezus, I've had ten" Mac laughed, after a pause to let the laughter die down, he added "tonight."

"Ah, Mr Valton, I zink your problem is zat your ball bag ist too full, zer body is releasing der sperm through ze application of der vet dream. If you are to be masturbating more often, zen der problem vill disappear."

"OK Dr. Bernie. I'll try"

Just then the SSM walked in, "Strange conversation you are having here boys" he was smiling, we smiled back "I need two men for GD and guard duties tomorrow, any volunteers?"

My mind did a few million calculations in a microsecond. It compared the journey to the airfield and the inevitable boring day with staying in bed and having a lazy day. "Yes Sir, put me down."

TC looked at me and knew that I had a good reason for saying yes and took a chance "And me Sir, I'll do it as well"

"Well, that was easy" the SSM smiled even more "Thanks men, Guard starts at 0545 hours on the rear ramp, one man on guard, one man in the galley, sort it out between yourselves" he tittered to himself and walked out.

Friday 11th February

GD starts @ 0545. We got there at 0730. No matter; captain's inspection so cleaned up the gruel. Went to see Spunky, he is happy 'cos of all of the nurses about. Sister is very nice. I saluted a WREN cadet officer in Stanley high street. I said "Good Morning Marm" and I'll swear that she blushed and coyly saluted back.

MALE DOMINANCE RULES

Got pissed on 'cardi and coke.

TC and I lay in bed until just gone seven o clock. We washed and shaved and went and ate a leisurely breakfast. Over a slow cup of tea TC and I worked up the energy to talk to the cooks. The Captain was having one of his inspections, so we were immediately put on to washing up the pans and plates. We had a quick discussion and I got GDs and TC got guard.

By nine o'clock I was stuffed.

Let me explain. Being a soldier in a 'supposed war zone', (OC's words not mine) we didn't know what was around the corner, so we ate anything that we could, just in case there was no food tomorrow. That was our excuse and we stuck to it. Any sausages that were on the serving plates, any eggs that were going cold on someone's plate, any rashers of bacon that had congealed in an inch of pig fat went into our mouths. Wash this down with a gallon of tea and you now know what I mean when I say 'stuffed'. After the 'General Duties' (pan wash) was finished the time was my own until tea time when the guys came back.

I decided to go and see Spunky, or the nurses, either would do.

I caught the first boat that graciously touched down on our rear ramp and bobbed my way over the Port Stanley's main jetty. Berthed next to the large wooden jetty was the Sir Tristram. It was bombed in the war and was burnt out. The hole in its side where a bomb entered was on show for all to see. Living on the Tristram was a Squadron of Engineers. In amongst the burnt out decks were living quarters for a score of men for six months. I talked to a couple of them who were sitting around smoking. They had moved from living in the bombed out houses to the ship. To them the ship was paradise. I then realised how lucky we were on our ship. It was all relative. At the end of the tour we moved into a beautiful floating hotel. When our replacement Squadron arrived all they did was moan at the conditions. To us it was heaven. Life is all relative.

I walked to the hospital and saw Spunky. He was also in heaven. He had a hairline fracture and was going to spend some time in the hospital. Every night he joined the nursing staff in their bar that was at the rear of the hospital. For hospital, visualise a one storey, wooden community hall. It was bedded out with Army issue beds and had an office for the staff. Somewhere was an operating room, or a room that was used to sew up people. Toilets were outside and the food came from 75 Squadron's cook's tent. BUT out the back was a small twenty foot square storeroom that was kitted out as a bar. The place rocked. Any patient that could hobble was usually to be found there. In the morning they slept in to get over their hangovers. I bade Spunky farewell and after checking for mail in the Sqn office took a walk around Stanley. There was a definite lack of women. I was walking along the front which was a long road between the houses and the sea, it is always featured on the TV shots of the war, when coming towards me I saw a WREN officer cadet. They have a blue patch on their shoulders. She was around five foot nothing, I was six foot two. The gap closed and the inevitable eye contact happened over the last fifty metres. She saw me and looked down I saw her and looked at her tits, she looked up at me again and I quickly looked over her head in case she saw me looking at her tits. She looked down again and my eyes shot back to the tit region again, eyes up, eyes away, eyes down, tits, legs face (the order of the first two may vary but never with the third). By the time we reached saluting distance I had stripped her naked, made mad passionate love to her, smoked a cigarette, borrowed ten quid and left her life for ever. The path was not wide enough for us to pass without one of us moving to the side. I was the junior rank so it would have to be me. At ten paces she still had her face to the ground and was going to pass me without looking up. Tired of her body I wanted see her face, there was a way. I threw up a salute and finding my deepest Arnie Schwarzenegger voice said "MORNING MARM!"

She looked up, saw me saluting and waiting for her to pass, and blushing bright red, smiled, saluted, and looking to the ground again slipped past. The poor girl was going to have to go through that thousands of times during her tour of the Falklands. Most of the men were not Officers and would love to salute her. Some would even run round the block to salute her again. It takes a special type of person to put up with that.

Later that night, after writing to Sandra I visited the bar which had been set up on the tank deck. Many Bacardi & Cokes later I climbed up into my pit and fell into a deep sleep, and woke up at one thirty in the morning and threw up my tea.

Saturday 12th February

Spewed up my beautiful tea at 0130 this morning. Pinko is going to be a daddy. He got a telegram. TC said that his mum died, SSM laughed. We built the rest room, it was good fun. I got 2 letters off San. A Valentine and lots of bills. I started practising with the staff and German. The bar opened tonight but I didn't go, bloody booze only makes you sick. I'm really missing San, how am I going to survive 5 ½ more months??

The mail was handed out at lunchtime. The SSM came down to the airfield and got us round in a group and handed out the mail. I received a handful of letters, and a Valentine card. It was huge and smelt of perfume. I got a ribbing from the guys but it just made me happier, because I had someone to write to me.

We opened our mail and read it; Pinko kept his unopened in his map pocket. I did that once and the letter got wet and smudgy, so I always read them immediately. "Why don't you read your letters, Pinko?" Jock Asked.

"I ain't reading my letters here with you" he looked at us with distaste when he said 'you'.

"What's wrong with us then, Pinko?"

"Well look at you" we looked at ourselves. We were sitting on the ground which was all peat on the Island. TC was deep in thought and didn't look up, Jock let out a fart and Mac puffed away on his cigarette. "What's wrong with us?" I couldn't see the problem.

"I don't want to soil the memory of Susan with visions of you lot."

"He doesn't want to soil his pants with us in vision, more like" Mac chuckled.

"Well… maybe that as well" Pinko laughed.

The SSM walked over to our little group, "Everything alright lads?"

TC looked up at the SSM, his eyes were sad and empty, "No… Sir" he said quietly "my mother's dead"

The SSM laughed, turned on his heel, and walked away. There was a stony silence in the group. I stood up not knowing what to do but felt that I had to do something for my friend, I walked over to TC and squatted down next to him, his eyes were on the ground in front of him and he said nothing.

I put my arm around his shoulder, all the rest of the group were watching me, there was sadness in their eyes, and they felt Top Cat Furze's pain with him.

I spoke quietly "Is that what your letter said Top Cat? That your mother was dead?"

He looked up at me, I saw that there was deep pain in his eyes, when our eyes met I felt a shiver go through my body, Top Cat's face contorted and I could see that he was on the verge of crying "Haaaaaaa ha ha," he laughed! He was laughing! "No! Did it fuck, me mother's been dead ten years, but that bastard laughed, the SSM laughed when I said that me mum was dead. He'll pay for that"

"You bastard" I shouted and pushed him over onto his side, we wrestled for a minute, or to be more precise I wrestled him whilst he laughed uncontrollably

The joke was on me, and I joined in the laughter although I tried hard not to, it was infectious.

Back in the boat that night, I decided to give the bar a miss. I had spent the night before throwing up in the little toilets so I had no desire to do the same again. I lay on my bed and wrote to Sandra, I replied to her letters and felt very far away from her. It was only five weeks that we had been separated, but already I was missing her like hell.

Sunday 13th February

We had the morning off but had to catch the 1030 ferry (work) I did nowt @ 15 Sqn. resources, so we went to 15 Sqn. Plant where I found an armour piercing and some Argie 1" very flares. The rest of the Sqn. had to run up Sapper hill on their day off. Why can't

they just leave us alone? The dormitory is starting to get on everybody's wick. It's too cramped.

75 Squadron had the morning off today, but not us. We had to work. We were supposed to go in and prepare the plant for take over from 50 Sqn. Again, 50 Sqn weren't interested so TC and I wandered around the area that 15 Sqn plant was in, we found a cache of armoured piercing shells and Very flares. Not a fantastic find as they were littering the road all the way to Port Stanley, but it kept us amused for a few hours. When we got back on the boat we were in deep shit. Luckily I was just a lowly Sapper. There were full Cpls above me whose job it was to take the shit from those in higher places. We were supposed to join the squadron in a run up Sapper Hill. Sappers running up Sapper Hill. Good one, eh? Jock and Taff tried to explain to the SSM but he wouldn't have any of it.

Monday 14th February

We got a bollocking today (HQ) for not parading for PT. The fact that we were working has nowt to do with it. Apparently the OC wants us to do the Para yomp from Goose Green to here. 70 miles. He must be off his fucking head. We put the window in the hut and Top Cat lost his keys for the third time.

Today our contribution towards the war effort was to hammer a window into our hut, the Support Troop doss room. It was how we passed the time until someone up above decided what we were to do. Word came down through the grapevine that the OC reconfirmed that he wanted 75 Sqn to do the same march that the Para's and Marines did. I would rather break my leg first. We sat in the tea room and smoked and talked. We would talk about anything and everything. TC was in love with his girlfriend Ami. He hadn't had a letter from her yet. Neither had Mac had a letter from his wife. All of the other pads (A 'PAD' is a term used to describe a married person in the Army. They were given a 'PAD' to live in. Pad's Patch was the married quarters, a Pad's Brat was the child of a married person in the Army, Pads wife… etc) had had a few letters. We all thought that someone was porking her, but we didn't say that to Mac.

Tuesday 15th February

Happy Anniversary babe! God knows how we've done it. Its 3 years now. Wow! [← Written by Sandra before I left.]

I celebrated by not working too hard. The above really cheers me up when I look at it. We put the floor in the rest room and "Brown stuff" on one wall. Apart from that we did sweet FA AGAIN. Someone threw an air bottle overboard. The SSM bollocked us for dirty rooms. A RMP stopped our wagon for no indicators even though on the front was written "NO INDICATORS."

Written in my diary was the above text from Sandra. She had written it before I left and I only saw it when I turned the page. It warmed my heart. It was like Sandra talking to me over this great distance. On the airfield we concentrated our efforts on to the hut. We broke apart a couple of pallets and put them in as a floor. No more mud for 75 Sqn Sappers. We found some brown paper that lined the ammo crates. That was nailed to one wall as wallpaper. It gave the room a certain 'Crappiness' feel that is so important in home made tea rooms.

SSgt Benjamin Byrne came looking for us, he saw Jock standing outside the hut and came across. We were sitting inside the hut smoking and drinking the tea that we had brewed up on a small wood fire. He walked up to Jock and started talking to him in the doorway, he hadn't seen us, "Jock, the SSM needs a working party, where are your guys? I need you to get a party of…"

"Oi! You're in the light, would you mind moving please, Staff?" TC called out from inside the hut.

"What the fu..?" Benjamin looked into the hut and saw twelve Sappers sipping tea and taking it easy. His face broke into a huge grin that showed off his large Jamaican smile. "Well, would you look at this, you POM's know how to take it easy"

"Do you like the wallpaper, staff?" TC nodded at the one piece of brown paper nailed to the wooden wall.

Benjamin looked at the paper after he had taken TC's tea off him, a chuckle escaped past the official face that he was wearing and his demur changed. Benjamin was the first son of Jamaican parents that had come to the 'Mother country' to get a better standard of living. He was born in Manchester and both his father and mother had worked on the buses. His father had wanted something better for him and so after he had left school with top grades he had applied for the Army. All of the Infantry and Guards units had refused him a place. The Royal Engineers had welcomed him with open arms. Racism is virtually unheard of in the Sappers. The way to get abused in the Sappers was to be a knobber. Benjamin was not a knobber, in fact he was the very opposite. He did so well that he was promoted to SSgt at a very young age. He tried to be a hard nosed Senior NCO, but loved to revert to his roots, which being Jamaican was to take things easy and enjoy life. With Support Troop, he found the atmosphere to be much like himself. We knew that and welcomed him to our clique.

"Man, you got it good here. We SNCOs haven't even got a kettle in the Secretariat. Everybody is running round kissing the OC's arse!" Benjamin told us between sips of TC's tea. TC was wide eyed and looking in turn at Benjamin and his disappearing tea, he had an incredulous look on his face. It was all put on, we all knew that and we played the game. Benjamin saw his look and asked him "Do you want your tea back TC, bearing in mind that I have to find a works party?"

TC laughed and sat back "No No, Staff, you can have it all. I just wanted to make sure that it was hot enough for you"

"It's fine thank you, TC." Benjamin refused the four mugs that were thrust towards him.

"What's the gen from the Head Shed then, Benjamin?" Jock asked.

"Oh, man. The OC wants to do the walk that they did during the war, all of the knocker SNCOs are telling him what a good idea it is.

If they do do it, I will have to change my library books or something. There is no way that I am going to walk eighty miles."

"We're with you there Benjamin" there was no way that I wanted to walk eighty miles either; the practise that we did in Germany was bad enough. This was the bollocks. Benjamin was always good for getting us the inside information from the Head Shed.

"Have you found out about the fishing yet Benjamin?" Mac asked. Benjamin was a keen fisherman, as were Jock, Taff, and Mac. "Oh yes, I did. I almost forgot to tell you, Jock." Benjamin looked towards Jock even though it was Mac that had asked him. "I have arranged a fishing trip for us; I'll get more details later. Are you on?"

"You bet there isn't much to do here right now"

"What you mean not much to do?" TC asked in mock anger "you have the other three walls to paper yet, and then lay the tiles" TC's arm swept across the cabin "put in the fireplace, clean the windows, plumb in the shower and install a WC. You ain't going anywhere until you finish that." Jock's answer was to grab TC round the head and wrestle him to the ground with a big grin on his face. TC was laughing as well.

Benjamin left half an hour later. He had told us all of the gossip in the Head Shed and had drunk all of TC's tea. We had gained a SNCO as a friend. We knew that because as Benjamin had left he had declared that he would find some Knockers for a works party. That suited us just fine.

Written in chalk, on the front and the back, of the Bedford truck that we had was, in large capital letters, 'NO INDICATORS'. It related to the fact that there was limited room on the re-supply ships and planes. Indicators were 'dues out', (meaning in true military parlance that that was the time when they were due in, and not due out? Er… OK) for September 1983. It was February 1983. We would not see the indicator bulbs during our stay on the islands. Our bulbs were all broken, hence the sign. This concept was all too much for a pair of Royal Military Policeman who saw our lorry parked on the potholed main road of Port Stanley. We had stopped off at The

Kelper Store, one of Port Stanley's main shops, and also the shop that the NAAFI was supplying. It was on one of the main crossroads in Stanley. For crossroads read cross tracks, the roads were in a terrible state. They were built for the occasional Landrover's. They didn't stand up to half the entire Argentinean Army tracking across them; they were covered in pot holes and certainly had no road markings. Outside The Kelper Store was a huge shipping container that contained a generator, which fed electricity into Port Stanley. It was run by a couple of Sappers. The Kelper Store had a green wooden front and two large white lined windows in the front; it was the most shop-looking shop there. The store on the other side of the road was called Kelvin Store. It had two small windows in one was a display of air fresheners in the other a row of baked bean tins nicely heating up in the sun. Its door resembled a toilet door and the whole store shouted "KEEP AWAY! DO NOT SHOP HERE!" so we didn't. In a wall to the right of The Kelper Store was a silver cigarette machine that had had the glass smashed. I wondered if the Argies had smashed it or was it errant kids on the island. We entered the store even though it had a notice on the door stating that there was No Unauthorised Entry Allowed Unless on Official Business. "What the fuck does that mean?" Taff asked his hand on the door knob. "It means no Welshmen allowed, now get the fuck in" Jock laughed and pushed Taff in through the door. "Are we allowed to shop in here, then?" Taff asked one of the two women behind the counter. She looked puzzled until Taff pointed towards the notice. "Oh yes, of course you are, that is just to keep people out who only want to look at the goods and not buy. "It's a fucking NAAFI" Top Cat's voice came from behind me. "Oops, sorry missus" he put his hand over his mouth when he saw the two women standing behind the counter. They smiled at his embarrassment, TC was correct in his observation. It was stocked with NAAFI goods. It had the survival type of barmy stuff that was found in NAAFIs all over the world along with NAAFI labelled biscuits, coffee etc. even the girls had on NAAFI uniforms. We had a look around and I bought Dhobi dust (NAAFI), biscuits (NAAFI), Marmite (Non NAAFI), and boot polish (KIWI).

On coming out there was a RMP standing behind the truck writing in his notebook. He was taking the number of the truck. He might have let it go at that had it not been for us lads getting into the back of the truck. A steady stream of helpful comments flew towards the policeman.

"Hey look guys, a Monkey that can write"

"A bit young to be out at this time isn't it? Does your mother know that you are out?"

"What are you doing, Corp? Collecting truck numbers? Couldn't you find any trains out here then?"

The RMP ignored all of the taunts and carried on writing. Only when the truck's engine started did he show any sign of panic. He quickly walked around to the cab and shouting to Taff, who was driving, climbed up onto the footplate. I was in cab with Jock and Taff.

"Did you know that this is a double yellow line, no parking zone, Cpl?" the RMP Cpl asked Taff.

Taff's answer was to burst out laughing, as did Jock and myself. "Where's the yellow lines then Boyo?" Taff looked out the front windscreen at the muddy potholed track that served as the main road in Port Stanley.

"It has been on garrison orders and on all of the unit orders that outside The Kelper Store is a no parking zone."

"Ah, well we have only just got here last week. We haven't had time to read them yet, mate" the RMP twitched at Taff's use of the word 'mate'.

"No excuse, and what does 'No Indicators' on the front mean, Cpl?" the RMP was trying to regain control of the situation. It wasn't helped by the laughter and taunts that were still coming from the rear. Taff turned his head to look at us in exasperation. He had a 'Can you believe this idiot' look on his face. He slowly turned to look at the policeman and spoke slowly as if he was speaking to an idiot "It… means… that … we …have … no… indicators." The pitch of

Taff's voice rose on the word indicators as if it was a great discovery he had just revealed

"Why?" the RMP Cpl was now demonstrating his interrogation techniques.

"Because there aren't any indicator bulbs on the Island" Taff's voice was becoming strained. He was trying to stay amiable and was loosing.

"We don't have any problems getting any for our Landrover's" the Cpl argued satisfied that he had broken Taff's alibi.

Taff looked at the RMP short wheel based Rover before replying, "Your Rover is 12 volt, this truck is 24 volt" Taff raised his eyebrows and smiled in the knowledge that he had got one over on the RMP.

"Well use a brake light then!"

"They have double pins on the end, an indicator bulb has only one, and it wouldn't work. Any more ideas, Einstein?" Whammo! Got ya. Taff's smile was total. He turned round and looked at us in triumph. We laughed. That didn't help the RMP with his ego. He went into full military mode.

"Look, *CORPORAL*! You have three in the cab when it is only designed for two, you have no indicators when there is no excuse for it and you are parked in a no parking zone. What is your name, rank and unit?" he jumped down and got out his notebook. A mistake as he was now being looked down on by Taff.

"Cpl Davies, 75 Field Support Squadron, Royal Engineers, mate"

"Right I shall be putting a report in to your OC, now move on and get the indicators fixed" the RMP ordered.

Taff looked at us with a smile. Jock laughed at his predicament and managed to say "Best move on Taff before he arrests you" between laughs.

Taff drove off and spent the rest of the evening complaining about 'Coming eight thousand miles to get a parking ticket'. The whole affair amused the lads in the back of the truck immensely, who, to be honest, had started it all. It was around the Squadron two minutes after the bar opened, helped on by mine and Jock's highly exaggerated testament.

Wednesday 16th February

I worked with Two Troop today on a Muirhill. It bogged in twice; the peat is useless to work in. I had to fit a backactor on so I went up to the airfield and got REME to put one together and put it on.

I got to the boat at 10° 'clock p.m. The drunken Matlots from HMS Antrim nicked the Kiwi so I went by CSB.

Another nice day! It was 06:30 and we waited on the ramp of the Geraint for the first boat to come by. There were various types of boat flitting around the inner harbour, large Landing Craft, Kiwis and CSBs in order of size. A Kiwi phutt phutted up to the ramp and fourteen soldiers clambered on. These small boats were sailed by the Royal Navy Auxiliary Service. *After researching this, I really don't have a clue who these guys were. Either the RNAS or the RNR or the RNVR or maybe even the RN??? All I can say for sure is that they were Matlots who drove the little boats as opposed to the Matlots who drove the big ships.*

Anyhow they gave priority to the Navy and would refuse soldiers if there were [real] Matlots waiting. This boat had gone to Navy Point and found no one waiting so, begrudgingly, had come to us. We sat on the top deck and enjoyed the ride in; it was a beautiful summer morning. The Falklands is the other side of the world to England and, like Australia has its seasons in reverse. That is where the similarity to Auz ends. Taff sent me to 2 Troop. I was cutting the top soil off, again and again the machine bogged in to the peat almost as soon as I had broken the surface. Working construction plant on the Falklands peat was an art. An art, that 50 Squadron had learned but refused to pass on to us, all they were interested in was going home. In six months I would feel the same. The Knockers pulled out the Muirhill with a dumper and I drove up to the airfield to fit a backactor. I spent the day digging trenches with the backactor. At nine thirty it got too dark to work so I scrounged a lift from a passing RAF lorry and made my way to the jetty. The area was full of Matlots from the destroyer HMS Antrim. They were shit faced; being drunk in Port Stanley was an offence that the RMP would happily jail you for. Unless you were a sailor so it seemed. There was the usual RMP Cpl and Sgt in their little hut and they were conspicuous by their absence. I booked in with them, as all inhabitants of the inner harbour had to, and waited for a boat. The sailors were laughing and falling over. They had finished an **arduous** four week journey from UK to the Falklands and were now letting off steam. A Kiwi came in and I went to get on, the RNXS sailor put out his palm and refused me passage on to the boat, he then waved part of the drunken party on. There must have been thirty sailors crowded on to the top of the boat. Fourteen was the maximum that were allowed. I muttered under my breath and shuffled towards the rear of the crowd, there were still a large crowd of sailors and I was going to be last.

"Hey, Bernie, is that you?" a cockney voice shouted from the other side of the jetty. I walked over and saw Titch Fuller sitting on a CSB. It was getting dark and I hadn't seen him when I first walked up. "Yeah, it's me, what you doing here, Titch?" Titch was a cheerful cockney; he was part of 2 Troop but had been detached and sent to the CSBs. This proved to be a blessing for the Squadron for the entire duration of the tour.

"I've been detailed off to the CSBs. This is my job for the next six months"

"You jammy bastard, how did you get a job like that?"

"I did a course three years ago in Bremen, you need a ride to the Geraint?" he nodded to the CSB.

I didn't need asking twice. I climbed down the ladder to the CSB jetty and climbed on to the back of the small boat. There was room for four people in the back of the boat, I sat down there.

"Not there," Titch laughed "you'll get soaked, stand up here with me." The front of the CSB had two glass windows and a small roof. It had no rear but, as I found out later, it didn't need one. I stood up and started to walk towards the front, a walk of only three paces, "well let go rear then, Bernie" I looked at Titch, he was looking at me and then at the rope that was tied to the back of the boat. As I climbed over the engine compartments, Titch started the engines. I removed the rope from the bollard that it was tied to and immediately fell head first onto the last piece of metal between me and the water. The reason for this careless imbalance was because Titch had just opened the throttles on the mighty Jaguar engines that were now running at nearly full throttle underneath my belly. I looked forward to Titch who between steering the boat and monitoring the gauges was glancing back and laughing. The CSB had the acceleration of a motorcycle, staggering my way to the front Titch laughed "You alright?"

"No! I nearly went over"

"Look on the bright side"

"And what is that?"

"It could have been me!"

"You've been talking to Jock, that's his saying"

Titch pointed towards a set of red and green lights bobbing on the water "Isn't that the boat that refused to let you on?"

"I think so." I could only see lights.

"Watch, they hate this." a grin appeared on his face as he fully opened up the throttles on the two engines, I discovered what the bar was for at the front of the cockpit. It was for holding on to for dear life. If it hadn't been there I would have tumbled ungracefully into the back again, this time I stayed cool, grabbed the handle and stood in the macho manner befitting the occasion. We rocketed our way towards the lights. It was indeed a Kiwi and had a mass of sailors on the top. As Titch went past the boat a huge bow wave hit the side of the Kiwi and pivoted it through nearly forty five degrees. This was revenge and it felt good! The RNXS sailors shouted abuse at Titch but the RN sailors were too drunk to care and screamed with laughter. Within thirty seconds we had bumped our way over the waves to the Geraint. I thanked Titch and went to my room, a hot shower awaited me as it was ten o'clock and the water had heated up again after the six o'clock rush. I didn't even have the energy to write to Sandra, I just flopped up into my bed and immediately fell asleep. Another day in paradise!

Thursday 17th February

A good day at work today. Chris Lucas helped me get un-bogged twice, repair a split fuel feed pipe, get un-bogged again, fill the Muirhill up with diesel, get un-bogged again and put 10 gallons of OM mixed into the hydraulic tank. It's the hardest I've worked since I got here, and the most enjoyable day. I think I'll write to my beautiful wife as I miss her.

The SNCO that was on duty entered the small cramped berth where I and another twenty soldiers lay sleeping. "HANDS OFF COCKS, HANDS ON SOCKS. RISE AND SHINE YOU WANKERS"!

Lumpy Phillips shouted into the berth, he was a true old style soldier. Harsh and brash, he was a man who knew his combat engineering. I heard a few people stir, nobody got out of their pits, no one jumped immediately to the floor including me. "I'll be back in a few minutes" Lumpy hissed. The veiled threat in his voice was clear, it was 'be in your beds when I get back and I'll make your life hell'.

He would as well, no one messed with Lumpy. He was nicknamed Lumpy because he had a large lump on the side of his neck, you couldn't not, look at it, but you also couldn't let him see you looking.

I heard a sheet being dragged off a body and a few groans as that person stretched and stood up. Slowly, with a moan I rolled over in bed, 'just a few minutes more please' I pleaded to the God of sleep, I opened my eyes and looked at the roof of the berth that was eighteen inches above my head. Everybody had put string across their bunks and had strung towels across. It gave us a little privacy in those cramped conditions. I pulled the towel across and was confronted with a sight straight from my worst nightmare. Jock was standing in the middle of the six foot by three foot floor space totally naked. If that wasn't enough he had the remains of a seven o'clock hard-on parading between his legs. You didn't have to be gay to notice that it was huge.

Jock noticed that I had opened the curtain but pretended that he was doing nothing out of the ordinary. He was hoping that someone would comment on the size of his knob. Being a good friend I didn't let him down; "Fucking Hell Jock! What is that?" I pointed towards his member. He smiled his wide, chin out smile and innocently answered "What?"

"That!" I shrieked "That currywurst that is hanging between your legs, where did you get it?"

TC was usually the last to rise in the morning. It used to take a small nuclear explosion to get him out of bed. This morning his head popped out from his towel curtains to stop six inches from Jocks' member. He spluttered, trying to find the words to over come his shock at seeing that monstrosity so early in the morning, "What the f… do… it… get… get that 'Thing' out of my way Jock"

Mac had his head out into the aisle now "Jezuz Jock, did you get that transplanted from a donkey?"

Jock's chest had expanded by around two inches now, he laughed with pride, but still he stood there, stark bollock naked with a semi-lobon.

"Hey Jock, move to the left a little bit will you?" I asked "you are blocking the light from the porthole." Laughter all around! "No wonder your wife is so short sighted, if you stick that monstrosity up her."

Jock enjoyed the comments; he bathed in the glory for a few more minutes before walking out the room to the heads, still naked and still looking for praise. I guess if you have it, you flaunt it. I noticed that everyone else put on a towel to get up me included, no chance of comparison then.

It was a long and hard day at work, but very enjoyable. Time flew when you were occupied. Sitting in a shanty built tea hut doing nothing, made each second last three seconds and each minute last an hour, but when we worked, we would often work through our tea break because we were enjoying it so much. That made time fly.

I slowly discovered what it is like to work on the peat of the Falklands. A good analogy would be to say that it was like working on an old BLANCMANGE. If a tyre broke through the crust the machine would immediately bog in. Trying to drive out only resulted in the machine getting deeper and deeper in the gluey peat. The next week was spent seeing how far one could push the peat. The peat had been there a million years and didn't care if we spent two hours digging out a Muirhill only to turn too sharply when driving out of the quagmire and bog it in again. During this first week the Plant Operators' name was mud, or more appropriately Peat.

It is an unwritten law in the British Army that if someone gets your vehicle out of the mud you buy him a few beers, usually a crate or a six pack. The Oggies loved to remind us of this and we had to pay our dues at the bar in the evening, this blancmange was costing me my salary.

I drove the Muirhill down to the location of the road and saw 2 Troop's Bedford. I parked up behind it and saw SSgt 'Homer' Simpson. He walked over to me and the scenario went something like this:

"Ah, LCpl Beirne, we've been waiting for you," wow, I thought, I'm important, they've been waiting for *me!* "Do you see the pegs that the surveyor, Cpl Tasker, has put in?"

I nodded "yes Staff"

"Well dig out the peat between the pegs until you get down to the rock, Ok?"

"Yes Staff, Ok"

I positioned the digger perpendicular to the road, everyone from 2 Troop is now watching me. The Muirhill slowly creeps forward as I point the bucket teeth into the peat. The bucket starts to take a large cut out of the soft peat, the wheels are still on the roadway. As the bucket cuts a large swathe into the ground the front wheels come off the road onto the peat, spin through loss of friction and bed themselves up to the axles, into the soft caramel-like soil.

Everybody bursts out laughing except two people, Homer Simpson and me. Homer was cursing me to hell, and I was waiting for the earth to open up and swallow me so that I didn't have to face the taunts of 2 Troop. The earth being the bastard that it is fails in my simple request and I have to climb out of the Muirhill amidst laughs and taunts and I pointlessly look at the large four foot wheels buried in brown goo up to their middles.

"You fucking dickhead Beirne, can't you get this simple task right?" it wasn't a question.

"Sorry Staff, it just went in"

"You'll fucking well go in if you do it again, you wanker" he looked around "Lucas, get the Bedford and pull this prat out."

Chris Lucas was a driver from MT or Motor Transport. MT was part of HQ Troop and he therefore was classed as 'one of us' and not a Knocker this aside, he was still laughing when he got into the truck.

The truck was attached to the rear of the LWT and it pulled it out. I tried again and this time took a very small cut with the bucket, not wanting to put too much strain onto the peat. As the rear wheels hit the goo all four started to sink. I stopped immediately, endured the laughter, and was pulled out again. Back I went in again. I got a bit further this time, but when Chris tried to pull me out he got bogged in as well. This time I laughed as well. Homer, well known for his temper, or rather his lack of it, blew up, and cursing us all to hell, got into his Mercedes jeep that had been left by the Argies, and sped off towards Port Stanley. We stopped a passing truck and used that to pull Chris's Bedford out. After finding a tow rope we pulled out the Muirhill. I didn't want to get bogged in again so I started to dig out the peat with the backactor bucket. I had just started to get going when the engine died. Air had got into the fuel system and I bled the air out with the help of Chris.

The fuel gauge was broken, as was the front brake system, the handbrake, front windscreen, heater, drain tap on the left air tank, the left air tank, crab steer system and the bucket self levelling device. All in all it was a piece of shit, but it was a working piece of shit. All of the others were u/s [or unserviceable]. By the end of the day I could hardly keep my eyes open, even the open topped ride in the Bedford back to the jetty didn't bother me. Inside my head I was already asleep.

Friday 18th February

The Muirhill bogged in again today about a million times. Friday the 13th Part 2 is on. A LCT lost its ramp the other day so we have to load from the side. A Sapper found an A/T mine just outside 15 Sqn. resources porta-cabin. He was kicking it as you would kick a tin can. The OC managed to get a 75 Sqn. flag on the ship. Sapper (smelly) Benny pissed his bed and sleeping bag and consequently is banned from the bar for 1 month. Good.

Sapper Benny was sent to us from another Squadron that was on the Falklands. We weren't told why, but we soon found out. He was a Plant Operator and therefore was sent to our Troop. He was a six foot four inch bumbling giant. Taff took an instant dislike to him, probably because he was as tall as Taff.

He was sent to work on the airfield with Jock. Jock soon discovered that he was hopeless at servicing and fixing plant so Jock put him into the quarry with 15 Squadron, he was too slow working the excavators, and they sent him back. Everybody has a forte in life, Benny hadn't yet discovered his. He did that night; most of the Squadron were in the bar in the Geraint. It was set up on the tank deck. The usual routine was to get back from work, shower, eat and bar. I tried to fit in some exercise. I had started to learn karate in Germany and had set up a punch bag on the deck. I would kick hell out of the bag, shower, write home to Sandra and if I wasn't too tired, go to the bar. Spr Benny was there this night; he was the sort that didn't fit in. He was on the edge of the bar and was laughing at all of the jokes and fun but would never chip in. Occasionally I heard him join in only to be immediately shot down by the bar smart ass, so I guess he had learned to keep quiet. He never seemed to get too drunk and on this night it was no different. We were discussing the size and names of penises. Harry was a small thin clerk from the Squadron office. He had a dry wit. It was out gunned by Jaffa's. Jaffa was a Yorkshireman, "and fukin' proud of it lad." He had that Yorkshire way of saying things. A way that I will try to replicate here, but being from the Fens myself will probably fail. My apologies, to all Yorkshire men out there. (Not really).

*****

Harry: So Jaffa, how big is your cock then?

Jaffa: Cock? Cock? Who's got a bloody cock? Not me mate, mine is far too large to be classed as a 'cock'.

Harry: Well if you haven't got a cock, what have you got?

Jaffa: A fukkin wanger.

Laughter across the bar.

Harry: (laughing) A wanger? What the hell is a wanger?

Jaffa: It's like a cock only bigger, much bigger.

Bernie: (Walking up to the bar from the gym area) Jock's got one of those!

Jock is chuckling with pride at the edge of the bar; a beer can in his hand.

Jaffa: Does he have dizzy spells when he gets a hard on?

Bernie: It blocks all the light from the porthole when he gets out of bed.

Jaffa: Yeah, that's a wanger.

Harry: I got a wanger as well then.

Jaffa: (In a fatherly tone) No, Harry, if you had a
                <u>w</u>anger, it would take all the blood in your
                body to make it hard, you'd die the first
                hard on you got. You've probably got a
                widgey.

Raucous laughter across the bar.

Harry: What's a widgey?

Jaffa: Look in your pants Harry there's one there.
                It's like a cock only smaller, much smaller.

Harry: Ah yes, mines a widgey all right. (He looks
                at everyone in the bar) What you lot got
                then?

Top Cat: A wanger, definitely a wanger.

Pinko: (sardonically)A cock, just a normal cock.

Pete the Pay: That's what your wife told me when I last
                had her.

Pinko: (Smiling) Careful now.

Gus: A dork!

Laughter all round.

Jaffa: Damn, a dork! That's fukkin huge, what's
                yours Bernie?

Bernie: Cheers Jaffa, mines a pint of bitter.

Jaffa: Shit! (looking towards Ginge the barman)
                get Bernie a pint Ginge.

Benny: Mine's as big as a baseball bat.

Silence in the bar, all laughter stops. An embarrassing
silence follows where everybody tries to think of a suitable
follow up to that out-of-context statement.

Jaffa: So… what's the gossip in the Squadron office then Harry?

*****

At around eleven o'clock every evening the bar was closed by the duty SNCO. When it was SSgt Purvis (3 Tp), SSgt Taylor (SQMS), SSgt Dyan (HQ) and even SSgt Simpson (2 Tp) they would always have a drink and get to know the lads. This night it was SSgt 'Lumpy' Phillips (1 Tp) he always cleared the bar within seconds. No chat, no drink up time, just get to your bunks and get to sleep. No one ever argued with him. We all went to our bunks; Benny's was above Spunky's bunk. In the middle of the night Spunky woke with water dripping down onto his face and chest. He got out of his bunk and switched on the light only to find that Benny had pissed his sleeping bag and the pee was dripping down onto Spunky's face. Furious, he dragged Benny out of his bed and threw him out into the corridor with his wet mattress and sleeping bag. Spunky had a shower whilst Benny put his sleeping bag into the tumble dryer. The whole of the upper deck, which housed the Officers and the laundry room, smelt of hot cooked piss. The only way that I can describe this revolting smell is that it is like the smell that comes from a pile of rotting carrots. We had a lot of them in the Fens. Not many in Yorkshire though.

Benny became public enemy No. 1.

Saturday 19th February

Wes got arrested and Toddy was spread-eagled when they were diving by RAF Stanley. A RAF Sgt with a SMG asked Wes for his ID, he had a wetsuit on. We had 1 tipper supplying sand. It had a turn round time of 50 min – 1 hour, so we didn't work too hard today. Chris Lucas did his foot in yesterday and has a plaster on it like Spunky. A pioneer lost his arm in a cement mixer on Thursday. He had two weeks left.

Part of the Engineer team, were the divers. They had a tin shack in the middle of Port Stanley. The divers of each Squadron did a tour in this shack. They carried out all of the diving work on the Island. Three from our Squadron were Cpls Wes Hardy, LCpl Toddy and the Second in command of the Squadron, a Capt Ball.

The divers were putting in a jetty right up on the end of the inner harbour, called the Canache. It was three hundred metres from the RAF security hut for the entrance gate for RAF Port Stanley. Their job was to place the bases of the scaffold on the sea bed and to secure them in. They would suit up in their hut on the waterfront and speed up to the Canache in their Rigid Raider motor assault boat. This morning was different; they had been diving for around an hour when Wes came out of the water to look into the barrel of a 9mm Stirling sub Machine Gun. On the other end of the gun was a mean looking 'Snowdrop', the RAF's name for their military police. Their hats had a white top, hence the name, Snowdrop. "ID!" the ape with the gun growled at Wes.

"I haven't got it on me" Wes tapped the sides of his wet suit to show that he had no pockets.

"I tried that but they won't listen" Toddy shouted to Wes. Wes looked over towards Toddy and saw that they had him spread-eagle on the ground with another ape standing over him, gun pointing at Toddy's head.

"Get out of the water and no funny tricks" Wes, having an Engineers' sense of humour, found this cliché hilarious, and couldn't help laughing as he climbed out of the water. As if he was going to do a funny Tommy Cooper trick whilst climbing out of the mud in a wet suit. The gorilla with the gun didn't like this weedy looking guy laughing at the serious situation that he had created and so, in order to reclaim the seriousness of the situation he pulled Wes out of the water by the top of his wet suit and threw him into the mud. Again the ape tried his new found skill of communicating and repeated the order "ID!" but screamed it louder this time, as if the louder that he shouted the quicker it would appear.

"I told thee, I haven't got me bloody ID card, 'ave' I, there ain't no pockets in me bloody wet suit is there?" Wes came from Yorkshire and when under stress his accent intensified. His accent had just gone from Southern Yorkshireman to Compo from Last of the Summer Wine. The ape saw the logic in this statement and realised that the silly man lying in the mud might actually be correct. Just to check he shouted "Cover me" to his mate and dropped his knee into Wes's Back. Wes's air left his lungs in a hurry and refused to return whilst the RAF policeman frisked Wes's wet wetsuit. Finding no pockets he stood up and asked "Who's in charge here?" Wes was totally unable to answer as the air was still refusing to return to his lungs until he reassured it that it would not get kicked out again. Toddy on the other hand was now glad that Wes had two stripes to his one and he made that quite clear to the gun totting morons that had spoilt their morning, "HE IS!" pointing to Wes "he's the Cpl, I'm only a LCpl"

"You're under arrest" the gorilla picked Wes up by his wet suit and at gun point and with his hands on top of his head, he marched Wes up the bank to the guard hut. Toddy on the other hand was allowed not only to get up but to get back in his boat and to speed back to their hut to get Captain Hall the Captain took Wes's and Toddy's ID cards to show to the Snowdrops. For some reason Wes's and Toddy's view on the whole incident was totally different. Toddy found the whole incident a scream whereas Wes didn't stop complaining about RAF police for … well… the rest of the tour.

I was working on the road to the Coastell 2 landing bay. It had just started. SSgt Simpson had made a serious mistake in cutting the top soil off the peat. He intended to cut down to rock, but gave up after three feet. So we put down the geo fibre matting on the gooey peat and started to fill the mat up with stone. Drop stone from a ten ton dump truck, push it out with a bulldozer and then roll it. The time it took a dump truck to drive from us to the quarry and back was around an hour. That usually meant that we worked for ten minutes and then waited for fifty.

8 Squadron were building permanent accommodation called 'Lookout Camp'. It was on the edge of Port Stanley and comprised of rows of porta cabins. They had Royal Pioneer Corps attached to

them. Great workers, salt of the earth, not too bright in the IQ section as this incident shows. A group of pioneers were working a large concrete mixer. One lad, in order to check the mix, put his hand in and grabbed a handful. His hand was caught in the agitators in the drum and it picked him up and threw him around and around. By the time the others had stopped the drum rotating his arm had been completely ripped off at the shoulder. As the diary stated he had two weeks left. As from that date all of the so called 'intelligent' Sappers that I knew, (myself included) stopped the practice of grabbing a handful of concrete to test its water content. Ouch!

Apparently Chris Lucas damaged his leg by jumping down from his Bedford onto the peat.

Sunday 20th February

We worked from 0700 hours but the Haulamatic drivers didn't start until 1000 hrs. We had two loads all morning. I didn't bother going to sports but I did get a letter and a "Miss you" card off San. I found out that I start night shift tomorrow night. Watched porno movie/ some bloke spussed into scrambled egg and the bird ate it. Yeuck. Did a pointless job for 52 and got bollocked for it.

Nice quiet day today, hardly any trucks turned up. We can't do anything until we have stone to push out. Seeing as we had no work I agreed when 52 Squadron asked me to dig a small pit on the edge of their Rubb shelter site. Homer Simpson went berserk when he found out, apparently I had to sit in my dozer and wait for the stone. Helping others was not acceptable. At the end of the road construction it took a bend to the left, the surveyor, called Ginge for the obvious reason, went to the Military Works Force (MWF) office and got a list of co-ordinates to plot on his theodolite. The numbers came from a computer. It would place the road to within a millimetre. As Ginge was plotting out the numbers and placing reference pegs for us operators to follow, Bignose came down the road and started shouting at Ginge;

"What the Hell are you doing, Cpl Newton?"

"Plotting out the corner Sir" he had a quizzical look on his face. It was bleeding obvious what he was doing and he couldn't see where this was leading.

"Well don't waste time with the theodolite, use a peg and a piece of string"

"Wh… what Sir?" an absolute incredulous look on the Cpl's face by now.

The OC stomped over to the theodolite and pushed it round, "Get a piece of string the length of the inside arc of the corner. Put a peg on the end and stomp the peg into the ground, then pull the string tight and mark out the corner." He spat.

"Er. I know how to do it Sir, but."

"Well why the hell, am I telling you?"

"Sir, I have got *numbers* from the MWF, I put them into the theo…" he tied to explain emphasising the word 'Numbers'. His eyebrows were raised and his voice had gone up an octave, he, a Cpl was trying to explain to a Major, his OC, why he shouldn't use the Major's method. He was on a loosing wicket from the start because the Major outranked him by about thirteen and a half miles.

Bignose grabbed the papers that Ginge was offering to him and threw them away into the wind, thereby stating quite categorically, that the argument was now over and that Ginge had in fact, lost. The torrent of abuse that followed only achieved three things. One, it made the OC feel more powerful. Two, it made Ginge Newton feel wretched and added fuel to the hate that he felt for him, and Three, it taught me an important lesson on man management. (Or woman womanagement.) Hey if you want to get PC, why can't women put the toilet seat UP when they have finished? Don't you hate those toilet seats in women's houses that have the fluffy toilet covers on? You put it up and start to pee, and half way through when you are marvelling at how the blue water is turning green, it falls down and twats your bell-end with such an almighty 'Thwack', that you can't wank for a week. Anyway, back to the story, Ginge carried out the

OC's polite request, using Argie D10 wire that was littering the Island. He then spent the rest of the day complaining about Bignose's stupidity.

Sundays were sports day, most of the guys went to Stanley and played either rugby or football. Some nutters ran up Sapper Hill for FUN! Me, I stayed on the boat and danced around Karate style. When the mail came there were two letters for me. One was the blue aerogram that had free postage for all servicemen and their families, the other was a card. I had a piece of string along my bed and put the card over the string. It reminded me of home. Perhaps not a good thing! We were told that there will be a night shift and that I will be on it. Great, I don't have to get up in the morning, a lie in. As I had a lie in, I went up to the canteen where someone was showing a blue movie. It was gross; it started to turn me on until the scrambled egg came out. I think I'll have fried egg tomorrow just in case the cooks also saw it.

Monday 21st February

I had a lovely sleep in this morning and did my laundry. Stanley shops (both of them) are shut 'cos of the celebrations. There is a Union Jack flying down the main road. It made me feel proud to be here. Mac thinks he has broken his toe. It was 1745 and I was sitting @ tea wondering how I was going to eat my tea and get to the stern gate in time for the 1800 boat when Brian Clunn told me "NIGHT SHIFT IS CANCELLED." Thanks for the day off Maj. Smythe.

What a nice day. All days should be like this one. I had a nice lay in, the best day to have a lay in is when everybody else is going to work. Then you hear them get up and you can stay in bed. The other half of our cabin is populated with Signals guys and a couple of Sappers. They are all on night shift and so come in a little before we usually go out. Everyone in the cabin has put a piece of string along the length of the bunk. Along this string we have all put towels. This gives us a little piece of privacy. Not enough! This morning I am alone in my half of the cabin with no other Sappers here. In the other half, all I can hear are snores. It is a good time for a wank. Stuck up on the bulkhead of my bed space is a series of pictures that I cut out of a Mayfair magazine. It is a big breasted girl, in red undies, peeking through red venetian blinds on a black background. Lying on my own I start to fantasise about her I take my tadger in my hand. Soon I can feel that sensation coming from wherever it comes from, and being totally unprepared, I frantically look around for something to come into. It has to be my curtain. Just in time it saves the day, (or a sticky tummy) and I lie back and savour the sensation. After a few minutes I realised that I now needed to do some Dhobi (an Indian word for washing. Actually it is an Indian word for the caste that does the washing. It has been kept by the British Army since the Indian Raj. 'Doing one's Dhobi.'; 'Dhobi dust'; 'Is that your fucking Dhobi on my bed?' etc) so I rolled up my towel and jumped / fell the six feet to the floor to be confronted with Timmo. Tim Turner was one of the Sappers in the other half of the cabin. He is sitting on his bunk reading, not four metres away from where I just had a wank. 'Did he hear me?' 'Will he say anything' 'Can he see the spussed in towel that I am holding?' I turn the towel so that the wet patch is facing towards me and say "Woto Timmo, not tired?"

He looks up from his book and as if he hasn't seen me before replies "Oh! hello Bernie, you not working today? I thought everybody had gone to work." Whether he had heard me I will never know, but he never let on. That's comradeship for you. Later on in the tour we were so blasé over wanking that Spunky used to do it in front of us, we had to turn away until he had finished. He refused to go into the toilets, told *us* to go into the loos whilst he had a wank. He had a good point actually.

I made polite talk whilst I thought of a way out, while I was listening to Timmo, I grabbed my Dhobi dust, made my excuses and left the cabin. The laundry room was empty; it still smelt of Benny's piss from where he had tumbled-dried his sleeping bag. After all my Dhobi was finished, I grabbed my camera, and caught the boat to Port Stanley. The first film that I had taken of Port Stanley, just after

I had arrived there, had been taken with the film not loaded, so I had to take all of the photographs again. The two main shops in Port Stanley were closed, The Kelper Store and the so-called supermarket. I had a roll of film so I walked around Port Stanley and photographed everything. As I mentioned before it is like a disrupted Rubik cube. It is very colourful, but quite often the colour of the roofs do not match the walls. I found some other shops in Port Stanley, a wool shop for instance (hmmm, useful) and I found Port Stanley radio station. The most photogenic object that I found was an old fire-hydrant that been painted up. We had the same sort of fire-hydrant in the village where I was brought up, except the ones in Burwell were not painted like this one, also the fire hydrant in Port Stanley had a lion as the nozzle. I popped in and saw Spunky, he was enjoying himself immensely. He invited me and the guys to a darts match with the medics, I accepted immediately. We would have a few beers that didn't come out of cans and then sleep in the hospital. Unfortunately I am on night shift on the road, still the other guys can go. I got back to the Geraint quite late, I had to get changed, eat tea and then get on the boat at six o'clock. It was twenty past five; I wasn't going to make it. Something had to be forfeited, I had a meeting with myself and decided to forfeit work in favour of food. So there I was eating my tea at a quarter to six and along comes Cpl Brian Clunn, one of the Cpls in 2 Troop, and he tells me that night shift was cancelled. Talk about making my day! A wank, my Dhobi, a day trip ashore, tea AND the evening and the next day off. More power too your planning, OC.

Tuesday 22nd February

Tonight night shift is also cancelled. Thanks once again OC. Taff, TC, Tadger, Dave, Mac, Peter and me went to the medics bar to play darts, we won. I WON!!! There were these men with funny chests, nice bums, sweet smelling after shave, long hair and high voices. Fuck being a medic if that's what it does to you! A Matlot gate crashed the bar, he was drunk, he was beaten up, he was thrown out, HE WAS A PATIENT! Is this why there are no beds?

I can't remember much about this day; it was a very lazy day. I seem to remember being bored stupid when I had a couple of days off. This must have been them. When I was working the days went pretty quick. Not quick enough for getting home, mind you. But when I was sitting in my bunk, with nothing to do, the day stretched out into infinity. There were no amenities on the boat for recreation besides the bar which was shut during the day, and a small multi-gym, there is only so long that one can work out. Add to that a leisurely wank, doing one's Dhobi, and writing home that would take up four hours. That left the rest of the day to get bored. There was no food on the boat at lunch time, not that I can remember. I always got on well with the cooks throughout my Army career. There were two sets of people that you looked after in the forces, the ones that paid you and the ones that fed you. The latter was usually highest on the scale. Because of my philosophy on life, I was able to go into the kitchen and grab toast or the bacon that they always cook themselves after brekky. I do remember taking a trip back into Port Stanley again. I had taken all of the photos that I needed, so that was out. I visited The Kelper Store and put in my rolls of film and complained bitterly about the fact that they had lost my other films. I met Mick the NAAFI in The Kelper Store. We talked and I discovered that The Kelper Store was being supported by the NAAFI. That would explain where the assistants got the knowledge on how to micro cut cucumber. Only in the NAAFI have I ever seen cucumber cut so thin. If it wasn't transparent it could be cut in two. My in-laws ran the NAAFI club in Hildesheim. Being ex REME (it's a crap Corps, but someone has to do it) (joke!) (I have to put that in because REME don't have a sense of humour) (Also a joke) (REME = Royal Engineers Minus Education) (Actually I was too thick to join the REME so they put me into the Sappers!) they realised that the men would rather have a large 'fuck off' sandwich and pay the extra than pay the normal price and have to hold the cucumber down to stop it blowing away. So they loaded up the NAAFI sarnies with extra cucumber, tomato, lettuce meat etc and charged 30 Pfennings extra. I believe the lads and lassies of 1 RTR in Hildesheim appreciated it. Mick the NAAFI was working in the warehouse, and was living on the Rangatira. That is the ship that doesn't have a sewage system. It pumps the raw sewage out into the propeller. The idea being that when the ship is sailing, all the little fishes come along and eat the poo, then Mr Fisherman comes along and catches the little fish, and we eat the fish. I don't eat fish!

A gang of us went to the hospital for a darts party. For hospital read; a small wooden school hut. Out the back of this wooden hospital building was an even smaller brick out house. It had been converted into a bar by the enterprising medics. We all traipsed in and were given dirty looks by the people in the bar, until Spunky saw us and shouted to us. Which looking back was a bit unnecessary due to the size of the small room, but it pointed out to the medics that we were with Spunky. We were immediately accepted and after getting in the largest beer that I had seen since we left Germany, (on the boat we were allowed only two cans each) we set up the dart board and started. I am hopeless at darts; I just throw them at the dart board and hope that they stick in the bit that I want. Usually they don't, this night they all did. Everybody in the bar thought that I was a professional. I won the match and was so proud! As the second pint of beer quickly flowed down the gullet the first was starting to relax me. In the bar were the first women that I had seen since Germany. There were a few in Port Stanley, but the winter weather is harsh on skin, and these women in the bar had not spent their years on a wind swept island. They were beautiful compared to the locals and were the focus all of my sexual thoughts for the next three weeks. Twenty minutes later the second beer took effect and the body was waiting for the alcohol in the third beer to filter through the stomach before letting me know that I was drunk. It always does that on me, lets me drink too much and then makes me pay by dry vomiting early in the morning. The bar didn't have too much beer and I stopped at three, two is my giggly stage, three is stagger stage. Somewhere between three and five beers I reach vomit, hangover, and feel sick all morning stage. I can't understand how these men claim that they have drunk thirteen pints and driven home, shagged the wife and kicked the dog. I bet in the morning, (or afternoon when they get up) the wife has a large bruise on her leg, the dog runs away from him and the wardrobe is full of piss. Close to the end of the night a drunken sailor barges his way into the bar and starts to abuse the nurses. Taff and Jock being true gentlemen smack him a couple of times around the head and drag him outside and throw him into the street. When they return we are all laughing, Taff asks "What are you all laughing for?"

A male nurse tells him that the Petty Officer that they have just beaten up and thrown into the street is a patient of the hospital; he is there to dry out. He wasn't having much luck, so it seems. Taff was six foot four inches of solid Welsh gristle, there was nothing to him. He was usually laughing, but like many soldiers had a violent side that only needed the right situation to bring it out. He was in a bar in Nunburg, Germany, when a Turkish man took offence to one of his Welsh jokes and pulled a pistol on him. Taff grabbed the pistol with it still pointing at his stomach and punched the man full in the face. The Turk let go of the gun and Taff beat him with the butt of the gun. When the German police arrived they had to pull him off the bloody mess of the Turk. Luckily the barman had seen the whole thing, and the German police arrested the Turk and commended Taff on his bravery. Taff told us that he was just furious that this man thought he could pull a gun on him; bravery didn't come in to it. Taff is now a policeman in Wales.

After the drunken promises from us that we would have a rematch on the ship, we were shown to our beds, *hospital beds*. I slept the sleep of the dead. Early in the morning we ambled over to the jetty in order to get a boat back. I saw Taff Adams, who was from 75 Squadron and he gave us all a lift back to the Geraint. I was still very drunk. I had a wash and shave and then caught the boat back. Spunky, the lucky bastard stayed in bed in the hospital whilst we went to work.

Wednesday 23rd February

Slept in the medic's porta cabin, in sheets last night! Got Taff Adams to give us a CSB ride back. I was still drunk. The D6D is a beaut. Jock found a bullet proof vest yesterday. It weighs as much as a Hymac!! Simpson shaved off his 'tash, he looks like a PIXIE. The tea tasted like OM33 again, it's good for cleaning the mess tins and unblocking drains. Any offers to buy?

We were given a new bulldozer today. A Caterpillar D6d, if that means anything to you. In the terms of a Sapper POM, it was beautiful. We all wanted to be the one to drive it. Heaters, windscreen wipers, tinted glass, cigarette lighter (only joking). It would also push the entire world if it was given the chance. It is so powerful compared to the small wheeled shovel loaders that we had been using. It was so powerful that, we all started to dig up the fabrics. On top of the peat was laid Netlon, a plastic mesh like fishnet stockings, on that is the Terram which is the fibre membrane that allows moisture to permeate through, on that is two foot of rock and on that is twelve inches of sand. We were laying sand and were digging up the Netlon and Terram! If Homer Simpson found out we would have been for the high jump. It would entail digging a hole in the rock and sand, repairing the membrane and then relaying it all again. We go to Jock, he is our guru. He says, "Fuck it, and just cover it up so that the Terram and Netlon don't show." We cut off the material that shows and push a foot of sand over it. We thought that Jock was the most knowledgeable construction expert that we had. I now know that he knew little more that we did, but he was an ex Para Engineer (9 Squadron Parachute Engineer Squadron) and didn't fuss over little things. SSgt Simpson would have gone ballistic. Good for you Jock, I learned a lot from you.

Thursday 24th February

What a totally non-descript Day. We got a Hamm roller at work. Simpson threw a wobbly over dump trucks and we shovelled sand.

Knockers <u>are</u> thick, all the way up to the top. Every POM has his own views on how to build the track. No mail. Sea is too rough.

Well, it might have been a non descriptive day for me, but other soldiers in Port Stanley were having fun and excitement. Operating in the inner harbour were Mexefloats, Mexefloats were large floating pontoons that were powered by a large engine that was stuck on the deck. They were totally flat and looked like huge green chess boards floating across the harbour. Nearly everybody used them. Ships were unloaded by Mexefloat and Haulamatic 10 Ton dumptrucks were transported across the harbour on Mexefloat. Well I have never got to the bottom of what happened, but the end result was that one sunk. It was loaded with eight brand new Haulamatic dumptrucks. Sorry, that was a typo there; it should have read 'it was *over*loaded with brand new Haulamatic dumptrucks'. One corner of the Mexefloat started to dip under the water. All of the drivers were in their uniforms and were sitting in the cabs of the trucks. Like a piece of ice in a lake when you step on it, the Mexefloat upended and dumped the Haulamatics into the harbour. All of the soldiers managed to scramble out of the cabs only because the water pushed in the windscreens. They were lifted out of the water and sent to REME to get the salt water out of the gearboxes, engines, electric's, hydraulics and ashtray. It's nothing but excitement in today's modern Army!

There was a big argument on the Coastell road today, Taff and Jock, were arguing over the way to construct it. Homer Simpson (minus moustache and looking like a little pixie) had a shouting session at us POMS, because no trucks had turned up with stone or sand. Taff operates the D6d all of the time and when he isn't operating, he always lets TC operate. I was put on a Hamm roller. It has a really neat diesel heater, but is minus two windows. I found some polythene and with BMT or Black Masking Tape, taped it across the broken windows. It was to prove a good move when the bad weather came. The heater burns diesel and has its own little exhaust pipe. It's really cool and really hot, if you see what I mean. Because there were no trucks for us Homer got us to shovel sand by hand. Oh, the shame of it all, reduced from a 3 m³ bucket to a .0025 m³ shovel. Three years of training for this?

Friday 25th February

I got 4 letters off San today. Isn't it great how she can cheer me up 8000 miles away, she's great and I love her so. No Haulamatics turned up for work so we knocked off work early at 3

ºclock. After we left two turned up! The 8 that ditched in the sea are called Aquamatics now. The OC. doesn't trust us L/Cpl's. There must be a Cpl on site on Sunday. Ha Ha!

Good.

My bottie is still marked from sit-ups done on the 29/1/83.

No mail yesterday, but today four. Sandra and I have a numbering system on our letters. There are two to three week delays on getting a reply from the letter that you sent. Also sometimes they would be mixed up. For example letter forty five would arrive before forty four. I would read them immediately and then again in the ship. It was like I was talking to San when I read the letters. It took me away from Falklands and put me at home. Pinko however refused to read his letters on the site. He said that he wouldn't read letters from his wife in front of us because we would ruin the ambience. I told him that I wouldn't touch his ambience if he told me where it was. He then called me a philistine and I told him that I've never collected stamps. Jeeves is getting letters from his girlfriend Yvonne but he is also getting letters from someone else and he won't tell us who it is. It is definitely a woman going by the suggestive laughter that comes from his curtained bed when he reads his mail.

We have to work seven days a week, up to now the LCpls, of which I am one, have had to pull Saturday and Sunday duty, whilst the Cpls had a day off and went fishing. Well Bignose the OC has put a stop to that, there has to be a Plant Corporal on duty on the construction site on weekends. As there are only two, Jock and Taff, that narrows it down a little bit. Remember the Supersports that we did on the Uganda on the way down? Well my arse still had an open sore from doing sit-ups on the wooden deck, one month later. We were knocked off work at three o'clock today as the trucks carrying the stone and sand never turned up. The Knockers stayed so we had no transport back. We set out walking back the four miles back to Port Stanley and watched the RN trucks passing us. It wasn't until a RAF truck came past that we got a lift. Those matlots were a snotty lot in the Falklands. They would never pick up us Sappers. The RAF and Army would always stop. We waited like automatons on the jetty and got onto the chugga chugga boats that transported us to our ships in the harbour. Hot showers today, a bit of a treat! Write home, go to evening meal, take a piss and then go to sleep. That was the general routine.

Saturday 26th February

Not much happened at work. I can't be arsed to do anything anymore at night. I'm so lethargic at night all I want to do is write to San and go to bed maybe in the hope that the days will pass quicker. They are I think. I started off with karate every night, now writing and taking a shower is a grind, besides they are always cold. I must start doing things at night, but first I must want to do something. I'll start tomorrow.

The rut had started to set in. It had been a month since I had left Germany and my wife, and I was starting to forget what she felt like. The light at the beginning of the tunnel was still there but it was getting smaller and smaller. It was disappearing into my memory like the details of who you insulted on a good night out on the piss. All we did was work. Sometimes as much as eighteen hours in a day. The usual day was fourteen hours. What was worse was that there was no light at the end of the tunnel to be seen. It was as yet too far away. Despondency started to set in. Another five months of this. Writing a letter was all I could persuade myself to do. This brought on feelings of guilt, but the problem was that I was always knackered.

Sunday 27th February

Spunky's birthday, was pissed. When we got in from work Spunky was pissed. Shit! I just said that. We did a lot of work today. Finished at 1930. Showers are cold again. Everybody is sitting in the room with hi-fis on, who the hell do I talk to? This heap sailed out of harbour today to test its engines. Nearly everywhere was out of bounds. The divers found a round painted bottle. Jock and Mac put dirt down Mongol's bum at work. I fell over laughing.

Steve Stigsson, Stig, or Mongol, after the film 'Blazing Saddles' was seen as being a bit of a fool, a village idiot. He was large and slow. He even talked slowly. We were waiting on the end of the Coastell road. (The 'road', being a few hundred ton of stone and sand.) Where the sand ran out was the ten metres of compacted stones that we laid the sand on. Where the sand run out was the geo-textiles and that was on the virgin peat. The D6d bulldozer was sat on the road, and we were waiting for the next dump truck of either sand or stone to turn up. We never knew what was going to come next. Mongol was spreading sand to the corners of the stone with his shovel when Jock and Taff grabbed him and shovelled sand down his trousers. It was like the Tom and Jerry movies where the cat and mouse are a tumble of arms and legs. Taff and Jock are large men but they were having a problem holding Stig. It was all for laughs and I sat down in the sand laughing, my sides hurt with the laughter. It was great medicine for the blues, we sat on the sand talking and joking after that. It turns out that Mongol has eight O level certificates and so many CSE's that he couldn't remember them all. It just went to prove that one should not judge a book by its cover.

After waiting for another hour, two Haulamatic dump trucks turned up. One was being driven by Sandy Shore. Sandy was from 75 Squadron and knew us all. He jumped out his cab and stretching his four foot eight inch body walked over to us, sitting in the sand.

"Where ya been, Sandy?" Taff asked him "Had to change your library books?" he added.

""Fuckin' Bignose" his face was red with rage. I smiled; my nickname for the OC, from the long walk had stuck.

"What's he done now?" Jock asked with his large smile, we all knew that the story was going to be a good one, and we waited patiently for Sandy to expand. Sandy knew that he had our undivided attention and took his time to explain. "You know that we have the priority on the Stanley Airport Road?" We all nodded, it had been on orders two days previously. "It is because if we leave the road with a load on our tyres sink straight into the peat and we have to get pulled out" Sandy didn't have to explain, but it added to the story and soldiers are good story tellers. "Well I was coming here with my load of stone" he nodded over to his truck. The driver of the truck that was behind him had jumped out of his cab and was walking over. We didn't recognise him as he was probably RCT. One could tell that he was RCT because of the way in which he was dressed. 75 Squadron had to wear the same uniform as we did in Germany. All of the other Corps wore a mish-mash of winter warfare, Silverman's, and Bob's second hand Army Surplus equipment. This man that was walking towards us resembled the Yeti monsters off the first series of Doctor Who. Sandy was regulation perfect except that he didn't have his beret on straight. "Well, I was just passing the minefield, you know, the one by the RAF entrance, when in the distance, I saw a Mercedes jeep coming towards me." The Argentineans bought Mercedes jeeps before the war, (oops sorry, wrong verb. It shouldn't be 'bought', as that suggests that a sum of money passed hands, when in fact it did not. The Argentineans took a delivery of Mercedes jeeps, during the war they were captured by the British. The Argentineans, as they no longer had the vehicles, refused to pay for them. Mercedes then went to the British and told them that they had to pay for the jeeps that they captured in the war, whereupon the British government replied, 'Sorry we didn't order any vehicles off you, the only ones that we have, we captured from the enemy. Take it up with them'. Mercedes lost that one!) Sandy continued "As it got closer I saw that it was the OC's," by some means, the OC had got the Mercedes jeep which the Argies had numbered '01'. It was a highly sought after jeep.

Everybody knew that it belonged to the OC of 75 Sqn. "I thought, I ain't gonna move over, the OC made the rule that we had priority, so he was obviously gonna move over. Well he didn't! The fucker stayed right in the middle of the road! I had to swerve off the road at the last minute; the front wheels went into the verge and sunk up to the axle. The fucking bignosed bastard didn't even slowdown; he just carried on and left me there!" We all laughed at that, the OC was renowned for taking up the whole road in his 01 jeep. He used to swerve across the road and make other vehicles slow down. Now he was forcing ten ton dump trucks off the road. "I had to wait for Dom here" Sandy nodded to the other driver who had reached the small gathering of Sappers listening to Sandy, "to drive past me and then he had to go back to REME and get a tow bar"

"You had a chance of killing Bignose and you missed," Jock made out that he was not impressed, " you wimp, don't talk to us" Jock turned his back on Sandy "now get back on that road and this time do the job right or don't come back." We all joined in to taunt Sandy, "You were driving a dump truck and you missed him?"

"Sandy, you had the chance to be the Squadron hero and you failed." TC joined in "Typical MT, bloody wimps"

"Ah come on guys, what could I do?" Sandy joined the game and came up in his defence.

Jock answered "If the OC put on orders that you had priority, you had priority, what more excuse do you need? You wimped out!"

"I would've killed him"

"And then the Squadron would have brought you a crate of beer." This went on until Homer Simpson Landrover was seen approaching, we all jumped to our shovels and dozers and made like we had been working. Homer threw a fit with Sandy over the number of trucks that hadn't turned up at his site, Sandy tried to explain that there were other sites in and around Stanley that needed sand and stone and he took his orders from the quarry manager. Sandy being a Sapper and Homer being a SSgt made the winner of the argument a foregone conclusion. A fact that the small Homer used to his advantage. In Civvy Street he would have his face smashed in if he talked to truck drivers like he did then. We finished work late at seven thirty in order to catch up for the late trucks. When we finally got back on the ship, it was to find Spunky on board and drunk. He had been released from hospital and it was his birthday. The bunk was quite dead except for Spunky. I was lying on my bunk and writing my diary, Spunky and TC were drinking a bottle of wine. Nothing unusual in that except that they were not letting the bottle of red come closer than twelve inches to their mouths. It was going all over their faces and the floor. It was the most excitement that I had seen in the ship for a couple of weeks and consequently I wrote the piece about Spunky again. They left to find another bunk with more people and everyone went back to their personal hi-fi's. All that I could hear was the tinny "boom boom tiddly boom" coming from the headphones. Jock, Taff and Mac were in their own world, and left me to mine. Ah well, sleep takes me to any part of the world and so I embrace it with open arms and closed eyes.

Monday 28th February

We got a Summerfelt eating 580bt Hymac today, what a heap!!! No windows, no heater. I dug out a ditch and the bucket fell off. The pins are too small. When asked for the hours, I looked no numbers in the gauge. The Hymac ate the track way. Mac's doing hair cuts for 30 p. On Stanley it is £1.10. On the wagon Jock Allen asked "What happens to the people not going to the show?"

"They catch the boat, stupid," said Homer "Who isn't going?!" he asked, hands went up all round "right, sort out that matting" he said.

There was a Forces Entertainment Show on in Stanley this night. Lots of pretty girls in tight leotards, cavorting around in front of seven hundred horny, soldiers! The toilet system was blocked this night with one hundred and seventy five gallons of semen. Sod that for sexual torture, I already knew that I was separated from the woman of my dreams; I didn't need to have women taunt me and rub my nose in the fact that I cannot have sex for the next five months. I stayed in the room. When Homer Simpson asked who was not going to the show, I was not that stupid that I couldn't see what was coming next. Hence, I had a hot shower whilst the rest were either working or trying to hide their erections in the Forces Show

Notes for February

The days are going very quick now, we don't know what day it is most of the time. Spunky and Chris did their legs in. Mac suffered numerous injuries, a Pioneer can't do press-ups any more and Homer Simpson is losing air from his ego balloon. Spunky is starching everybody's towels, Jock is turning into a hamster and TC and Pinko are going to be daddies. We are at extra awareness, the stern gate sentry has to look for bubbles, floating objects and Argie subs. One of the RCL's had its ramp knocked off in heavy swell. A chief (Navy) noticing the Generals cross swords when he walked in, said "Al right, clubs." On 11/2/83 SSM said to me on Gd's, "Take the gash through the galley, to the stern ready to put on the black pig" I said "Is that CB talk or what."

This was our first month on the Falklands. Not a whole month, mind you, March had the dubious honour of being called that. I am now a Safety Officer for a construction company and I can't believe the accidents that we had for such a small project. Two broken legs and an arm ripped off at the elbow. I also remember Mac injuring him self in many ways and places, if those injuries were on the site that I am on now I would be instantly fired. At this time the Forces had Crown Immunity from prosecution for safety violations resulting in injuries. That has now been repealed. The Pioneer would have probably got around £2000 compensation, if he was lucky. Outside on a normal construction site, £50,000 would have been nearer the truth. When I was in Kuwait a man lost this foot in a minefield, he received £500,000 from the insurance company. Crown Immunity was a way that the British Army could put your life at risk doing anything, training, peace time work or war, and not be prosecuted.

Thankfully those days have gone. Breaking your leg in the Falklands in 1983 only meant that you got a cushy number whilst it healed. Spunky was wanking into his own towel and anyone's towel that he picked up by mistake; we all used the green Army towel. Jock spends all of his time in the evening, lying on his bed and drinking from a wine bottle, Pinko and TC both found out that that they were going to be daddies. Pinko was married and happy about the event, TC wasn't and wasn't. We believed, (and told him so) that Ami, his girlfriend, was pulling the wool over his eyes about being pregnant.

The extra awareness had something to do with the time of the year. We all had to do gate duty now and again. I was told to look out for untoward bubbles.

"LCpl Beirne, you are on gate duty"

"There isn't a gate on this boat Sir"

"It is on the rear ramp, Corporal"

"Ah"

"The Argies are likely to attack now, so you are to be extra alert"

"Extra alert Sir, OK Sir"

"Look for submarines, drift wood that might hide divers and untoward bubbles, LCpl"

"Sir"

"Yes LCpl Beirne?"

"What shape is an untoward bubble?"

"Ignoramus!"

"Did you say Rhombus shape Sir?"

"Beirne!" walking away so that I cannot see him smiling "any more and you will be on gate duty all week"

"You mean I won't be able to work fourteen hours a day in a Hymac without windows or heater, get freezing cold and wet and work my fingers to the bone, I'll have to stay on board in the warm next to the cookhouse, Sir? I'll take the gate duty Sir, please Sir, thank you Sir."

"Shuttup Beirne."

"Yessir."

A Matlot was on gate duty when General Thorpe came on with his entourage. Generals in the British Army have crossed swords on their shoulders. Royal Navy PT instructors have crossed clubs and are known as 'Clubs.' The Matlot saw the crossed swords and nodded to the General saying "Wotcha Clubs." He was instructed about his faux pas by the CRE, CO, Adjutant, OC, 2IC, RSM, SSM, and anyone else who thought that he was important. The Navy have a complete language that has been built up through the years. I refused to use it, the SSM embraced it. I called the toilets 'Toilets, or Bog, or Shitter, never the 'Heads'. When the SSM said to me "Take the gash (rubbish) through the galley (kitchen), to the stern (back) ready to put on the black pig (rubbish boat)" I pretended not to understand him. He explained it to me in plain English and lowered his opinion of my IQ by another forty points. My IQ was now so low that I owed him points.

My beautiful Bambi

Tuesday 1st March 1983

I worked on the Hymac 580 to get it working and finally did. I dug an anchor pit and froze. Taff was told on an 'O' group for a night shift. He put himself and TC on, Oh dear. That leaves me and Mac for day shift. Yahoo, we might get some operating in, correction we will. Taff was going to move out until he found out that TC wasn't. So he didn't. God how I miss and love San. I really do.

I must have been stupid. I repaired the Hymac excavator and then sat on the wet seat with the wind blowing straight through the cab and froze! I have just read the diary before writing this and my first thought now (16 years later) was 'Well that's your fault for repairing the Hymac! Now I would leave it broken. There is a lot to be said for the wisdom that comes with age. There is the joke where a young and an old bull are standing on the top of a hill looking down on a herd of young cows. The young bull shouts "Hey, look at them, let's run down and fuck one." The old bull replies "No, let's *walk* down and fuck *ALL* of them." The anchor pit was a huge hole where an ISO shipping container was to be buried. It was around three metres deep and ten metres long. We were to fill it up with concrete and the Coastell would use it as an anchor point. There was a small problem. Where the OC had insisted that the surveyor, Ginge, use wire to mark out the corner instead of computer generated numbers, it had created and error, due to the fact that wire stretches and gives a different reading depending on how much you pull it. The road was in the wrong place, only by one foot but that foot of soil belonged to the anchor pit. CRE (Works) went ballistic. Not with us I might add. He did talk to Ginge the surveyor and ask him why he had made such a cock up. He wasn't happy with the explanation. The Coastell was on its way down to the Falklands. When it arrives the anchor must be ready, the anchor could not be put in until the hole was dug, the hole could not be dug until the road was moved, etc. The OC didn't bother us for some time after that.

The strain of living with each other was starting to show. Sapper Steve (Top Cat) (TC) Furze had grown to hate Cpl Taff Davies, which was unfortunate as it seemed that Taff was in love with Top Cat. In order to get away from him he arranged to move out of our bunk and into another. When Taff found out he said that he was also going to move out with Top Cat. This was great news for me as I 'bagged' Taff's bed. It was a converted sofa. Mac had the top and Taff the bottom. Instead of being stacked three high, it was only two. When TC found out he cancelled, and so did Taff, so you can understand why TC wasn't happy when Taff put TC on night shift with him. I was on day shift with Mac and that suited me just fine. We always shared the operating. I am really missing Sandra. It tears at my heart to be so far away from her. I now wish that I had volunteered for rear party like Holly Hollywood, at least I would be with her. It is not something sexual either, it is pure love, but it hurts so much. Shouldn't love make us happy? When you are in love it only makes you unhappy when you are not together, you might only be in the next office but it still has that effect. Sandra and I had a whirlwind romance, the type that one usually reads about in woman's magazines. We were married three months after we met, and it was only that long because we had to book the registry office. When I met my wife to be I was shagging any woman who crossed my path. I was nicknamed a slag by the women of the estate, and yet they still queued up to bed me. It was the peak of my womanising days and I loved it. "I'll never get married" was my slogan. I was living with one of Sandra's sisters, not sleeping with her but just sharing her flat. Sandra came back from Germany to see this slag that was living with her sister. I picked her up from Andover bus station and being a tit man and Sandra being flatter than Heathrow runway, she was definitely not my type. But being a woman she trapped me into dating her. (That's my version of the event… well it is MY book!) There was something different about her. She was independent, her own woman. She relied on herself and only herself. I admired that greatly. I had never seen it in a woman before. We also had fun in each others company. We had an argument and I went back to her and apologised, which surprised me as I had a policy that at the first sign of a crack in a relationship, I would leave. There were so many single mothers in the London overspill estate that I didn't need to go through all of that emotional stuff. Life was too short and I was too much in demand. Suddenly, here was a girl that I went back to after an argument. That was like the sun rising in the West instead of the East for me. I couldn't understand why I had gone back. Sandra had always had boyfriends that had done anything that she had asked. They bought her washing machines, rings, anything that she wanted. Here was a boy that said "No" to her. This was something different to her, someone who was more independent than her. We started dating, it was November. In the New Year which was a Leap Year, she asked me to marry her. Apparently it is an English custom that women can ask the men in a Leap Year. Whatever, I said "No way!" A week later I was kneeling in the corner of my bedspace, a bedspace that I didn't live in, with a toothbrush, trying to clean out the corners of the skirting board. I was doing this because a Sergeant had told us to do it, and I thought 'Fuck this for a game of soldiers, if I get married I will get a house, I can always get divorced, what the hell!' I went to Sandra that night and told her that 'Yes' I would marry her. I phoned up my parents and my mother answered the phone,

"Hi Mum, it's Julian"

"Oh, Hello Julian"

"I'm going to get married, Mum"

Silence

"Mum?"

"Is she pregnant?"

My parents had never met Sandra and I had never met her parents. We all met outside the registry office. "Hello Mr Dolan, I'm Bernie, I'm marring your daughter in five minutes."

Everybody asked us if we were doing the right thing, no one thought that out marriage would last. Well twenty nine years later they are still wrong. This was the first real separation that we had been through. A few exercises and courses but nothing too long and it was killing me. For the last three years I had slept cuddling up to her, spooning, (when my front is against her back.) I had woken up next to the woman that I loved and now, nothing, on my own. I had forgotten what she felt like and I hated it!

Wednesday 2nd March

I operated the Hymac all day. Well it broke down once at dinner. RH track motor pipe burst. We nicked one from the broken Hymac. Pins keep sheering, air cleaner fell off, fan belt was loose, no windows, bucket twisted. I could go on and on all day. Best thing today was no Taff Davies, he is on night shift with – yes, and you guessed it TC. TC wasn't pleased.

A good day, I was occupied all day and the time passed quickly. Could be worse, I could've been on night shift with Taff. I used to get on so well with him, but now it is great when I am away from him.

Thursday 3rd March

It's a bad day today. I've been a bad mood all day. I had to work 'till ½ 7. The CSB was late; I had to beg a tea off the nips. (It was chips and pie, good!) then the real kick in the teeth, orders:-

Quote:- No hanging of clothes in dorms. No kit bags in dorms. No one in dorms after 0715 on Friday. One more person for cons and to cap it all, fucking polish. ENTER 75 TRAINING SQUADRON.

I got up this morning and hated it. I didn't want to talk to anyone. It must have been all of the reminiscing about Sandra that I did last night. I bit TC's head off because he moved my towel. "Hey is that my fucking towel that you got?"

"It was hanging on that locker door, Bernie" TC looked concerned, he was pointing to his locker. (All towels are the same colour green)

"WELL IT'S MINE! DON'T TOUCH MY FUCKING STUFF! ANY OF YOU! "I shouted to the cabin. TC was visibly upset. I realised that I was being a wanker but I couldn't snap out of it. All these years later I can still see the hurt on TC's face, he had no idea of what he had done. He hadn't done anything wrong; being separated from Sandra had really got to me on this morning. I stormed out of the cabin not caring, I didn't want to hurt TC or any of the others, I think that I wanted to hurt myself. I sat on my own during breakfast, I really didn't want to talk to anyone. I shovelled the food into my mouth not caring what it was, my head was bowed and I didn't look up. During the boat trip to the jetty I stood on my own. I was terrible company and thought that it was better if I didn't talk to anyone. It was a long day, twelve hours of hard graft. The divers were building a small jetty by the Coastell Road. It was where Wes had been spread-eagled by the Snow drops. The CSB's would be booked to take us late workers direct from the worksite to the RFA Geraint. The CSB was late. My bad mood had slowly diminished throughout the day. I had even made it up with TC and we were back on laughing terms. That all went when I got back to the ship. First there was no food for the late workers; I had to beg some from the Cantonese cooks. Then the coup de grace, on Squadron orders it was ordered that we had to polish the floors of the cabins. Good idea for moral, OC! Get the men working twelve hours then make them polish the floors! And they wonder why Officers get shot in combat!

Friday 4th March

Hymac broke down, TC had to track it to REME, he got in at 10 o'clock. I heard of a 59 guy who lost his leg out here. He was in hospital in England and his mates sent him a parrot! I heard from Mick that San has got a job in the NAAFI, so I bought a bottle of wine and celebrated. Jock got a parcel from his wife with a nose with a rotating fly on it.

A better morning, I got out of bed and strangely TC was already out. Usually he was harder to wake up than the dead and yet he was already up. I spent many weeks with 'Top Cat' Furze on exercise in a CET. The Combat Engineer Tractor was a small tank with a bucket instead of a gun. Not a smart move really. A type of moving target, that can't shoot back. I could never wake TC up. If I shook him he would wake up punching. Many a time I shook him and parried a sleepy right cross from him. He must have had a lot of brothers who were trying to steal his bed. I would have to wake up, put on the BV (Boiling Vessel), start the huge Rolls Royce engine, heat up water on the exhaust, wash, shave and cook brekky , prepare hot water for TC's wash and then present him with food and a large black mug of tea in his sleeping bag to get him up. I jumped down from my high bunk to be presented with TC in a dominant butler pose with my towel folded neatly over his left arm.

"Er… Good morning Sir, did Sir, sleep well? Will Sir be carrying out his ablutions now?" TC asked in his best 'Jeeves and Wooster' voice. I laughed. I had been a total wanker the morning before and like a married couple it was now forgiven and forgotten.

"Er… yes please Jeeves, have you beaten the staff this morning, yet?" I put on an affected voice. It was now a competition to see who could keep a straight face for the longest.

"Er…yes Sir, especially that Henderix, he is a lazy bugger Sir," Jock's towel curtain shot back and his large smiling face joined the fun. "I have prepared Sir's razor for Sir, and a bowl of tepid water awaits Sir in the ablutions" TC held out my razor, it had toothpaste on the blades, "Your toothbrush, Sir" TC then presented my toothbrush from under the towel, it had shaving foam on. I was loosing the battle to not laugh. Jock burst out laughing. Mac's head appeared from around his curtain.

"Very good Jeeves, have you had a pee for me yet" this would make him laugh I thought, I would ask him to shake the drops off for me next; he would either laugh or capitulate at that request. TC turned around and picked up *MY* large black mug from his bed, " I took the liberty of having a pee for Sir in his mug thereby saving Sir the trouble of processing the tea, just drink it and it is already processed" he smiled.

"OH NO!"

"Will that be all Sir?"

"You grotty bastard" I laughed as I grabbed my mug, I looked at the edge, and my name was painted on the side. No mistake there, it was *my* mug. Jock was howling with laughter. Spunky popped his head around his spunk stained towel. "Someone call my name."

It was filled with water like substance. Being a black mug, I couldn't tell if it was pee or not. TC's face was still as straight as a ruler. I had lost completely. I put the mug to my lips and pretended to take a drink, because of the size of the mug they couldn't tell if I took a drink or not. Jock went "Eearhghh," Spunky laughed but my eyes were on TC. He laughed which meant that he knew that it was water.

"Hmmm, nice vintage Jeeves, order two cases" TC laughed, we were quits. Now all I had to do was to get the shaving foam off the toothbrush.

The Hymac travelled at only three mph. It had no suspension and rattled. It was designed to travel around construction sites. To drive it a mile was complete madness. There were no large transports on the Island, so we had to drive the thing to the workshop for services. When we did the oil in the hydraulics, which drove the tracks overheated and came out of the track overflow pipes. What this meant was that there were always two lines of OM33, the hydraulic oil leading the observer to the Hymac. It also meant that when one got to ones destination one had to top up the hydraulic oil as it was probably empty. The only redeeming feature on this 580 machine was that the travel levers, two levers that controlled the forward and reverse motion of the tracks, stayed in the forward and reverse position. Not important unless you had to sit in the machine for ninety minutes holding the levers forward. There was a short cut which could be taken. It was a 'as the crow flies' route. On the route was a fence that had to be held down so that the excavator could cross it and not get tangled. TC got out of the Hymac whilst it was still travelling and held down the fence, it trundled over the fence and TC not wanting to get back into the bone shaker, walked alongside the machine, only getting back in to make steering corrections.

We had a new SSgt for Headquarters Troop, Mike Bolan. He was shipped over to join the Squadron in late Feb. he was a very calm man; nothing seemed to get his back up. He was liked from the beginning. Our Troop Staffy stayed in Germany, probably didn't want to leave his hooker girlfriends. They would have lost a lot of money if he had left for six months. Mike Bolan came down the track today and walked up to me, "Cpl Beirne, I have some good news for you"

"My pools numbers have come up and I now own more money than the Army?"

"No not that good" he laughed "Your wife, Sandra, has got a job at the NAAFI in Nunburg"

"Hey! I'm married to a NAAFI tart" this was a standard joke. I was now qualified to say it, "How do you know this, Staff?" I asked.

"Apparently, I now live next door to you, my wife and yours are good friends"

"Oh god, the neighbourhood has taken a dive now" I laughed dodging a slap around the head.

When mail call came, Jock got a parcel; in it was a pair of plastic glasses without glass in. Attached to the frames were a plastic nose and a moustache, on the end of the nose was a black fly. Jock put the glasses on and played with the something in his pocket, the fly started to rotate. His wife had sent this trained killer a joke pair of glasses. These glasses would keep us amused for months. I bought a bottle of wine from the bar and drunk it all to celebrate Sandra getting the job. It would mean a bit of extra money for us but most of all it would give her a social life.

Saturday 5th March

Knockers bogged in the Thwaits. They tried to lift it out, pull it with another Thwaits and string, and push it out. We finally helped them. Found out 'Operation Ironworks' starts mid March. I hope I'm one of the two to do it. The lads have just hung TC's Animal. 1 Tp are digging fuel bonds with a 100b and carrying away the spoil with stretchers!!

We had learnt the lesson the hard way about the peat. There was no way that you could break the surface. Do that and the tyre or track would sink into the peat up to the axle. Trying to drive out would only dig the wheel in deeper. The knockers took a lot longer for this lesson to sink in. There was also a lot more of them and they would take it in turns to drive the dumper. Each driver had to learn this lesson the hard way. Operation Ironworks will be a cushy number. Two Sappers and a load of Boffins. I don't normally land this type of easy number so I'm not too hopeful. 1Tp are out in the sticks and Andy is their operator. He was using the backactor with a ¼ cubic yard bucket to dig the hole for the rubber fuel bladder. There was no dumper so they used their ingenuity and two guys held a stretcher whilst Andy dumped the soil onto it. They would then carry it away and dump it. You have to give them credit for that.

Sunday 6th March

Taff and I worked, didn't do much until ½ past 6 when Simpson wanted a ditch dug. I ran over 3 profile boards. Jock caught a 18 lb. mullet, supposedly pretty big. I found out the secret of eternal hot showers and I was filmed by Brian Hanrahan for news at 10

Monday 7th March

Worked ditching on the Hymac all day. TC is not going to be a daddy. It is costing him DM 100. We let Stig in the Hamm, he thinks it is great. I told the rest of spt. troop about the showers except Mac. The Hymac 590CT's are here along with the Haulamatics (new). Brewsters start on the road today, thank god.

Tuesday 8th March

A 14 hour day again. Just when we thought we had finished the left hand track came off, and we couldn't get it back on. Jock has lost his socks in the wash and god knows how. We seem to only get tippers when we finish. Bloody knackered again. It's that stupid Hymac 580bt. It's crap. We had a look in the containers that held the dead bodies. Guess what we found. NOWT.

Wednesday 9th March

Homer didn't like the fact that one of our lads had yesterday off, even he lets one of his lads off everyday, it should be my turn tomorrow. Mac was the only guy to operate today. The rest of us sat around getting bored. Taff said me and him are on 'Ironworks'. All the tippers came after we leave so we are kicking up shit. TC thinks he has a hernia. The knockers have found out about the showers. The civvy poms are getting £1000 a month.

We got in from work at seven thirty tonight, opened the door to our cabin and walked in chatting and laughing, we were all happy to be back at home, so to speak. The other half of the cabin was still in bed, they were on night shift. Tim Turner shouted from his pit and told us to be quiet, or to be more accurate "Shut the fuck up you bastards, I'm trying to get some fucking sleep, how would you like it if we made noise when we left for work, now shut the fuck up!" Bearing in mind that there were two full Cpls with us, Mac and myself were LCpls and Tim Turner was a Sapper, he was a bit out of order with the tone of his voice. He was quite correct in asking us to be quiet but went about it in the wrong way. Mac took offence at the way that Tim Turner spoke to us and went over and started to argue with Tim. The argument was based on the fact that we should be quiet when we come in; Mac's response was that if asked nicely we would. Tim Turner was renowned at his ability to upset everybody with everything that he said. If you were married to a German he would slate the Germans in front of you. One of the guys had a disabled sister, Tim picked on this guy to tell him that all spastics should be put down at birth. Tim couldn't understand why the guy beat him up, even after he was told the reason. Even though he had just been woken he was in top form at upsetting Mac, Taff told him to leave it and to come back over to our side of the room, Taff obviously realised that we were at fault and told Mac so.

It was around ten thirty pm and everybody was in bed. The other half of the cabin was getting up to go for night shift, through my sleepy haze I heard them, but was able to screen it out and carry on falling off to sleep. In my half dream state I didn't realise that the room went quiet as they left. Through my dream I heard somebody shouting not one yard from me, "See how you like it, huh, not very nice when it's done to you is it you bastard."

I realised it was Tim's voice and was no dream. I opened my eyes, listened and heard two feet landing on the deck floor and an argument start up outside my towel curtain. I popped my head past my curtain and saw Mac and Tim Turner arguing. Tim was in full uniform but Mac was naked except for his underpants. The argument went something like this:

*****

Tim: See how you like it, huh, not very nice when it's
           done to you is it you bastard
Mac: What the fuck do you think you are playing at,
           Turner?
Tim: I thought I'd show you fuckers what you sound
           like when you come in after work! I work night
           shift and have to sleep through...

*****

Tim, well known for his ability to talk the hind legs of a donkey
now stopped talking. The reason that he stopped talking was because
Mac had just punched him squarely in the mouth. Tim hit the deck
on his back, like an old black-and-white movie where one punch pole
axes the opponent; Tim went rigid and scribed a beautiful ninety
degree arc to the floor. Here he lay for a full three seconds totally
silent. The speech part of his brain, which took up the largest part of
Tim, wanted to carry on talking but was held in silence by the rest of
Tim's brain as it estimated damage from the attack. When Tim's
brain realised that there was no lasting damage to Tim's body it
allowed him to start talking again. Tim was renowned for talking his
way INTO trouble. The two most commonly used phrases in 75
Squadron were 'Giv'us a Fag' and 'Someone's punched Timmy
again'. His first words were "You didn't have to do that, why did you
have to hit me?" There was real hurt in his voice but the tone was
completely different from what it was five seconds ago. The
aggression had gone out of his voice. Somewhere along the line Tim
has missed out on a valuable lesson. Even though he got punched
regularly he didn't realise why. Mac told him to shut the fuck up,
which he didn't, and he went out the room still talking and moaning
about Mac 'over reacting'. Mac took the two steps to be back by his
bunk and I asked him why he had punched him.

"I was having a wank and was on the vinegar strokes when he
shook me, it scared the hell out of me, and I thought you guys had
caught me wanking. That's why I punched him." We both laughed.

Jock, Spunky and Taff were looking from behind their towel curtains, but no-one had bothered to get up to stop the fight. It was good entertainment. TC was still fast asleep!

Thursday 10th March

Got up at 0500 to do the washing. Last night Mac punched Tim Turner, stupid sod asked for it. I start Ironworks tomorrow. In Stanley today all the Bennies were very 'offish'. Some even giving me aggressive looks, I reckon they resent us being here. Rumours of a young girl giving head for £1. I wonder if she gives discount for bulk buying. Also rumour of a nurse giving the lot for £17. I'll do it for £16.

TC was pissed that he missed the fight last night. He told us that we should have woken him first.

The only time that one could get to the washing machines was early in the morning. Throughout the rest of the day they were full, either that or there was someone's washing in the machine, a sort of 'reserved' sign. It would go on to the top of the machine and mine would go in. I found that if I just piled the washing on to the top of the machine in the same way as it came out there was a good possibility that when I came back my washing would be thrown all over the Dhobi cabin. It was safer to fold up that washing and put it neatly on the top, and then my washing would still be in the machine when I got back. I can remember doing the Dhobi but cannot remember where we ironed our clothes. We obviously did as there was no way that we would have got away with creased clothes in this 'normalisation' period.

Project Ironworks was the name given to the project to clear all of the mines that the Argies planted in and around Port Stanley. Straight after the war 59 Independent Commando Squadron, Royal Engineers were making an attempt to clear the mines when one exploded and a Commando lost his leg. So Maggie Thatcher said," No more soldiers must die in The Falklands, the war is over." The Argie minefield fences were a single piece of barbed wire, usually lying on the ground. The Brits put another fence thirty metres outside this. It was a proper, three stranded barbed wire fence. We, the British , had no records of where the Argies had laid the minefields and so a call went out to Porton Down, the Nuclear, Chemical and Biological… er… 'testing' establishment to devise a mechanical minefield clearing piece of equipment. I suppose it was given to Porton Down because they have the greatest concentration of Boffins, or scientists' in the Army. Six months later they had devised a cunning plan to get rid of the mines and they went out there to test their ideas. We in Support Troop had all attended a training course in Chattenden and Porton Down and two were to do the actual thing in the Falklands. For some unknown reason Taff chose himself and me? Me? What had I done to please him I will never know? It was going to be a bit of a skive, I had hoped.

Today I was preparing to start the project. Everybody was envious of me and Taff. This was something big, something that might go down in history and I was on it. Being a Leo and a total extrovert I revelled in it. Everybody else was trying to get on the team, from Officers down to the dirty unwashed. No go, just me and Taff. EOD (The bomb disposal guys) were furious. They wanted to do it all. Who were we to go walking around on their minefields?

I went into town today and noticed a difference in the townsfolk. Why, I had no idea. Maybe a soldier had raped one of their young girls. More like one of their young girls had raped a young soldier. We used to see the girls, aged around twelve to fifteen, hanging around the soldiers outside the few pubs. The soldiers were always laughing and joking with the girls. Who knows? I felt uncomfortable in Port Stanley for the first time. I was stared at and avoided like I had the pox. The girls at the cash register in the 'Supermarket' were very curt and offish. I bought some provisions, like soap, toothpaste and Dhobi dust I walked all round Port Stanley again and bought some stamps and a couple of liberation coins. They are now worth … nowt. Good investment Julian! The second part of my diary entry probably answers my question. I had never thought about it until just now, twenty nine years later. The young girl, who was giving head, was most probably 'young'. If her parents had found out then that would explain the stares and aggression towards the ones who had liberated the Falklands from the Argies. The nurse was a different matter. If I had found out who she was I would have spent my whole months pay on her... or *him* knowing my luck. Many of the nurses were men. Imagine your horror when you find out that it is Nurse Smith that does the lot for £17. You enter the hospital with £17 clutched in your sweaty paw and walk into Nurse Smith's office only to be confronted with a 'him'. It was also rumoured that the house at the top of David Lane was a knocking shop. We went past it every day and it looked more like a chicken shack to me. Even if it was a brothel I would not have wanted to enter the house. Occasionally I saw a man or woman around the house and there were always kids playing outside so I guess it was also malicious gossip. The only sex that 99.99 % of all the males had was with their hands. No wonder the rear of the ship Rangatira stunk! The sewage wasn't processed.

I have already mentioned how heavy a sleeper TC was. He slept through all of the shouting and scuffling that went on between Tim and Mac last night. He was really green with envy that he hadn't seen it, and he asked Mac to hit him again tonight. Mac was happy to oblige but Taff put a stop to it.

Friday 11th March

Taff and I tracked the 590CT's up to the minefield 110. After dinner went to 15 Sqn. Throttle stuck on County. Clutch seized on Bambi. Bombardier wrecked. We've been given a free hand to carry on and put the kit together. Lumpy Phillips asked 75 Sqn. for floor polish and a cutlery set. He put floor polish in top preference above fuel, food, etc. A sigs guy pulled a SLR on a Benny; he's in nick, for not giving him water.

Taff and I reported to B jetty. It was where all of the heavy equipment was unloaded. It was also the location of two beautiful, brand new Hymac 590CT's. The Hymac 590 was a newer, more up to date version of the 580. The 'CT' model was a special for the

Army. It had huge two metre wide swamp tracks. Each track plate was a pontoon box. It could almost float on top of the wettest marsh. It would have no problem going where man's foot couldn't. The other distinguishing feature of the 590 CT was that it was totally armoured. It had a blast proof cabin, and three inch thick shatter proof glass. I immediately fell in love with them. A love that was to last ten years! I could never have guessed at that moment that ten years later I would be sitting in the very same vehicles clearing the minefields in Kuwait. As a Civvy! We checked the vehicles over and tracked them up the hill to Port Stanley common minefields. We discovered the step backwards that Hymac had made. On the old 580 the travel levers stayed forward and one could relax and steer using the bucket and boom levers. On the 590 the levers snapped back to the neutral position when they were released. It meant that you had to hold them forward all the time. On a long journey it was knackering on the wrists.

On the project were two Boffins from Porton Down, a photographer and two Sappers. The Sappers were Taff and I. That was it, no head sheds, no SSMs, and no other Sappers to get the good jobs. It was a dream job. There were two other people that had an input in what we did on the minefield clearance in Port Stanley and that was the EOD Warrant Officer who was in charge at the time, His nickname was Q Mines, and a Major from the EOD and trials team, called Major Mukos. His name aside he was one of the best Officers that I ever met in the Army. Major Mukos met us and gave us a welcome talk. I had met the Major before when we were running a trial on anti-tank ditch digging machines. After the initial introductions we were given a nice new Landrover. It was an EOD Rover with red wheel arches. The Rover was for us and us alone. We were met by Q Mines and I immediately knew that all was not well. He was not happy to see us, and that included the Boffins. He told the Boffins, deciding not to talk to us Sappers, that between the time that they had liberated the Island and now, they had found all of the maps to the minefields and therefore didn't want us messing up 'his' minefields with our machines. We saw our easy number line up on the runway in order to take off out of our life for ever. The Boffins stepped in, and in their educated tones suggested that we should still go ahead with the trial. The Q, still pissed off that we had the task of clearing up 'his' minefield and not his guys, grumbled something about finding a 'bit of ground' for us to play with. If he had pushed it too far the Boffins would have pulled rank but it wasn't needed. The Q begrudgingly took us to the minefield on Port Stanley common and showed us the old Argie fence and the nice shiny new British fence, which was thirty metres outside the Argie fence. A few months later Margaret Thatcher, (God bless her glorious name) would stand on this hallowed land. A few weeks after that, Q Mines would stand on the same piece of soil and blow his foot off. So much for maps eh? Right then it was the first real minefield that I had ever seen and it was … disappointing. There were no dead bodies or blown up tanks, no large black mines or huge holes in the land, only a single piece of rusty barbed wire and grass. Nevertheless it was a minefield and we were on the edge of it.

After this moving occasion Taff and I drove up to 15 Squadron Resources to see the kit that we had to play with. We shouldn't have bothered, it was all knackered. There were three Snowcats, called a Bombardier, a Muscat and a Bambi. The Bombardier was a four man Snowcat as was the Muscat, they had a covered cabs and rubber tracks. The Bombardier had been dropped by a Chinook helicopter from a thousand feet and was wrecked, the Bambi had not been looked after and when we tried to start it, it lurched forward. The clutch had seized due to lack of use. We also had two County tractors. These were fitted out with remote actuators and cameras so that we could operate them from outside the minefield. The throttle on one of them was stuck closed and would not start. We disconnected the actuators on the other County and freed up the stuck throttle. Then we caused more than a few turned heads when we drove the tractors up to the ground that Q Mines had graciously allotted us. The reason heads were turned was because we were driving two brand new tractors through a farming community. Taff commented that it would have been more fun if we had left the actuators on and drove the tractors up with no one in the cabs. We transported the Elk wheels up to the laydown area. The Elk wheels were a round metal framework that had wooden slats bolted on to it for traction. The idea was that when we drove over a mine it blew off the slats and allowed us to re-weld the frame back together. A good idea which had only been put to the test in Porton Down! Ten years later in Kuwait we found that bulldozer tracks kicked ass when it came to mine explosions. They were virtually invincible. (This statement does not include the Royal Ordnance 9kg barmine which can totally ruin your day, your hearing, and your life!).

Rumour of the day was of a Signals guy who stopped a Benny from entering an area by holding a gun to his head. That was allowed because it was a classified area and the war had only just finished and the Benny had no identification on him, but he refused to give him water and was subsequently thrown in jail. He wasn't humane enough for the British Army. A bit ironic when you take into account the way that the British have hacked and murdered their way through history. Apparently the British are the favoured nation to be tortured by, every other nation tortures you mercilessly, and the British stop every hour for a cup of tea.

1 Troop worked out in the sticks, they had run out of diesel and were running their generators on aviation fuel which is basically paraffin, Lumpy Phillips put in a requisition for stores. It was requested in order of priority. On top of the order was floor polish! Second in order of priority was a cutlery set and eighth on the list was diesel. I was in the Squadron office when the Squadron Quarter Master Sergeant (SQMs) received the order. His comments on the intelligence of field SNCOs was noted and distributed throughout the Squadron by yours truly.

Saturday 12th March

We got an EOD Rover. Goody! A Benny stopped me asking me to clear his house. I told him I would pass the message on. We tried to find 4 David Lane. Try 34 Sqn. office. The Chinook dropped the

Muscat knackering the suspension. San wrote to me saying that she wanted a kiddie. I feel very depressed now. Why can't I be with her to talk to her? I don't know what to think. Do I or don't I? I best write to her but what do I say?

Where does the RAF get their Chinook pilots from? All they had to do was to hook up the Muscat Snowcat and carry it to the laydown area, but no that was too simple, they cut the load in mid flight and dropped it. The suspension wasn't too happy at the ground when it met it at one hundred and twenty mph and smashed its way through the body of the Muscat. We were severely pissed off. The Muscat was going to be our little toy. It was the only vehicle bar the tiny Bambi, which could sail across the peat without fear of getting bogged in. (Not taking into account the Bombardier which the RAF wrecked previously).

We were driving out the top of Port Stanley when a Benny (nicknamed after the Crossroads' village idiot) flagged us down. We pushed forward the window and he stuck his head in, "can you come and clear my house of bombs, there are a lot in the living room." I looked at Taff and he at me, "Where do you live?" he pointed towards a house, "OK we'll get the teams down to you as soon as we get to them, Ok?" I said with more authority than I felt. There was no way I was going to start poking around in Argie booby trapped ammo. If I was in an Army that had just had its ass kicked I would take great pleasure in booby trapping everything that I left behind. Taff and I had time on our hands so we drove around Stanley trying to find 4 David Lane. That was the house that was supposedly the brothel. We found a rundown shack that passed for a house on this Island but we both agreed that if it was the brothel, anyone that went there was to lazy to wank. Germs in there could probably jump twelve feet! I got a letter from Sandra in it she wrote that she wanted a child. I was always the single guy. Getting married was as much a surprise to me as it was to my parents. When I told my mother she went silent and asked me if the girl was pregnant. Having a kid was a big step, and meant that our "staying out all night" days would come to an end. I felt terrible at not being able to talk to her. A phone call would have made it better; at least I could have had an immediate conversation with her. Our communications had a four week delay, which made any kind of discourse other than I love and miss you, impossible. Anyway, as far as I could remember, I needed to be there for San to get pregnant, so her wanting a baby was a little bit academic.

Sunday 13th March

TC's hernia (suspected) is playing him up. We got the Bambi going, the rotavator on and other such boring things. No mail on Sunday. I showed Bruce Lee how to use a rota-gym, it was amusing. Everybody wants to get on the project. Fuck em, get our lads on first. 15 Sqn. plant operators are working on Coastell Road.

TC is considering going sick with his hernia. It is restricting the way that he is walking. He can only wobble. He thinks that he must have lifted too much a few days ago and either pulled a muscle in his leg or got a hernia. No one knew what a hernia looked or felt like so we were no help. Taff and I had a lazy breakfast and made our own way up to the site. Everybody else was in their usual rush, wash, dress, eat, boots and out on to the boat. For Taff and me it was as and when we felt like it. When we finally arrived at the site, (which was a few pieces of equipment in the middle of a field,) at around nine o'clock the Boffins still hadn't arrived. They were living the life of Reilly in the Canada Goose Hotel. We got to work with putting the rotavator on the rear of the tractor and putting on the Elk wheels. At around ten o'clock the Boffins turned up with their photographer. They were impressed with the work that we had done. We thought that we had been idle, still, no point in popping their little bubble. I got to work on the Bambi. It was a Ford car engine with a simple four speed gearbox. I jumped the battery off one of the tractors and slowly engaged and disengaged the clutch. After a few minutes I was able to put the Bambi into gear without it shooting forward or the gears grinding. Now came the ultimate test, I engaged first gear and let the clutch out, the Bambi shot forward and I was in motion. The Bambi was no more than six feet long. It had black rubber tracks and a yellow body. It was around five foot high and had two seats. In between the two seats was the engine so there was no room in the cab, everything had to go outside. It also had a trailer with the same tracks. Without the trailer it was a cabby little machine that could go almost anywhere. I drove it up to the top of Sapper Hill, (the only way to ascend a hill) and found a large 150mm recoilless anti tank gun. It resembled the old British Wombat. I had a coil of rope so I tied it to the rear of the Bambi and towed it down to the camp. The Boffins and Taff thought that it was the bee's knees. Whilst they were buzzing around it I got into one of the Excavators and starting it up swung round and picked up the gun, lifting it high up into the air I drove the barrel into the earth. There it stayed as a monument and landmark for all. When we left five months later it was still sticking its Ventura up towards the clouds. The Boffins declared that they were finishing for the day, it was only three o'clock!

"What are we to do?" Taff asked Jeremy the head Boffin.

"Well… er it's up to you, finish for the day if you wish" came his uncertain reply.

"We'll work for a while longer" Taff stated and went back to torqueing up the bolts on the Elk wheels. I looked at him with concern. This wasn't like Taff, had he turned over a new leaf? I hoped not!

The Boffins got into their Argie Merc and sedately bumped their way over the hill, when they had disappeared Taff stood up and smiled at me "Right, Boyo, lets fuck off then." I needed no explanation and threw the tools into the tent and jumped into the Rover whose engine Taff was gunning. Taff shot off over the hill like a rally driver, far from complaining I held on for dear life and giggled like a little girl. This wasn't our Rover and EOD had it in for us. If we fucked up their Rover! Oh dear!… Sorry… giv'us another. All throughout the short working day groups of soldiers had been visiting us trying to get onto the project. Every body saw it as a cushy number and for once in my life *I* had landed it. We weren't about to give it up. If we did need any more personnel then we would recruit from Support Troop and nowhere else. The Army is very tribal. We are trained that way. Even in PT the instructors put us into teams and we compete against each other. Even if our best friends were in the other teams we would try to beat them. We were Unit proud, Regiment proud, Squadron proud and Troop proud depending on who we were competing against. I have found that we take this attitude with us into Civvy Street. I have shocked many civvies by polishing their boots for them because they had no idea on how to do it. That is our way. If one of our own is lagging behind on a run we will all take his kit so that he can keep up. This camaraderie is what is missing in civilian life. Many servicemen and women drift into military style jobs when they leave the Forces. Jobs like the Police, the Prison Service and Security. It offers them the same style of friendship that they had in the Forces. Servicewomen (and men) (thought I'd do it the other way round this time) in civilian jobs can be as loyal as a dog if they are treated in the right fashion, but civilian employers use the wrong motivators and therefore get the wrong response from service personnel. One of the best bosses that I have so far had in civilian life was an ex RAF Vulcan pilot. Using loyalty he got the best out of me and I would have done anything for him. (Nearly, anything). The bottom line was that there was no way that we would have allowed another Regiment to put a guy with our little project.

We got back to the jetty and it was empty. We were so early it was unreal. We were even able to park the Rover right next to one of the shops next to the jetty. Titch Fuller was on the lower CSB jetty. We climbed down the ladder scrounged a lift off him to the Geraint. A quick, hot shower and first in the dinner queue and I was free for the rest of the evening. 75 Squadron had set up a multi gym on the tank deck of the landing craft. I changed into shorts and went onto the deck to work out. The crew of the LCT were Chinese from Hong Kong. One of them we'd nicknamed Bruce Lee because of the way that he liked to copy me practising karate. As I was working out he came over and watched me, I indicated to him and asked him if he wanted to have a go. He did.

Monday 14th March

REVELATION TIME

TC's HERNIA IS A ZIT!

He said he was going to wind us up so Taff and I wound him up. The lost packet of fags really done it. 'Horses Mouth' is longer than WAR + PEACE. Sgt REME rammed the Bedford with the county. I'm gonna sack him! We've got a tent. Must nick a heater. £1,000 a fucking week.

TC threw back his towel curtain, there was a beaming smile on his face "Hey, guys" he shouted "I'm cured!!"

"Cured of what?" Jock asked trying to stretch his Y fronts over his seven o'clock hard on, failing and looking at the end peeping at him from his waist band.

"My Hernia, it was a fucking zit!" TC raised his eyebrows and smiled as if he was stating an obvious fact.

"A ZIT?" Taff laughed "you have been making all of that fuss over a zit?"

"Hey" TC's face adopted a serious expression "this was no ordinary zit, this was an Argie undercover zit that was trying to take over my body"

"Sounds like it has already taken over your mind, you dopey twat" Taff stood up and saw Jock trying to stuff his knob into his pants; he rolled his eyes towards the roof and dropped back into his bunk.

"How do you know it was a zit then Top Cat" Spunky called up from his pit. After the Benny incident Spunky had moved back into our room.

"Because…" TC paused for effect "I have just squeezed it, and it was fucking huge"

"Where is it?" Spunky climbed out of his bunk bed and stood up to look into TC's.

"Oh no, this is getting too gross for words," I felt my mind recoiling against the image of TC squeezing a zit whilst Spunky looked on "I'm off for breakfast." As I left the cabin I heard Spunky say "you call that a zit? This is a zit." That was enough, my mind shut down for the morning; it was receiving no more calls from any of my senses, especially the hearing and sight. I stumbled blindly up to the cookhouse (or Galley to give it the nautical term) and my nose persuaded my mind to accept the smell of cooking bacon. Happy that I had something to visualise other than TC's zit, I enjoyed a full Army breakfast.

Taff joined me up in the canteen, "TC reckons that he is going to wind us up, he told Spunky that he was going to tell us that the OC was putting us on the Road and him and Mac on Project Ironworks, so I nicked his fags out of his combat jacket, lets see who gets wound up first, eh?"

"Has he gone" I asked him.

"Yeah, picked up his jacket and got on the boat, didn't check for his fags though"

"I think he is going to be a bit pissed off when he gets out onto site and finds that he hasn't got any fags"

Later that night TC had a sense of humour failure when Taff told him that it was him that took his fags. TC sulked all night and didn't talk to anyone. Apparently he spent the day sponging rollup fags from Mac.

We had a SSgt visit us up at the mine clearance site every now and again to check and service the equipment. He was so proficient at driving that he drove the brand new County tractor into the back of the Bedford lorry. His excuse was that he didn't realise that there was a hand throttle; we have banned him from driving the equipment.

We spent the afternoon putting up a large one hundred and sixty eight pound tent. It was a canvas monstrosity from the First World War. It takes a lot of common sense and an old soldier who has put one up before to erect it. There are poles all over the place. Our first attempt finished with the canvas inside out. After a few hours of fumbling we had erected the canvas cavern, it was bloody freezing inside it. At least the sun warmed up the body outside, inside the tent it was permanent shadow and cold. As you can probably tell by the diary entry I was still a little pissed off at finding out that the civilian construction companies that were out there, Brewsters and another whose name I forget, were paying their plant operators £1,000 a week to be there. We were getting just under that on a long month. What added insult to injury was that a lot of them couldn't hack the conditions and were getting on the mail plane and flying home again, the ones that stayed were mainly ex-forces! Jock knew some of them as they were ex-Airborne.

Pinko has had an idea that we are all following. He has written to some large companies that have connections to the Army and he has told them that he is in the Falklands. He buttered up the letter and told them how good their kit was. He wrote to Allis Chalmers, Muirhill, Caterpillar and Aveling Barford, all makers of the construction plant that we use. As an afterthought in his letter he put that if they should decide that should be sent some form of company merchandise then here follows his vital statistics, and with that he put all of his body measurements. Cheeky bastard! I wish I had thought of it first. Now Pinko has all of the best companies. That is why he told us after he sent the letters. I would have done the same! I wrote to Goodyear, as I want some new tyres for my VW Golf GTI, The Sun, because they have got loads of money and claim to support the services, and Winget. For those of you who don't know, Winget make vibrating pedestrian rollers. Pinko gets Caterpillar, I get Winget. Heaven help me. TC wrote to Volvo saying that all of our equipment in the Falklands is falling apart, if we had Volvo it wouldn't be. Please send me some Volvo freebies.

Tuesday 15th March

Some knocker filled the lighting tower engine sump with diesel. The OC found out! No mail again. Bignose told Lt Slovey that the road was too high. Lt Slovey just agreed! I'm getting pissed off with that bloody airfield road. I found out today that although I put a film in the camera I never loaded it. 36 pics wasted. What a Pratt. I was filmed again this morning getting off the RCL.

Bignose went to the site today. He parked up his Mercedes jeep and walked down the site. He stopped at the lighting tower and unscrewed the crankcase filler cap. The cap was red. "Cpl Henderix, Come here a minute please" he shouted to Jock. When Jock got to the lighting tower the OC pointed to the engine crankcase. Jock looked at the lid in the OC's hand, looked into the rocker cover and burst out laughing. "Who the fuck has done that Sir?" Jock was on the attack. The best means of defence is attack.

"I was just about to ask you the same thing Cpl Henderix"

"It must have been one of the Knockers Sir; it has a red cap on the rocker cover so a Knocker has probably filled it up with petrol thinking that is what goes in there. Red is for petrol, yellow is for diesel."

"Well get it sorted Cpl!" the OC stormed and plonking the cap on to the top of the engine walked off to annoy someone else.

Jock walked over to Spunky and laughed "Bloody Muppets!" That was Jock's favourite saying. If anyone fucked up, they were 'Bloody Muppets'. The OC was always being called a 'Bloody Muppet' by Jock. We were laying a road onto peat, it was waterlogged. As I have said earlier it was like building on blancmange. In the normal course of events ditches would be dug at the start so that they could be draining the ground as the project went on. Well we didn't. The Clerk of Works couldn't persuade the OC to dig ditches. We will dig them at the end! He would remonstrate to the poor SSgts. They went to the CRE, the Commander of the Royal Engineers, usually a Brigadier or some other semi god with red lapels. We weren't allowed to spread the huge piles of peat that we dug out and the water pooled up in gigantic lakes. The CRE clocked this and wise to the OC's antics told him on a weekly meeting to flatten the windrows. Come next meeting he was asked on record if they had been levelled and he straight faced answered "Yes, of course they have!" All the CRE had to do was to drive along the road and see for himself, which he did and was not pleased. So, the Squadron hated the OC, the tipper drivers hated the OC and now the CRE hated him as well. Although that was by no means everybody on the Island the OC still had lots more time to piss them off, which to eliminate any stress caused by this suspense I will now tell you that he did, Officers, SNCOs and even locals.

I took my camera to the site and took some pictures of the mine clearance train, which consisted of a tractor with Elk wheels and a rotavator on the rear followed by another tractor with a Dutch stubble burner on the rear. The whole effort was driven in reverse. The idea being that the rotavator smashed up the plastic mines and the burner set fire to them. After finishing off the roll I opened the camera only to find that I hadn't loaded the tab into the roller. All of the photos that I had taken of Port Stanley were on that film! Or not as the case was. To make matters worse, one of the Boffins was a professional photographer. Photography being a macho thing, (the "my lens is bigger than yours" thing) I failed to tell anyone there of my oversight and made plans to re-photograph the site the next day.

Wednesday 16th March

I had the afternoon off, so I did a lot of washing. Listening to Roger Whittaker makes me feel so far away from my heart. When will this separation end? I haven't spoken to a woman since I left except to say "I'll have this" and "I think I've got the 3 p." I don't think I know how to talk to them any more. "For fucks sake don't fucking fart in here again, Pratt" doesn't seem right somehow. Come to think of it what is a woman? Is it one of them fat Bennies with spots and a high voice that I've seen about?

The strain of the separation was starting to show. It wasn't so bad for most of the single soldiers as they slept in barracks, usually on their own. Although I do remember walking into the block on a Saturday morning as I was on duty and saw Spunky fast asleep at the top of his bed. I started to walk out when I did a double take that is normally only seen in the movies, I looked back. Spunky's legs were sticking out the end of his bed. The distance from the soles of his feet and his head was around eight feet, also his feet were on their side and his shoulders were flat on the bed. He was stretched and twisted. I stood and stared for a full minute trying to figure out what was happening. I had two theories. I tip toed up to his bed (although the occupants were sleeping the sleep of the shitfaced, the room stank of booze and cans littered the room, a rifle shot wouldn't have woke them!) and I lifted his bed covers, not a very heterosexual thing to do, but I just had to know. Under the blankets was Tiny Westminister, a small guy from MT. Both he and Spunky were fully clothed and were fast asleep. Apart from the occasional drunk sleeping partner the single soldiers slept alone. The married soldiers on the other hand slept with a woman every night. Their every evening and morning was spent interacting with the woman and kids that they love. They are then taken away from these people and put with men, smelly, farty, rough, unshaven, macho men. It took a lot of adjusting. When we were working or interacting with the others we were able to think about other things, but on days off, it was think about home time. That hurt! The fond memories of home were getting more and more distant. End Ex was a dream in many many weeks time. The light at the end of the tunnel wasn't even visible. It was a very depressing time. When I thought about Sandra it gave me a terrible yearning that I couldn't satisfy. I couldn't even telephone. We got one call every three months. I hadn't yet learned how to cut off the thoughts about home and they just made me miserable.

Thursday 17th March

We lit the burner today, we had the pilot flame on and Taff stood on the burner to turn it on to run, he immediately disappeared in a flash of flame. It runs! What heat, it's great. We dropped the engine oils on the Hymac. I wrote Ode to Airbridge. Taff wrote state of the support troop.

Bignose threw a wobbler because there was no plate for him at dinner. Petty bastard.

Everything was ready at the minefield clearance project. The Elk wheels were on. The flat bottomed ditching bucket was on and had been turned backwards so that the blast from a mine would be sent away from the man in the cab. The rotavator was on and working and the tractors were fully operational on servos and cameras.

It was light the blue touch paper time, Taff started the tractor engine and I lit a wad of cotton waste on the end of a long steel rod. I put the flames into a hole and lit the pilot flame. The Boffins were all happy and so were Taff and I. It all worked. The Boffins had to scour the country side for the stubble burner, they found it in Holland. That is a lot of scouring. "Well let's get a flame going then, Boyo" Taff stated as he stood on the burner and grabbed the lever that opened the fuel vent. That was the last that I saw of Taff for the next minute. He disappeared in a huge conflagration. The Boffins took a step backwards from the heat and I tried to take a step forwards to help Taff but was pushed back by the heat. "Is he alright on there?" the lead Boffin asked the concern clear in his voice. Suddenly Taff appeared from the front of the tractor, he was jumping around and laughing and there was steam or smoke coming from his lightweight trousers. "I think it works boyo."

"How the fuck did you get out Taff?" I laughed, he was laughing so I felt that it was alright for me to laugh at his close shave.

"When the flames shot up I jumped through the rear window, look at this" he showed us his jumper, it was singed up the back. The hairs on his hands and his eyebrows were singed and there was that awful smell of burning human hair. "It could've been worse" I launched into Jock's second favourite saying "It could've been me"

"It will be next time Bernie, because I won't be turning it on again" A Boffin approached us with concern on his face, "er, I think it is designed to be turned on from inside the tractor." We walked round so that we could see through the side window. "Er, yes, that might have been a good idea, that's why you get paid so much more money than I do," Taff turned to the Boffin, "You spot things like that"

"I can assure you that my pay is not all that much better than yours the government paid scientist spoke with sadness in his eyes. It seemed that there was better money to be had in the civilian sector but it was hard to transfer into that sector. The blower was kicking a lot of heat and the grass underneath was starting to burn away from the area under the flames. "Well, lets try it shall we?" the Boffin shook himself out of his forlorn thoughts and got to grips with the task in hand. We set the burner moving slowly over the peat. We had an area set out in the common. On the area were plastic mines that were dug in at different depths. The Q Mines had complained bitterly when the Boffins had told him that they had wanted live mines to play with. They were, after all, *His* mines. The Boffins simply went over his head and he turned up at the site with his tail between his legs and a cardboard box full of plastic mines.

These we played with, much to Q Mines' chagrin and eventually buried them in the peat. He had made a big issue over marking the area where we planted them. The mines had no detonators in them so they were only a lump of plastic explosives. The stubble burner was driven by remote control, slowly over the area. Nothing blew up, there were no large explosions. Nothing exciting happened. We left the area for an hour in case a mine was slowly burning and decided to explode when we walked up to it. Nothing happened in that hour. Q Mines decided to be the hero of the day and be the one who walked up to the mines to see if they were safe to extract. There was no discussion on this. No "Don't go Q Mines, let me take your place" shit. We were more than happy to let this prat put *his* life at risk rather than ours. He brought back the mines. Some were charred, some had some of the plastic melted, but most hadn't even been touched by the flames. A distinct failure by anyone's standards! Later, the Boffins put thermometers in the soil and we ran the burner over it again. On the top it was 3000 ° C. one inch below the surface it was down to a few hundred and two inches below the surface it was the normal temperature of the soil. The stubble burner was designed to so just that, burn stubble. We wanted it to burn mines up to a foot under the surface. Quite rightly, the burner refused to do this. The burner was regarded as not suitable. I am sure that we could have discovered this in the UK. The next test was the rotavator. The idea behind it was to drive it backwards and chop up all of the plastic mines. When we told Q Mines of what we intended to do he went from red to purple and blew a fuse. We wanted to chop up *his* souvenirs. He came up with a million different reasons why we shouldn't chop them up. While we were still digesting those million excuses he came up with another million and although we accepted one of the second million he was quite clearly thinking up another million to throw at us. He did agree to get some mine bases and fill them up with Plasticine and they would have the same characteristics as the real mines. These we would not get until the next day so it was knock-off time. A great idea!

That night there was the message on Squadron orders that we hated to read. "Due to technical reasons there was no Airbridge today." Airbridge was the name given to the aircraft that flew from Ascension Islands to The Falklands. Usually Hercules C130, they carried among other important things all of the mail to the Islands. If there was no Airbridge then there was no mail. I composed and wrote the following Ditty.

*****

ODE TO AIRBRIDGE
As I sit here with a cold heart
Counting the days that we're apart
I dread to hear that terrible sound
That our mail in Ascension never
Left the ground.
Don't they realise what it means
To have a letter from the woman
Of your dreams
Left in the sack, on the bottom rack
3000 miles from here.
A letter from home warms the soul

Keeps us happy, content and consoled
Makes us cry, makes us laugh
Sends us crazy, sends us daft.
The only thing better than a
Letter from you
Is two.
*****

Friday 18th March

We changed the buckets round amidst torrential rain and mud, and then I knocked off for the afternoon. I did my washing. The second CSE show was on. I didn't go to that either. Weather was bad this morning. Jock should have been out of the Army today. 75 Sqn. wives club video on tonight.

VERDICT: - had a good time guessing whose wife was who. The best bit was the sensible bit from Spacers and Mac's missus.

Oh dear, the good weather has left us. Today it rained and rained and rained. The area where we were doing the mine train trails was a sea of mud. It was named Port Stanley common. Apparently it was the picnic and dog walking area for the people of Port Stanley.

The Boffins have a new idea. We dig up the peat with the mines in and store it and let it dry and then at a later date, set fire to it. As do the Falkland Islanders. The Boffins figured out that the soil could be dug out with the excavators but in order to protect the machine and operator the bucket should be facing outwards instead of inwards. Someone in the heavens thought that this was bad idea and tried to let us know by making it pour with rain. With rain running down the back of my 'Waterproof' I realised that the peat would never stay dry in the Falklands, a bit like British Soldiers in their 'Waterproofs'. These were combat coloured dustbin bags. Obviously non porous, they didn't let a single drop of rain in or for that matter a single molecule of sweat out. Your clothes would be soaked in sweat if you wore the waterproofs for longer than twenty minutes. That is standing on guard, if you were doing heavy manual work then that time was reduced to minutes. Rain, doesn't smell, sweat does! It was considered preferable to get soaked to the skin with rain than wear the waterproofs whilst doing heave manual work. Gore-Tex® was out but it was so expensive that each jacket cost the government half the defence budget. Trident missiles took the precedence over keeping the soldiers dry and comfortable. Something that would never be used, costing millions of pounds was where our Gore-Tex® waterproofs went.

If any British government had a backbone they would have made the Trident program a huge bluff, and spend the capital elsewhere. Tell everyone that the system was so secret that it was being built elsewhere. Where ever you worked and who ever you were was not secret enough so it was elsewhere. Leak some false papers to the Soviet Union stating the Russian cities that they were pointed at and spend the money on Gore-Tex® Waterproofs for the services. Politicians are obviously not poker players. Therefore, we were soaked to the skin but happy in the knowledge that if the Russians annihilated us with nukes, we could annihilate them. A comforting thought, thank you British government. Remind me not to vote for you again. One advantage of being soaked through was that the Boffins, who were standing in the one hundred and sixty eight pound tent, drinking tea from their issued unbreakable metal flasks, took pity on us. After we had reversed the one metre flat bottomed ditching bucket so that it dug away from the excavator the lead Boffin suggested that we knock off and change our clothes. "Bye then" and we were off. It was only ten o"clock.

Finishing work at ten am instead of seven pm meant that I was able to get not only a washing machine but a tumble dryer as well. The little room had never smelt the same since someone dried their pissed in sleeping in the tumble drier. It always had that rotting carrot smell. The CSE show was on that night so I prepared by deciding not to go. The Combined Services Entertainment (CSE) was the second show in Port Stanley. I didn't go. The last thing that I needed here eight thousand miles away from my wife was sexual stimulation by some cabaret hopeful in a leotard and mini skirt. Rather than go through all of that sexual frustration I stayed in the boat. Besides the wives club video was on in the bar. This was a video of all of the wives of 75 Squadron saying little messages to their loved ones. It was embarrassing when it was your own wife but fun when it wasn't. Mac's wife's message was quite nice. She told him that she missed him and loved him, normally not a message that should surprise. Only in this instance, we had just learned that Jeeves had been porking Mac's missus in Nunburg before we left. When we started to receive mail Jeeves had a lot and Mac had none. Jeeves was getting mail from Mac's wife, we all knew this and thought that there was nothing to it. Well there was something to it. He was bonking her. Apparently she also propositioned Spunky, which would be like a model propositioning a beach bum. Spunky declined because Mac was his friend and it was Mac's farewell party, Jeeves had no such scruples. Maybe she was having regrets. Jeeves had a girlfriend called Yvonne.

Sandra gave the standard message but it didn't matter. It was her message from her to me. Plus she was one of the best lookers there. She made me proud that she had chosen me to be her husband.

Saturday 19th March

Had a day off today. So I got bored. I wrote 'Apart' and 'If I was a little bird'. Got three letters off San. Need I say more? I love her so. Jock is turning into a wine guzzling hamster. TV eye was on tonight. The camera crew made this gaff look great

*****

Apart
Today I saw a happy couple
Walking hand in hand,
For they are as one
In this foreign land.

I am but half a man
My other half is you
For my heart is broken
And is now split in two

Although we are miles apart
And your body I am denied
When I read your letters
I have you by my side.

To say that we're apart
Is not strictly true
You are always in my mind
And my love is just for you

When we go to heaven
Many years from now
I will still love you
As much as my soul will allow.

If I was a little bird
If I were a little bird
I would fly across the sea
To sit on your window
And sing of my love for thee
I'd sit on a tree
And of our love would sing
But I'd make damn sure
Not to shit on your washing.

*****

The poems might not be that good but they show the effect that Sandra's letters had on me. They made me write bad poetry!

Sunday 20th March

Jem's birthday. Well what can I say? Another day off. Too many are bad, the day goes too slowly, and I much prefer working.

Monday 21st March

It seems that the cooks have got it right at last, they put the packed lunches in air sick bags.... to save time and effort and double handling, we just leave the food in the air sick bag. Q Mines took Taff through the minefield. Bloody silly! Now we won't hear the last of it. Two Mirages came close to the exclusion zone, we were on yellow alert.

PACKED LUNCHES. The British Army's, answer to psychological torture. The idea was that your lunch was packed in a bag. It was a filler and saved the trouble of driving back to the canteen. It was supposed to be a balanced diet. The can of drink that was supposed to go with the bag was always omitted. The idea was that if they didn't put in a can of carbonated sugar water (cola), they the kitchen could use the money allocated to the drink somewhere else. It was usually to boost the soldiers' daily allocation from half an egg to a whole egg. The sandwiches were often cheese and some kind of Spam, just that, bread, thin marge and a microscopic lump of cheese. No pickle, no onion, no tomato, just cheese and bread. More often than not the bread was thrown away and the cheese eaten. Same went for the Spam. To save time the cookhouse now put the food in seasick bags. I am still mesmerised by the many choices in most sandwich bars. "Mouldy Brie, Danish salami, salad, mayonnaise, butter not marge, rye bread, cut into triangles please." I ask before adding "Twice." We were waiting in a line, called a 'Stick', to get on a Puma helicopter. I was at the front (I love flying) with strangely enough, the RAF Officer Pilot. In his hand was a 'Nose bag', or packed lunch. Both of us, being bored with waiting to get on the Puma the conversation went like this.

Me; "What you got in there then, Sir?"

Pilot looking at the bag in his hand; "My packed lunch!"

Me; "I bet they give you smoked salmon and Beluga caviar."

Pilot laughing and turning to face us; "No I get the same shit as you."

Me; "What cheese and Spam?"

Pilot; "Cheese and tuna I think, I always take them home to my dog."

Me; "Do your cheese sandwiches have pickle in?"

Pilot; "Why yes, of course!"

Me; shouting to everybody else in the line; "HEY! The Pilot has got pickle in his cheese sandwiches!"

Pilot; laughing and holding out the bag to me "Do you want them, then?"

Me; grabbing the bag before anyone else "You bet Sir." I unwrapped the cheese sandwich and pushed the whole thing into my mouth so that no-one else could get it.

Pilot; laughing but concern on his face "Leave me the tuna, you'll make yourself sick."

Me; mumbling through a mouthful of cheese and pickle on NAAFI white bread, sandwich; "I bet you couldn't pull three 'G' on that and make us all sick."

Pilot; looking towards the Puma helicopter; "I couldn't pull three 'G', but I could make you all feel sick."

Everybody in the 'stick'; "MAKE US SICK! MAKE US SICK!"

I'm sure that every manoeuvre that he carried out had a name to it, to us, strapped in the back it was hell and heaven. We were thrown all ways and purely due to the fact that we didn't crash and die, (which I thought that we were) it was the best helicopter ride that I have ever had in my life.

Taff was befriended by Q Mines. I think he wanted someone on the inside. He took him in a Rover up to the Stanley Common minefield and by foot, *in to* the minefield on Stanley Common. I don't know whether Taff was mad or not but Q Mines certainly was. He didn't take him in with a mine detector. He just walked him in, there are things called 'nuisance mines'. They are mines that are laid out of pattern in order to deal with situations just like that. The Officer of the mine-laying, when the pattern is laid, then grabs a handful and lays mines willy-nilly. It not only catches the enemy when they try to lift the mines but prevents his own soldiers from sabotaging the mines. Taff was full of it when he got back. Full of shit! He couldn't believe what the Q had done with him.

"Why did you go with him then you Welsh tit?"

"Well, he's the WO and the expert isn't he, besides, I'm now the only Sapper on this boat who has been in a minefield" Taff smiled with pride.

"You're the only Sapper on this boat who needs a lobotomy."

Pinko walked into the room in mid conversation "Hey guys, have you read orders yet?"

"No, they weren't up when we came in. Why?"

"We were at yellow alert today, two Argentinean mirages flew close to the "exclusion zone.""

"Nice of them to tell us Sappers of 75 Squadron, with effect from this order you are all now in the Argentinean Army. Spanish courses will start immediately. Signed: - Colonel Miguel."

"You weren't told either?" Pinko asked.

"No but we were out on our own on the Common, do you mean that you weren't told either?"

"First I knew about it was when I read it on orders"

"I didn't realise the 'Fog of War' started so early. I thought that shooting had to start before the hierarchy stopped telling us stuff."

"So how is the glorious mine clearance going then?" Pinko asked.

The sentence had been formed in my mind, my mouth was open and my tongue had placed itself in the correct position to form the first word when Taff interjected "I was in the minefield today" like a kid who had just been to the zoo. I rolled my eyes to the heavens and jumped into my pit, "I've heard this one before." It didn't stop Taff from relating the whole story again. I noticed that a few items in the story were enlarged, endorsed made more dangerous. I didn't say anything, just noted this for when I listen to a story from Taff next time.

Tuesday 22nd March

*A Harrier crashed into the sea today. The pilot ejected safely.
Taff lost my mug in a wagon, I had to go and chase after it. I must
remember not to lend it to him, in fact don't lend him anything.
Rumour that POM's are getting 'T' pay. I hope it's true.*

It's not. [Author. Actually it was and we did]

*****

"Hello Smiggins how was the flight? Why are you all wet? What is
that in your hand?"

"It's a joystick Sir."

"Looks like a Harrier joystick to me."

"It is Sir"

"Are you fitting it to your Harrier?"

"It is my Harrier, Sir. Can I have a new one please? I…er. I don't
need the joystick bit, just the rest. All, of the rest…. Sir"

*****

'T' pay was technician pay. Helicopter pilots got it, Helicopter
mechanics got it, and Plant Operator Mechanics didn't. But, POM's
left the Army and went to work for civvy companies instead. In
order to keep them in the Army they eventually paid us 'T' pay, much
to the chagrin of all of the rest of the Corps.

Wednesday 23rd March

*Rumour has it that two Mirages came within 45 miles of Stanley
at low level. 20 more miles and they could have released an exocet!
3 minutes is all exocet takes to do 20 miles. Booked a call for 0945
tomorrow. My mind is all a turmoil, what can I say. Christ!
Who'd've thought that I wouldn't know what to say to Sandra.
What it'll be like after 6 months? Damn am I love sick and horny. I
better have a wank before I have a wet dream. OC on the Coastell
2 told Jock "Stop Bluffing."*

The Argies were really trying it on during this period. We had already lost a Sea Harrier and they didn't have to fire a single shot. Calls to home were made through Cable and Wireless who had a little hut on the hill just outside Port Stanley; it was a small hut with a huge antenna mast. The mast was so tall that if you stood on the top you could see Germany. (This is of course an exaggeration. Did you notice?) Phone calls had to be booked and we had to pay for them. The calls were usually around a day's wage, stress making events and unmemorable. By unmemorable I mean that ten minutes after the conversation you couldn't remember what was said. Leading up to the call was like going on a blind date. What would you say? What did we now have in common? Do you tell her how you hate it there? The worst part was what do you say? Two months away and we were like strangers. I wrote to Sandra every day, and although that was like being with her, it wasn't. She didn't reply immediately to my ramblings, on the phone, it is immediate. I REALLY didn't know what the hell to say. Everything that I thought was in the letters. Jezus was I nervous over that phone call. It was all that I could think about, and that led to thinking about Sandra, which led to sex which led…..Ok God, must think about something else.

Bignose went to the Coastell site today as he normally did every day. He was in a bad mood, as were the rest of us, and took it out on the Troops. TC was in the D6 bulldozer and Jock was standing on the road that we were building, waiting for a truck to come so that he could direct it on where to dump its load. The OC came striding down the road and went straight up to Jock, "Cpl Henderix. Why isn't that bulldozer working?"

"We're waiting for a dump truck, Sir. When it comes we'll …" Jock never got to finish the sentence, the OC wasn't interested. He was only interested in shouting at someone who couldn't shout back, a lesser rank, "STOP BLUFFING CPL HENDERIX GET IT WORKING NOW!"

Jock was not a man to turn away from a fight but he could see that there was no reasoning with Bignose. He muttered a contrite "Yessir" and walked towards TC in the dozer.

The OC stomped off down the road to the Groynes where the Knockers were working. Jock, now fuming, climbed up the tracks of the dozer, opened the door and *asked* "TC, will you drive up and down the track to make it look as if you are doing something for the OC."

TC, seeing the seriousness of the situation burst out laughing, "You're fucking joking." This made Jock laugh and the tension left his body in an instant. He got in the dozer and they tracked up and down the road in first gear on tickover at a speed of around a quarter mile per hour whilst making unfriendly remarks about the OC. I was taught a long time ago by my old Army Cadet Officer, who was an ex Ghurkha OC that leadership was the ability to make someone do what they didn't want to do, and enjoy doing it. Even at thirteen years old I thought that that was real power. I have expanded it. Leadership is also the ability to make people do what *you* want them to do and yet make them think that it was their idea. That is really fun if you can do it. Some Chinese General called Tso Tsung-t'ang said that when the leader has finished his task, others will say "I did that." That was two thousand four hundred years ago. You would have thought that the human race would have learned from others in that time. The OC has been in a time warp, either that or he was asleep during Leadership training in Sandhurst. (IF they have time to fit such a menial lesson in in-between their etiquette lessons.) Good leaders amongst the British Army Officers are very few and far between. A Colonel Bide, the Commanding Officer of 220 Engineer Regiment, was one. I was bust because of an administration hitch during my time there; it was the second time that I had been bust in the Sappers. During that time one did not get re-promoted after the second time. I was standing in front of the Old Man (He was in fact very young with a damn horny German wife) I felt that my life had finished. I was full of despair and probably close to suicide. I had let everyone near to me down. The CO reduced me to the ranks of Sapper and then added "LCpl Beirne (I was still a LCpl until the scissors came out) I have reduced you to the ranks of Sapper, but if you keep your nose clean (funny terminology that, but I didn't laugh)

I will re-promote you in three months. I will get your OC to write a report on you in three months time, if you are worthy then you will get your rank back. Is that understood?" He had just changed my depression to happiness. I was elated. I knew that I was going to get bust but here, now, was a chance that I could get re-promoted in three months. I smiled and was sincere when I said "Yes Sir. Thank - You Sir." I would have followed that man into battle anywhere. He didn't have to do that. It cost him only a few words. In three months he could say that the report wasn't good enough. But he was a true leader. He made me happy even though I had just been bust. I HAD HOPE, something to strive for. And strive I did. I strived and strived until I ran out of strives. Three months later to the day I was in-front of him again (no escort this time) and he handed me back my stripe. I now would not only have followed him into battle, I would have actually gone in front of him! Still this if this man was white then Bignose was black, CO hot OC cold, CO Salt OC Pepper. They were complete opposites.

Thursday 24th March

The burner idea went out the window. It's no good for what we need. A lot of young girls are running about in tight jeans teasing us. It's playing havoc with my loins. I tried to phone San to say I Love You, but German lines were engaged, so I booked for the 31st. It's Thursday already. Time is really flying. I wish it was going quicker.

The town of Port Stanley is heaving with little girls in tight jeans and short skirts. It must be school holidays, they were all under fifteen and jail bait. This didn't stop all of the infantry from chatting them up and it didn't stop the girls from hanging around outside the pubs waiting to be chatted up by a soldier. It has probably been happening like this since English girls flirted with Viking soldiers.

I went up to the C&W hut with fifteen minutes to spare and had to sit in a government issue, chair listening to the other conversations before it was my time. I didn't take in anything that went on around me. I was thinking of what to say, abruptly it became my turn. I entered the little graffiti covered booth and wondered who had the time to write graffiti whilst paying their days wage on a telephone call. I picked up the receiver with my heart pumping in my ears. How would I hear Sandra with all this noise in my ears? I dialled and put the receiver up to my ear. I was prepared. I would start with "Hello Babe, It's me" Fucking stupid really, who else would be calling her from the Falklands? It was all I could think to say, I would adlib from there. I heard the clicks of the phone connecting the numbers and then came a silence and …. The engaged tone, "FUCK!" All that stress and adrenaline was pumping through my blood and it was engaged. I tried again, and again and again and again and there was a knock on the door of the cubical. I opened the door and there stood a small fifty ish lady who had been standing in the wind and sun for too long. Her skin was seventy ish "I think that the lines for Germany are all engaged. It's nearly the end of your fifteen minutes. Why don't you rebook?" I looked at my watch I had been the cubical for twelve minutes trying to get through to Germany. I gave up, rebooked and left. Happy in a way that, I didn't have to talk to Sandra, but frustrated that I still didn't know what to say and would have to go through it all over again.

Friday 25th March

The OC directed the wives club video at the Coastell 2 road. They interviewed Stig, he said it was a good job except that the OC keeps coming down and talking about what he don't know. Jock had to talk about the D6 and Mac about the grader too. Don 2 Tp had an escape committee through a culvert. OC told Simpson to move APB as it was bending the scaffold, it was refraction. OC bollocked 1 Tp for not wearing their berets under a Chinook, he refused to listen to Porky Scratching telling him not to come aboard a ship at Goose Green because a Chinook was loading. He then bollocked Porky Scratching in front of the troops.

OC called Stig a twit!

The Buffoons' contribution to the war effort today was to direct a video that was to be sent back to the wives. He came down to the Coastell and videoed the people mentioned above. The lads had to give a spiel about the job rather than say their 'I Love You's'. Jock had to talk about a bulldozer as if it was something interesting to the wives. They wanted to see their men, hear them speak, preferably about how they feel about their wives, not about a bulldozer. Taff and I were on the Port Stanley common plain with mines so we were missed on the video. The ability to get a list of all of the Sqn names and tick them off was beyond his ability. They interviewed Stig. The OC was standing behind the video camera. He told Stig to say what he thought of the road building job. Stig said that it was alright but spoiled by the OC who keeps on coming down to the task and talking about things that he didn't know anything about." The OC snorted "TWIT!" and stormed off. I have always thought that that was very brave of Stig. It took a lot of balls! I wouldn't have had the nerve to say it. It was round the entire Squadron by that evening. Beer flowed in the bar and Stig got plastered even though he didn't buy a single drink. Some of 2 Troop had an escape plan, when their lookout saw the OC coming with Harry from the office carrying the video camera; they all dived down a culvert and crawled to the other side of the road. They had no intention of being made to look a fool on video. After the filming was finished the OC had his daily nose around the site. The main road from Port Stanley to Port Stanley airfield was around two miles long. It was along a spit of land and followed the Canache, or internal harbour. That's the bit that was nicknamed 'Bomb Alley' during the war. The intention was to float in two huge floating hotels up to the end by the airfield. We were building the tracks from the main road down to the Groynes where the Coastells would be berthed. We also had to dig in two twenty one foot ISO shipping containers, and fill them with concrete to act as anchors; everything was within a few inches tolerance. When the OC made the surveyor use wire cable instead of a theodolite the track was one foot off and even ran to the hole for the anchor. We couldn't move the anchor so we had to move a one metre high by ten metre wide rock road instead. This day the OC walked down to the APB or Air Portable Bridge, this was a floating bridge and it was tied up to a scaffold framed jetty. The OC looked into the water and saw the poles bend in the water. He told Homer Simpson to move the bridge as it was bending the poles. SSgt Simpson was now wise to him and just said "Yessir" and did bugger all. (Apart from telling the entire Squadron, that is)

After he left us the OC went down to the other areas where 75 Squadron were working. One of these was the infamous Goose Green. Our lads were billeted on a ship in the harbour. One of the few overworked Chinook helicopters was in the process of loading stores when the OC, in a CSB driven (sailed? Raced is a better word) by a 75 Sqn LCpl, LCpl Slanders, approached the ship. The LCpl saw the Chinook and asked on the radio if he had clearance to approach, knowing full well that he didn't. Helicopters have air intakes. The only take that air intakes are designed to take in, is air. Not twigs or leafs, not sweetie wrappers or drink cans and certainly not Royal Engineer berets with a stay bright cap badge lodged in the front. All headgear has to be removed when working near helicopters. It tends to save the lives of not only the helicopter crew but all those people underneath and around it. It is also a general rule that when a heli is flying above a ship, all boats are to stay away. This is for the protection of the personnel in the boats. If the Heli crashes, then the surrounding boats would get covered in burning aviation fuel. (Avgas)

You now know as much as the dimmest Private in the Army about helicopter loading.

LCpl Slanders got the reply that he knew he would get. He didn't need to be told. Normally he would just wait until the Heli had finished loading, but the OC was on board so this made it official. "I can't go in just yet Sir, the Chinook is loading" he explained to the scowling Officer. "Don't mind that, just get in there!"

Slanders looked at Harry, who was sitting in the back of the CSB. Harry had no intention of getting covered in Avgas either but between them they only had two tapes on their arms. The OC had a crown. The Queens crown. The Queen had given this man a crown, similar to her own, to wear on his shoulders thereby making him one of her Officers and able to pass her orders on to us. Therefore the Queen wanted them to endanger their lives to get the OC onto the ship. Slanders grabbed the radio and with a slight quiver in his voice spoke "Er Echo one this is Echo Charlie two, we are coming in, over"

The reply was instantaneous "No, Echo Charlie two, you are not, repeat not, allowed to approach the ship, there is a helicopter unloading, can't you see!"

LCpl Slanders looked sheepishly at the OC. The OC grabbed the microphone and shouted into it "This is the OC (good radio procedure, mate. Nice security) I'm coming aboard! Get in there Slanders!"

So, picture the scene. A million Pound helicopter hovering over a million Pound ship, crewed with soldiers that cost a million Pounds to train and the OC of 75 Field Squadron Royal Engineers in a £700,000 Combat Support Boat, orders the lowly LCpl to break all standing orders and approach the ship so that he can get on with his business. What would you do dear reader? No you wouldn't. You would say "Yessir" and sail the CSB under the hovering Chinook so that the OC could get out that is what you would do. You are a soldier. You follow orders, no matter how stupid. Even orders like "Charge up that hill and attack that machine gun post, men." After LCpl Slanders had dropped the OC and LCpl Harry off, he pulled back the throttles and stood the CSB on its tail getting the hell out of the area. He knew the dangers of the situation even if the RE Major didn't.

Major Smythe storms up the walkway and straight into SSgt (Porky Scratching) Brown. Who, in his error had a radio in his hand. Porky salutes the OC and stammers "Er... Sir... you are not supposed to... erm... approach the er... the ship when a er... when a... you know... helicopter is er... is loading and er," (Pay attention dear readers, this is the very second when Porky's career in 75 Sqn took a nose dive.) "Sir… could you …er … please erm… take off your ah your erm …er your beret… er you're not supposed to erm… wear them under… you know… under helicopters, Sir, please" he made a large large smile which showed off his crooked, tobacco stained teeth. Also unfortunately for Porky, as the helicopter was still loading, he had to shout. He had to shout so loud that all of the Sappers heard and looked, which didn't help him with what came next.

"DON'T FUCKING TELL ME WHAT TO DO YOU LITTLE CUNT! I'M THE OC! IF I WANT TO APPROACH THE SHIP THEN I FUCKING WELL WILL. IS THAT CLEAR SSGT SMITH?" it was quite clear to everybody from Goose Green to Buenos Aires. General Tso Tsung-t'ang turned in his grave so much that it caused a minor earth tremor in the Eastern Chinese region. You should NEVER- NEVER- NEVER, bollock leaders in front of their men. It has a detrimental effect on moral and on that leaders' effectiveness. Porky was a really nice guy. He wasn't handsome, his skin resembled a Pork Scratching rind (hence the name) he stammered, and gave out orders apologetically. He wasn't respected as a leader but the men really liked him and would carry out his orders because they respected the man, and didn't want to let him down. He would look after the Troops needs and so they would look after him. Something to do with Maslow's Hierarchy of Needs, for the more learned of you readers. He was a very easygoing SNCO. This little outburst did more damage to the OC than it did to Porky. I have a theory! It comes from an old 1940's black and white movie. The new Captain of a small ship had to enter the war and to gel the crew together, he was a right bastard. They all hated him, and with good reason. But it gave them a common goal, something that they could all identify with. It made them gel together as a crew. This is what the OC's attitude did for us in 75 Sqn, but I don't think that it had to do with any kind of obscure leadership qualities. The man was just an out and out knobber.

Saturday 26th March

I blinked and missed today, Sorry.

A knocker tried to prime a lighting tower with water in the diesel tank. He asked Jock where to put it.

We had water pumps on site, water pumps have to be primed with water. This entails opening a vent hole with a spanner that is always lost and pouring in loads of water until it fills the pump chamber. When the pump is started it creates a semi vacuum and pumps water. Don't prime the pump and it *doesn't* pump water. Are you still with me? It isn't rocket science. We had trained the 'Knockers', or non construction plant tradesmen, to do this simple task. Jock was walking up the road when he reached a lighting tower with a Knocker standing over it with a five litre oil can full of water. He was looking around the lighting tower with a quizzical look on his face. He saw Jock approaching and his face lit up. Salvation! "Jock. Where do I prime the lighting tower?"

"What?"

"The lighting tower, Cpl Green sent me up here to prime it for the night shift. I can't find the plug to remove."

"That's because there isn't one you dolt. You don't need to prime a lighting tower; it is only a diesel engine and a generator. What's there to prime?"

"That's what I thought, but Cpl Green said that there was and I had to go and get some water and prime it." It took that lad, months to live that one down. Jokes like that are common place.

The second day that I was in the Army we were issued our kit. We struggled back to our accommodation block in the Army Apprentices College in Chepstow, carrying a suitcase and sausage bag full of kit, two pairs of boots around our neck and a mattress over our head. We were pulling out the kit and throwing it on our beds. We were exploring, and discussing the varied pieces of equipment when a Steve Croton pulled two putties from his bag "What the hell are these?"

I and Jim Coke were both ex-cadets and knew full well what they were. I jumped at the chance "They're putties, but you have two left putties. You need a right" I held up my two and turned one round so that it looked different. (They are identical and are meant to be.) "Isn't that right Jim?"

"What's that?" Jim looked up at me.

"Steve has two left legged putties." Jim looked at Steve who was holding his up side by side and comparing them. They were truly the same. His heart must have dropped, his face certainly did. Going through the stores on the second day in the Army was hell. We were shouted at from the start to the finish. We would rather go into the gas chamber than go through there again.

"They're the same Steve, you'll have to go and get them changed" Jim confirmed.

"Shit" Steve nervously laughed "I don't fancy that. Oh well, the sooner I do it the sooner it will be over" and off he went on his quest for the right legged puttie. As soon as he left we told all of the other thirteen young recruits in the room. When Steve came back he was red faced and looking down at the ground. Everyone in the room was waiting for his return. "Did they change it for you?" I asked.

"Fuck Off" was all he mumbled. Fifteen recruits burst into laughter. One didn't. Sorry Steve.

Sunday 27th March

My heart rises like a dove. I got my second parcel off Sandra. 2 pairs of knickers. Really turn me on even if they do look brand new. "Am I a pervert yet mum?" Kinder eggs, marzipan, a magic yo-yo, toys and lots of love. TC went into town to make a phone call, he came back three feet taller, well worth the £14 he said. My call is on Thursday. He said the C&W girls listen in. Parcels make the days seem shorter. I feel guilty. She spends so much money on me but I spend none on her.

The Knickers Saga!!!

I cannot remember what I received in my first parcel but I can certainly remember what was in the second. There were two large salami's, German chocolates, German marzipan covered in dark chocolate, a championship yo-yo, a framed picture of Sandra and two pairs of sweetly scented knickers. I was the envy of everyone on the boat. To rub in the fact and to enjoy the items I strung the knickers out on the string that was across my bunk. When I sat up, (which was only just possible) my face was in the knickers. For a month, or at least until the joke got old, I would awake, sit up, inhale deeply and say in a loud voice "Aahhh, Sandra."

What I didn't know until I returned from the Falklands was that they weren't Sandra's knickers at all, they were her sisters! [So quite a result eh lads] When I got the parcel, we had a grand opening in the ~~room, bunk, billet~~ matchbox that housed twenty two men and all their kit for six months. Being a serious type of person I tried on the knickers whilst Taff photographed me (without my permission, I might add!) I also gave Mac a blow-job using one of the salami's and shared round the chocolate and toys. It is fair to say that the whole Troop enjoyed the parcel. It raised our spirits, which had been on a steady decline. When Mac received a parcel we went through the same procedure as we did when Jock got one. See the pictures for the grand opening of the parcel. *G

Monday 28th March

I didn't feel too good today as I had to rotavate mines with explosives in. I was told that they were completely disarmed but did they tell that to the mines? I've hung San's knickers above my nose on my bed. I now go to bed and get up with a massive lob-on. I got a parcel from San yesterday.

"Ok Bernie, you call" Taff tossed the coin into the air; I called "Heads" while it was still airborne. He let it fall to the ground. It was tails "Shit. I guess that means that I get to rotavate the mines." Q Mines had assured us that they were safe. The detonators were removed and the explosive was as safe as it could be. Explosive is activated by a detonator which creates a small explosion and ignites the explosive. Who was to say that a rotavator blade hitting the explosive wasn't the same? Q Mines had failed to find any Plasticine and therefore had to submit and let us play with his valuable 'real' ones. We had scrapped the idea of using remote control to drive the tractors. It was just too hard to drive them; a human is so much more agile.

I got in the tractor as the rest moved a safe distance away, all apart from Q Mines which made me feel better. I started the engine and engaged the power takeoff. The rotavator started shaking the tractor. I engaged reverse gear, upped the revs, and dropped the rotavator into the peat. The rear of the tractor disappeared in a shower of peat. I now had no idea of where the mines were and had to judge it by aiming for the main tent. Q Mines walked along side me and was watching his mines like a duck looks after her ducklings. Along side the track that I had to rotavate were yellow markers that indicated the placing of the mines. I passed one, two, and three, all off them with out an incident. I closed down the tractor and jumped out, "Wait there" Q Mines shouted holding up his hand "I'll make sure that they are safe" 'My hero!' I thought; that was quickly followed up with 'You mean that they weren't safe in the first place?'

After the Q had dug around for a bit he called us over with a wave of his hand. We approached the newly dug area and he showed us some pieces of cut up plastic mine in his hand. "We wanted to see them in situ Q!" The lead Boffin complained. "Well this is only one mine, you can find the rest."

We dug around and only found three. Four were missing believed dead. After much highbrow consultation the Boffins came up with the theory that the mines had been smacked so hard by the rotavator tines that they had been shot through the peat to a depth that was too deep for us to find. This didn't please Q Mines, who was still under the impression that it was all a waste of time in the first place. He had now lost more of his little souvenirs. Ah well, he had a whole minefield of them out there. He just had to go in and get some more.

He seemed happy with that. The Q started to walk away after stating "Well that's that then" when the lead Boffin shocked him motionless with "No Q, we have to carry out the trial at least three times before we have a satisfactory result. No amount of blubbering, wailing, shouting or excuses would be tolerated by the Boffins and with Q Mines' bottom lip dragging along the grass we carried out the trial again, this time with Taff in the drivers seat, and me on the camera. Same result. More lost mines and the Q now standing on his own chuntering and shaking his head.

Tuesday 29th March

Quite a lazy day today. The sheers on the groins collapsed at the Coastell2 road. No one hurt. 'What Car' magazine voted the MG metro the sports car of 1983. Stupid sods, how much has BL paid them? I haven't heard from Goodyear yet. Maybe they are making 5 tyres for me. Simpson on night shift ate pilchards when our lads wouldn't. At 0100 in the morning he was throwing up.

The Royal Engineers are pretty good with their knots and lashings. I can still remember most of them today and occasionally use them. What we aren't good at is maths, the type of maths which calculates how much weight a square lashing can hold up. We just pile on the weight until it collapses. And this is just what the sheers did on the Groyne. It was a proper three legged tripod that was lashed together with rope. It should have held up the whole world. But, we forgot to inform the rope of that and it gave up. In my job today as a Safety Officer this would have resulted in a large scale investigation. Down in the Falklands in 1983 it resulted in many laughs and a few red faces in the bar that night as the rest of us took the piss out of the Troop Cpls. I used to have a MG Midget which isn't surprising until I tell you that I am six foot two inches tall. When I had it I was in the MG owners club. They hated the MG Maestro, Mini and all of the rest of the pretend MG's. The Mini Metro MG was the worst. At this time the MG club had welcomed the pretend MG owners into their club. Now the 'What Car' magazine had voted this ugly box on wheels the car of the year.

We have a night shift running. TC is on it along with Jock and Spunky. Compo (composition rations) was bad enough but the depths of despair was the pilchards. If you were at war and you found that you only had a tin of compo pilchards left then that was the Army's cue that you had to surrender. NO-ONE ate them, sometimes we would feed them to cats and watch the cats vomit for fun, but eating them was out of the question. SSgt Homer Simpson wanted to prove that Support Troop were a bunch of wimps so he challenged the guys to eat a tin of pilchards. They, for obvious reasons refused. Homer proceeded to eat the pilchards and later on that night, for fun, the guys watched Homer vomit out the entire contents of his stomach including the bile and stomach lining.

Wednesday 30th March

CRE and CBF came to the site today, we threw a demo for them, with dets. It looks as if the kit will never go into the minefields. We had a look through the engine room, Mac and I, quite big. Maj. Mukos said that he might stay on for another week. Everybody went quiet. This place would be alright if it was accompanied. Monotony is ruling my life right now, with nowt to do at night; all the days are the same.

The Commander Royal Engineers and the Commander British Forces, a General Thorpe, came to the Project Ironworks. General Thorpe was a soldier's man. He had a field dressing strapped to his web belt. He used to hit his field dressing and shout "I have one of these and you should have one of these." He would say that everyone should be ready to fight as he was. He always wore combats and would take the time to talk to the men.

Strangely for once, Q Mines was only too happy to be there. He doddered around and continuously made sure that he was in the path of the top ranking Officers, so that they would have to ask him something. He bathed in his own glory and tried to present a macho

"Devil may care, but I'm a professional" attitude. He juggled two anti personnel mines in his hands to show his contempt of them but twice shouted to us to "Take care with them" when we had to place mines in the trail path. As young Sappers we were so confused, we came to the conclusion that when you reach the height of Warrant Officer Second Class, you become explosive proof. With great showmanship, Q Mines put some mines with detonators in the path of the rotavator. Taff and I stood on the side lines nudging each other in the ribs and giggling like school girls at his antics. Once he had placed the mines he casually strolled back to the top Officers and made a casual remark about the size of the explosion of the anti personnel mines. I don't know if they wanted to know this information but it was clear that they didn't want to have his nose shoved up their asses. They would politely nod at his comments and then turn away and continue their conversation, which when they passed me consisted of golf and wives' friends. They were soldiers and friends as much as we were. They were also probably as bored as we were and only wanted to go home to their loved ones. Q Mines on the other hand saw this opportunity to kiss some butt and enhance his promotion prospects. Sad!

The mines were rotavated with the tractor in remote control, which was hard to do but preferable to sitting in the unarmoured cab. One of mines with the detonators in exploded, the other didn't, which was worse, as Q Brownnose had to go into the wet rotavated claggy peat and find the bits. One of the bits would still have the detonator in and as it had been hit could explode at any second. Maybe it was hanging on with just a piece of dirt stopping it. Q kiss arse had to walk over the area where these pieces were and look for them. He clearly hadn't considered this when he turned up with live mines and told us that we would trial with the 'Real Thing'. After all of the bravado and telling us to keep away from the live mines as if we weren't responsible enough, and doing it loud enough so that the Generals could hear, he could hardly then send us in to find them, could he? I noticed that he was shaking when he came out, his face was white. I wouldn't see fear like that again until I worked in the

Kuwaiti minefields in 1992, and I then understood what he was experiencing. Major Mukos was the liaison between the civvie Boffins and the Army. It was he who the Boffins went through when they had problems. (With WOs for instance) He was most unlike an Officer. He was friendly. Too friendly! We weren't used to it. We always suspected a trap. He would come up to us and start talking about anything and everything. Maybe he was lonely, I don't know but when he said that he was going to stay another week our body language and our silence screamed in his ears "NO DON'T". He didn't.

The newness and the 'Boys Own' adventure bit of the tour had gone. We were into the start of the monotony period. We all had our routines now. We would get out of bed at different times in order not to over crowd the small toilets. I was in the middle after Jock. Mac being hyperactive was always up first, Top Cat being a night owl was always up last. We had a method of getting to our small lockers and a way of dressing without upsetting anyone else. I would always sit on the bed below mine which belonged to a nest of life jackets. Our lockers were so small that we didn't have enough room for our kit. So we removed the lifejackets from some of the lockers and used them. On an inspection the Captain of the Geraint went apeshit. After much ass kissing he allowed us to put the lifejackets on a lower bed where we could get at them and use the lockers. Above Jock the bedspaces were spare also. The previous occupants were scattered around the Islands. It wasn't too bad as we had room to move and sit. Our relations would deteriorate rapidly later when blokes came back from the Islands and reclaimed their beds. I was to phone Sandra the next day but it didn't feel real. Every day was too much the same. There were no weekends, no days off, although I had plenty through the Ironworks and enjoyed the insults when the rest of the room came back in after working a fourteen hour shift to find me showered, changed and fed. I was training with the Shotokhan Karate that I knew on the tank deck. I would be throwing kicks and screaming Bruce Lee chants and thirty metres away was the rest of the squadron in the bar. Occasionally, one of the Chinese crew would join me and we would train together even though his karate was as bad as my Cantonese. We would train using the international finger. This is an international language that enables one to communicate with any person from any country. The day myself and a chap called Stu arrived in Nunburg/ Germany we saw a Schnell Imbiss cabin opposite a bar called Blondies. We went in and looked at the pictures on the board behind the counter. We didn't know what the words meant let alone how to pronounce them, so I used the finger. "Two" I held up two fingers "Chips" I pointed towards the chips that were cooking "und" I knew that bit, "two" two fingers again "half" I bent a finger into half "chickens" I flapped my arms like chicken wings and made a cluck clucking noise. Everybody in the Schnell Imbiss laughed including me, but I got my message across, the girl answered in pure German "So, that's two chips and two half chickens, is that with mayo or ketchup on the chips" she smiled. This German is more like English than I could have believed. Blondies was a bar owned by ex British Sappers and everyone from the camp used it, and the Schnell Imbiss! They spoke better English than me!

Thursday 31st March

Phone San 1300 hrs today. Happiness. The phone call I made today really changed my life. I am so much happier. It didn't sound like San but it was her. She's great. It cost £9.75 and was worth every minute. Maj. Mukos gave us £2.50 for drinks. We (Baz, George and me) drunk it. Cheers.

I cannot remember a single word that was said during that phone call. I can remember the elation that I felt afterwards and the fact that I couldn't recall a single word when I got back on to the ship. Everybody knew that I had just had a home call, not by the fact that they knew where I had been but by the fact that I was a nice person again. Not so grumpy, so snappy. We were living on top of each other, into each others business; there was no privacy on the ship. We ate together, washed together and breathed each others' farts. Yes, think about that dear reader. When there are eight people living in a room the size of a large bathroom it gets very personal. If socks fall onto the floor, whose are they? We all wore green Army issue, they were all the same. It was a smell test. If the sock repulsed your sense of smell, then it wasn't yours. You can usually stand the smell of your own socks. There wasn't even any privacy in the toilets, or 'heads' as the matlots called them. The doors were three feet high and stood approximately two feet off the ground. If you approached them you could see the person inside over the top of the door. Doing anything else other than a poo (known as dumping stores, or a ground dump when done outside on exercise) was out of the question. (At the beginning of the tour, I won't spoil it for you, read on). This evening I entered the heads for a pee and whilst I was using the urinal I heard extremely quiet, tinny music. The heads were empty and I looked around for where it was coming from. It was so quiet that I couldn't figure out the direction so I looked all around for a Selfish Stereo that someone had left on whilst shaving. I eventually approached the shithouse doors and slowly walked up to them. Looking at your mate whilst he is having a dump was not a thing that blokes do. No male bonding in the shithouse allowed! As I peeped over the top I saw the top of Spunky's head, he was asleep. He had his trousers around his ankles, a Selfish Stereo on his head making that tinny music that I had heard and he was snoring! Being the good friend that I was, I immediately run back to the room and told the lads. We all crept in, trying to contain our laughter and photographed him. We didn't tell him; instead, when the photos were developed we put the picture on the squadron notice board. You can't buy friendship like that!

Notes for the month of March

This so far was the hardest month. I can neither look backwards or forwards. There is no light at either end of the tunnel. The month went quick. Only the OC sticking his nose in at the site has caused consternation. He is a fucking pain. He is after a medal or summink and we are suffering because of it. The other squadrons

call him the mad major. How can anyone so dumb be in charge of so
many people? God help him in a war.

As you can read we weren't impressed with our leader. It was
obviously his job to go round to the sites where his men were
working, but the idea is that he should incite his men to work harder,
to raise moral and to build a bridge between the ranks. His way of
achieving this was to come round to the sites and criticise. Criticise
and shout! Shout and Criticise! Never, a word of encouragement,
never a smile! He lacked the basic man management skills that should
have been taught at Sandhurst. They were certainly taught on Jnco's
Cadres. We all hated him. The truck drivers hated him, the squadron
hated him and the CRE wasn't too happy with his elevated truths.
For me, it was a hard month with out my wife. Earlier on I could still
remember what it was like to be with her. She was still fresh in my
mind. But now, it was a distant memory, like a childhood event it was
all foggy. So much had happened that home life didn't seem real.
Some men were taking it bad already. Scouse Barley would complain
bitterly about being in the Falklands every minute that he could. I
would tell him that after we returned we would forget the bad bits
and laugh about the good. He would snort at this vision that I had
and tell me that I was mad. I would not 'join' his peer group. He had
a lot of followers that also moaned about the conditions. I had
sussed out this kind of person on my second posting. My first was in
Tidworth in Hampshire. A town that had been an Army garrison for
hundreds of years, there were men in my troop that continuously
moaned about being in England and all that they wanted was to get
back to BAOR where the beer tasted good and people partied every
night. My second tour was in Nunburg in Germany. There I met
people who continuously moaned about being in BAOR and all that
they wanted was to get back to UK where the beer tasted good and
people partied every night. I though 'Hey, wait a minute, here is the
supposed to be the good place not there! Maybe these people are
never happy.' I was correct they moaned about everything. It was
always somewhere else that was better. They are probably right now

moaning about being in Civvy Street and when they were in the Army the beer tasted … etc.

There were many people like that in the Falklands. I was still enjoying the Boy's Own adventure but it was wearing very thin. The Operation Ironworks helped to split up the month but didn't help with the separation. I married Sandra because I loved her and wanted to always be with her, I enjoyed her company so much that I made a vow to spend the rest of my life with her, and then I bugger off for 6 months. Hey Holly, maybe you weren't so stupid! There was nothing to look forward to except too many days to bother counting. The end was too far away to even think about. One had to get on with your daily job and not think about home. A bit hard when we got letters in groups. Nothing for three days then eight letters.

Sometime during this period Top Cat Furze was witness to an amazing contest. This is how he tells the event.

"I was transferred to 51 Squadron because they had kicked out Spr Benny and 75 Squadron had taken him in. He had ripped out the ILA (Instrument Landing Aid) equipment for the runway and they didn't want him to touch plant again. I was sent to finish the job that he had started. I was on the D6C and Tony Daring, a Sapper from 51, was on the Hymac excavator. The harriers came in for their morning ear blasting" Every day for a month or so, four Harrier Jump jets would fly over the runway and carry out their air show display. All four would do this in unison separated by around two hundred meters down the runway. At first it was great to watch, but after a while it was just one hell of a noise. It must have cost the British tax payer one hell of a lot of money to do this, in fuel alone. We were told that it was for our morale. It did raise it at the beginning but then it got too much. I think that if the Argies attacked again the Harriers would put on a dazzling hovering display which would captivate the conscripts there by giving our officers time to get our soldiers off the boats to shoot them. "We were on the end of the runway so there was one around 50 metres from us. He slowly flew in over our heads and too up hovering position within ear splitting distance of us. Their first manoeuvre was to turn left towards us and as they did Tony turned the top of the Hymac towards the Harrier whilst flashing his boom light on and off and dipped his boom up and down. The Harrier pilot saw this and copied Tony by flashing his front wheel light on and off whilst slowly dropping the nose of the Harrier and raising it again. The other three Harriers had continued with their display and were now turning to the right. Tony then flashed his boom light on and off dipped his boom up and down and turned the top through 360o. The Harrier pilot copied, flashing his wheel light, dipping the front of the aircraft and slowly turned a 360o circle. Tony then flashed his light, dipped his boom, turned the top to the right 360o and the bottom of the excavator left 360o. There was no way the Harrier pilot could compete with this and he flashed his landing lights on and off and slowly climbed to catch up with the other three aircraft that had finished their display and were now circling the airfield. That was not the end of it. When the Harriers landed the pilot came over and met with Tony and took him over to the Harriers. He arranged and took Tony up in a training two seat Harrier. In this Harrier the pilot did things that even Tony couldn't do in a Hymac 580 BT excavator. He threw up in his mask and threw up over the runway when he got out of the aircraft, but he loved it"

Signallers getting very wet in the back of Titch's CSB

From left LCT, CSBs and RFA Tristram

Friday 1st April 1983

I got a load of Goodyear gifts from them today. The pens don't work. All the guns on the ship have been uncovered but there is nobody qualified to fire them on this ship. Maj. Mukos and Cecil went back today. Today is Wednesday I wonder if Argentina will be stupid enough to attack tomorrow. I doubt it. Q Swinton stood on a mine with a det in today, proof that Ironworks don't work.

Santa Claus came for me today, the letter to Goodyear tyres paid off. They sent a load of stickers, pens, key rings and bumf on their tyres. No tyres though. Pinko, who started the whole thing off, received a letter from the managing director of Muirhill. The letter said that he had read the letter to the board of directors and they thought that he deserved something for his neck if not for anything else. They sent him a Muirhill jacket, hat, gloves, key ring, pens, (that *did* work) stickers and a little dinky Muirhill A5000 Loader. We were all envious. Caterpillar sent nowt. It was April Fools day and maybe Goodyear was fooling with me and would send me the tyres later. In the Sappers we were supposed to be soldiers first and Sappers second, but we only got to shoot our guns (the thing that we were supposed to kill the enemy with, which if you didn't know is the whole point of the war thing) once a year. We had to 'qualify' with our own personal weapon. Mine was a SMG. Qualifying with it was easy. We shot it from fifty metres, and on one test even walked forward to twenty five metres. By the time that we were meant to fire we had to shoot two rounds. If one shot one then one could let rip with the gun at the twenty five metre point. To miss at that range was near impossible. It seemed that the Navy had the same procedure with their 'not so important' ships. Today the ship had to test its guns, but no-one was certified to shoot them. If they had let us have a go we would have made their guns go bang, no problem, doesn't take a brain surgeon. We have redesigned the time that we have to do here. To say that we have four months or one hundred and twenty odd days is too depressing. So each month is now a day. We came here on Monday (January) and we are to leave on Sunday (July). So by that new design, the 1st April is Wednesday and we have only four days to do. One of the routines that servicemen on the Falklands did at this time was to take the piss out of other servicemen who had longer to do than them. The conversation would go like this:-

"Hello Bob, not seen you in a long time. It's good to see you again old friend"

"Yeah hello Stan, how long you got to do here?"

"Eighty four days"

"Ha ha ha, no-one's got that long to do! Stag on you Turkey"

In a morose tone "How long you got then?"

"Forty six days"

"Shit"

"Ha ha HAAAAAAA days to do are getting few!"

"Wanker"

"Ha ha ha"

When anyone asked 75 Squadron "How many days you got to do?" We could now answer "Four days!" this would obviously not stick up to any kind of scrutiny but it was part of the fun. Part of the joy of your leaving date getting close was the ability to sing "Days to do are getting few" and "Going Home, Going Home, Going Home" ad nauseam. The other cry was "Stag on you Turkeys!" for god knows why. Someone must have shouted it when they left after the war and it stuck. Major Mukos took the hint and didn't stay any longer, him and the chief Boffin from Porton Down, Cecil, went back today, along with many other happy servicemen and a few servicewomen. All around Stanley were happy faces and those three chants echoing out to anyone who would listen. The joy and happiness on their faces was good to see. It was something that I wanted to enjoy. Our time would come. It was soon to be the anniversary of when the Argies attacked Stanley and we are on alert. What the hell we were supposed to I don't know. Throw stones at them? There were infantry regiments stationed around the Islands as well as small tanks and the occasional destroyer. I suppose a submarine was lurking around somewhere as well, that lot with the air cover was enough to protect me if they came. Just as well because unless the enemy came to within twenty five metres of me and stood very still, I wouldn't be able to hit them with my gun. Throwing it would have a better effect. It was full of pointy bits that always caught up on cam nets when on exercise. Q Swinton, if my memory serves me correctly was one of the RE WOs in charge of the minefields. The Q Mines chappy, he was walking over the area that we had completed the trials for the CRE and CBF and he heard a 'click' like they do on the movies. If you heard a 'click' and not a "Kerboom', and upon looking down, you still had two feet on two legs then the mine had not worked. Q Mines had stood on a mine that he laid and it hadn't been smashed, or burnt by our little mine train. The mine had the detonator in but it didn't activate, which doesn't say much for Q Mines' ability to arm mines. Just as well as it turned out!

Saturday 2nd April

All I did at work was to drive the Bambi up Sapper Hill. Jock was furious at the OC and very depressed so he went to the bar to drown his sorrows in a bottle of wine. I joined him not because I'm depressed but to cheer him up. I succeeded but got drunk myself in the process. This was wrote after two cans.

The Bambi was a little, two man Snowcat . It had rubber tracks and was around six feet in length. It had a Ford 998 cc Escort engine in and it went like stink. Operation Ironworks was more or less finished and we had the job of clearing up. I wanted to go souvenir hunting, as the equipment had been left in the same place as the Argies and the Brits had dropped it. We were only six months after the end of the war and the debris of war was still everywhere. I threw a toolbox into the rear of the Bambi and set off up the hill. This is the hill that the Squadron ran up for PT last month. I, drive up it. The only way to travel! It bounced, and dipped and jiggled its way to the top. There were a few positions up there and magazines and empty cases were all over the place. Compo tins and bits of clothes were scattered in and around the trenches but the pearl handled Colt 45 pistol with white leather holster was nowhere to be found. What I did find was what I can only describe as a Bazooka. It wasn't a Carl Gustav 84mm back breaker, or the nimble 66mm throwaway yank thingy. It was a true blue Bazooka, an Argie weapon that had been left behind. I threw it into the back of the Bambi. I sat at the top of the hill and looked down at Port Stanley. I couldn't imagine the feeling that the lads felt when they got to the top and looked down at occupied Stanley. It was too unreal and too peaceful to have happened here where I was sitting.

Sunday 3rd April

Like an idiot I walked to the penguin colony with Pete, only to kneel knee deep n penguin shit. Taff hooked a seal fishing today. Benjamin Byrne hooked a cormorant. I got 5 letters and another parcel. Someone has spilled petrol on the harbour. Mac was forced

to do the football and cross country. He came 161st out of 162. He... he. I got a parcel. In it were two tapes. 1 with speaking. Magic.

THE PENGUIN COLONY INCIDENT….

We all had a day off today. Taff and Jock went fishing with Benjamin Byrne. Mac was furious because he couldn't go. He was 'volunteered' to play football, which he loved as much as fishing, and to run the inter Squadron cross country, which he hated. On the grounds of the horse to water thingy, he pulled out all the stops on the run and came last but one. The last man was a roly poly doughnut. Mac said he couldn't walk slow enough to get behind *him.*

I was lying in my bunk bored to tears when I heard Pete the Pay (the pay clerk) stick his head into the bunk and ask "Anyone want to come to the penguin colony?" Like a fool I answered "Yeah! When you going"

"Right now, who's that, is that you Bernie"

"Yeah," I said jumping down from my bunk "Let me get my trainers on"

"We'll be at the back" meaning the rear of the ship. I put on my trainers, locked up my small locker and ran to the back of the ship. I was just in time to see a CSB roll up. There were two Officers standing in the dry area just behind the cab and that left the engine compartment for us. Oh, shit I thought. This is going to be bad. The driver was from our Squadron, and he looked at us and the Officers and then back to us and nodded. He set out at a slow pace and the wash behind the boat only flew six feet into the air instead of the normal eight, the spray still flew back onto us. My lips started to taste the salt and my eyes were stinging. I looked down at my light jacket and noticed that it was covered in a fine spray. Looking up at the sky it was clear by the total cloud layer that it would not dry out on this trip. The trip had started out bad and if I knew how much worse it would get I would have dived over the side and swam back to the ship. Devoid of the opposite to hindsight (er...frontsight? foresight?.) I didn't, I stayed in the boat. We got out on the jetty and walked over to a Landrover. As I was the lowest rank I sat in the back. The Landrover's at that time had a small moveable seat made out of steel tubing. It was hung over the edge of the Rovers and had a foam cushion for the seat and back rest. It wasn't too bad. The other type of rear seat was a long piece of PVC covered foam. Both, I noticed as I looked in the back, were absent without leave. I quickly looked behind me to see the CSB disappear away from the jetty in a plume of spray. It was too late to go back now. I forced my six foot two inch frame in through the small three foot opening, being too lazy to undo the tailgate. I looked around and running out of ideas sat on the metal rungs of the wheel arch tool bins. I had also forgotten how bad the roads were in Stanley and as soon as we started I realised that my error in coming was mounting up to be an error of considerable magnitude. I bumped and scraped my bottom around on the sharp, cold pointy bits on the arches. When it got too much to bear, (around two hundred metres) I squatted in the rear and held onto the roof bars. Not being Vietnamese, this was bloody uncomfortable. "How far is it Pete?" I asked.

"Around twenty miles, not far"

"AAAARRRRRGGGGGGGGGHHHHHHHH" I shouted in my mind.

Twenty bumpy, jerky, head banging, knee scraping miles later I undid the rear tailgate and let it drop. I knew that I didn't have the agility to climb out the same way that I had climbed in. I should have had, but the journey had taken all of the strength out of my leg muscles. I had spent the last nineteen miles alternatively squatting and standing in a crouch trying to get comfortable. I had failed miserably. I ached all over and stretched my arms above my head and stood on tiptoes as I stretched my back. As I did I looked around me. I didn't know much about penguins but I knew that they liked water. Sea water to be more precise and all of my five senses were telling me that there was no beach with its crashing waves within earshot let alone eyeshot. (Eyeshot? Is that a word? How about noseshot and tongueshot for taste?) "Where the fuck, are the pengwins?" I mispronounced.

Pete took out a compass and after turning around for a minute pointed towards an expanse of grass "That way" and he started to walk off with the pay Sgt walking alongside him. "How far?" I shouted after them.

Pete looked back as he walked off the dirt track road "Only a couple of miles, com'on."

Com'on? Com'on? A COUPLE OF FUCKING MILES! And he says com'on as if we are walking down to the corner shop. Resigned to my fate I started to walk after them now totally in a bad mood. When I got to the penguins I was determined to kick one because it was their entire fault. We walked over a hill and the grass changed. We were now walking, nay, stumbling over Elephant grass. For those dear readers who have never had the misfortune to walk over this grass that comes straight from the devils bottom, Elephant grass grows in little clumps. Each clump has a solid base of grass that sticks six inches off the ground. If you try to walk from clump to clump you will fall off the second clump and twist your ankle. So you have to walk in-between them. God does not sew them in a straight row, they are all higgledy piggledly, and with only six inches between clumps only barely enough room for your foot. The distance between the clumps also mean that when you stumble you can not shoot your foot out to catch your self as it is trapped between these clumps. One last bastard factor is that the soil between these clumps on this occasion was wet, soft, marshy, wet, wet peat. Within one hundred metres my socks were soaked through and my feet were sodden. I was so happy I felt like I wanted to sing.

Note: This is of course sarcasm, due to the loss of tone in the written word I thought that I had better let you know this, just in case you were under the impression that I was having anything even remotely connected to a 'Good Time'. I am also informing you of this in case this book ever reaches one of our American cousins. They have no concept of sarcasm. My large friend, Geordie Anderson and I came in from the minefields in Kuwait and entered the air-conditioned American office complex. We had been in an armoured excavator that wasn't air-conditioned, and could only stay in it for thirty minutes at a time due to the 50° C heat outside and the 70° C heat inside. You would climb into the cab, shut the solid steel door and strip off your overalls down to your boots and immediately track into the minefield and start to 'pop' mines with the bucket teeth. Within a couple of minutes you would be lathered in a sweat. I stayed in too long once and fell out with heat exhaustion. We were exhausted, dirty, parched and happy that we had survived yet another day. The American project manager saw us and patting Andy on the back asked "How's it going Limey One?" (Our radio call signs were Limey One and Limey Two) Andy immediately answered in a pissed off tone "Oh, great, fucking great, I enjoyed it so much I think I'm going to go back out after tea and do another few hours." The sarcasm was so thick that I was unable to make out Andy's features through it. The Yank boss looked startled and then concerned "O Hell Andy, don't go back out, leave it until tomorrow. Go and get a shower and have some tea. Andy looked at me in disbelief; I smiled as it was well known of the Yanks ability to miss dry humour. "Andy put on a tone of a child that had been told that he would have to wait until tomorrow to open his presents "Oh, Ok boss, I guess I do need a shower, Thanks" and before he could walk off the manager beamed in happiness at his triumph of man management and patted Andy on the back and stomach at the same time. "That's the way, Andy. Good man" Andy froze and nodding to his stomach whispered "Don't pat me there, I'm English." When we got in the lift (elevator) we broke out laughing at the manager's face and shock when he realised that he was patting a Victorian English gentleman's tummy.

I digress, only because writing about the penguin colony is only marginally more interesting than walking (stumbling) to it.

As I surmounted the top of each rolling hill there was always another one in front of me. All I could think about was the Bambi. That would have sailed over the grass. Eventually after falling over three times and plummeting my hands into the marshy peat I could hear the faint sounds of the breakers on the coast and could smell the salt air. We crested a hill and in front of us, the sea changed the colour of the ground from grass green to sea green. It was NOT a moving experience. Stuck in the middle of the last grass was a dirty patch of dirt and scattered across this dirty patch were penguins. "OK, we've seen them now, can we go back?" I begged. They laughed, they thought I was joking.

"What sort of penguin are they?" the Sgt asked both of us.

"Fucking stupid ones for living out here" was my educated answer.

"King Penguins" came Pete's, proving why he was in the Royal Pay Corps counting money and I was in the Sappers driving diggers. "Com'on lets go and see them" Pete spoke with enthusiasm in his voice, "Yeah, lets" I spoke without. We started to walk the two hundred metres to the colony when we heard an aircraft jet engine approach from behind. I turned to search for it. It sounded like a Sea Harrier and therefore was infinitely more interesting than the penguins. It came over the previous hill and flew slowly right over our heads and over the colony. Being a human and therefore the master race on the planet I turned my body as the Harrier went over head. The penguins, not being the master race and being as thick as the shit that I was about to discover that they were living in; didn't! They all turned to face the noise and followed the Harrier with their heads until it was overhead and then like a stack of dominoes, fell over backwards. I thought that it was the funniest thing that I had ever seen until I saw them try to get up off their backs with their stupid stubby wings. The Harrier pilot threw the Harrier in a tight turn and I saw his face in the top of the canopy, he was laughing and I'm sure that he stuck his thumb up as he disappeared towards Stanley airfield. It was the highlight of the whole journey. Pete didn't think so, he was mumbling about "did that on purpose" and "Bloody RAF". I was still laughing loudly when it hit me. "What the fuck is that stink?" we were still around a hundred metres from the colony so it couldn't be coming from there. It smelt as if someone had opened a bottle of ammonia. As we got closer the smell got stronger. It was coming from the colony after all. From fifty yards onwards the grass was scattered with large bird droppings. The closer that we got the thicker the shit until at twenty metres we were walking on three thousand years of penguin shit. "Thank Christ dinosaurs are extinct" I said through my nose. The entire ground that we were on was probably reclaimed land. Reclaimed by penguins! I have the useful ability to shut off my nasal passage and breathe through my nose. This comes in useful on occasions like this. I stopped breathing through my nose and therefore stopped smelling the shit. I spoke like a pratt but it was preferable to smelling this stuff. I was now able to concentrate on the birds. They had no fear of humans which is an amazing thing to witness in an animal smaller than you. I approached one slowly and crouching down to make myself smaller put my hand down on the mud. 'MUD! WHAT MUD! THIS ISN'T MUD' my mind screamed to me. I looked down to see the tips of my fingers disappearing into the shite. "Ohhhh noooo" I moaned. I had nothing to wipe my hand on and the sandy shore was not sandy. I had thirty metres to walk before I could get to clean beach. Hell, put up with it, I thought, I ain't coming back. I gently whistled and clucked and held out my hand to the King penguin with the Dennis Healy eyebrows. S/He looked at me with a "What?" look. You ever been at a gate to a field and a hundred cows have come up and looked at you? Well it was the same here. They were all looking at us and wondering what we were. Probably the same look that the last Dodo gave the human who killed it. "Hey pen-gwine," I called to it and all its mates standing next to it, "Did you know that there was a war here six months ago?" Nothing! S/He moved its head around and back to me. "Did you know that the price of housing is going up by two and a half percent in real terms in the South of England this year?" I heard two human laughs behind me.

The penguins looked at me and bored with this funny looking penguin in front of them, one by one turned away from me and faced the sea. They obviously didn't care about wars, the price of housing or whether I make full Cpl or not within the next few years, and it was then, kneeling in all that penguin shit that I realised that they were living life and we weren't.

We are living a false life that has been created by a thousand generations of humans. Human emotions are all that matters to the humanoid life forms on my planet. Greed, hate, anger, jealousy, they are all that people live for. They live to feed their human emotions. The millions of other life forms on this planet couldn't give a shit if I and every other human on this planet dropped dead. And come to think of it, it wouldn't make one iota of difference to the planet either. Life, time would still go on. We are given a life and to the most, we waste it striving after things. Houses, cars, automatic washing machines and worst of all… money! Fuck it all!

We worry if the public toilet isn't spotless and here are penguins that are living in the shit of there forefathers. If they are born without the antibodies to cope with the shit they die. I looked down at the shit, it was teaming with flies. They were making their living eating the poo. It was all part of life. Who put them here? No one! The same as the penguins, no human had a hand in their being here. We were visitors in their world, not only on this patch on the Island but also in this patch of time. I started to look at the world different from that moment on. I went to wash my hands in the sea and noticed that the sand was made up out of crushed up pieces of sea shells and tiny stones, billions and billions of them. As we walked back the Elephant grass that I had hated so much on my outward journey I now marvelled at. It would return to grow here every year until the end of the planet. It got its kicks from the rain and feeling the sun on its leaves. The hills were not bastard things to get over they were parts of the rock plates that were being pushed upwards by another plate that covered millions of miles and weighed so much that to calculate it would tax even Pete the Pays mind. The journey back was completely different to the journey out. The route out, I was cocooned in my human mind, the trip back I felt things that had been happening around me all the time but I was too engrossed in myself to see, hear, feel or smell. It was as if my senses had at last been turned on. Wow! What a rush.

Nowadays I get enjoyment out of feeling the rain on my face, on seeing dew on the leaves of trees and on hearing birds sing. Life is a trip man, but we are in too much of a rush to see its beauty. Well… you are mate; I've been enjoying it ever since that day. I talked to a friend who was in 59 Commando Squadron RE during the war and he said the same. Little things that used to bother him no longer did. He enjoys every day as if it was his last. Try it guys. It beats the hell out of marijuana

When I got back to the ship there were a parcel and five letters waiting for me. I listened to the stories of the other guys, the cross country run, and the fishing trip but realised that all I could tell them was the physics of the penguin trip. The change in me, I was still unsure about and couldn't tell the guys. They wouldn't have understood. Nowadays when it is pissing down with rain and someone walks into the office first thing in the morning and says "Miserable day, isn't it" I reply "Actually it's a beautiful day, it's only miserable in your mind..." I get some strange looks.

Monday 4th April

The track came off the Bambi and I put it on all on my own. Tim gave Stig a pen pal letter with a fairly good looking picture of a bird on it. The real author of the letter is a fat gobbing spotty lump of blubber. Joke of the tour, it must be. Taff did the bubble blowers initiation course. I saw Al Alanson today, it is his second day. Nobody's got that long to do.

"SHIT!" the Bambi had thrown a track and there was no-one in sight. Well, that was not strictly true. All of Stanley was in sight but too far to be of any help. There I was on top of Sapper Hill again. A Sapper with a Bambi with a thrown track at the top of Sapper Hill surrounded by Sappers (and a few other Regiments and Corps). I could walk down to Taff, a good hour away. I could run down to Taff a good fifty nine minutes away on this Elephant grass or I could sit down and wait for someone to pass. I took option four. I would put the track back on myself, macho or what!

I took out the toolbox (thank you me, for bringing it) and checked the tools. A twelve inch adjustable, a six inch adjustable, a few different sized spanners, a grease gun, two screwdrivers, a hammer and a brass drift. Yep I had enough tools. I could have done with a six foot pinch bar, a socket set, a set of elevating ramps, a ten ton jack, an eight ton winch, a fast car and a Swedish blonde, but I didn't have any of those. I was a Sapper on Sapper Hill and I had to improvise. Or walk! I let the pressure out of the front wheel tensioner and pulled the track to a position where I could manoeuvre it back on. I then drove engaged the track on rear drive sprocket and slowly drove forward to pull the track back onto the front. It totally ignored my plan and fell off. I tried again and in defiance it wedged itself between the front wheel and the body of the Bambi. I could swear that the track laughed at me. I wrestled the bastard track out of its hiding position and tried again, this time slewing left, (it was the right track) the track went on the roller, YIPPEE!, and straight off the other side and did it's wedging trick again. This wrestling match went on for an hour before I finally got the track on true to the wheels. I pumped up the tensioner and looked at the Bambi. It had taken me an hour and all of the strength in my fingers but I had done it. By buggery I had done it, and with a confidence that comes from facing up to a challenge, and beating it, I drove back down to the camp. "Where the fuck have you been, Boyo?" Taff asked.

"I threw a track on the top of the hill" I pointed up to Sapper Hill in the distance. "I put it back on myself." I waited for the praise and admiration to be showered on me. It was a long time in coming. Taff looked at my filthy combat jacket and simply commented, "Take your combat jacket off when you sit in the Rover, we don't want to get grease on the seats. Com'on, the others have gone and I have got that divers course to go on." He walked off towards the Rover. My ego took a crash and I ambled along behind Taff feeling like an unrecognised actor.

We parked the Rover up by the jetty and ambled on to see if anyone was on duty that we knew. On the jetty were a few different types of berets. Black ones (dark navy blue when new but we brush them with our boot brushes so they take on a Kiwi Black appearance) green Scottish ones and a couple of red RMP ones. We ambled over to the black berets, if we knew anyone it would be from these soldiers. "Bernie!"

I looked to the source of the voice, it was a friend from my previous unit in Tidworth. I ambled over and went through the normal Falklands greeting; "Hello Bernie."

"Hello Al, when'dju get here?"

"Yesterday."

"Jezuz, you must have 180 days to do. Nobody's got that long to do!"

And so the custom was passed from me to him, and no doubt from him to someone he knew and met. [A lot later. Haha! 180 days!]

Tuesday 5th April

A bit of a bore today. Waste of time getting up. Mac went to Fox Bay, Jock went bondu bashing. 2 dracones were dragged out and destroyed by the RAF & RE's because they were not repairable. Taff got a parking ticket for parking outside the NAAFI.

We had gone to the NAAFI in Port Stanley in the truck again. Taff had parked it outside on the rutted road and we had piled out the back onto The Kelper Store. (Incidentally, 'Kelper' is the name of the seaweed down South) when I came out I saw that Taff was having a heated discussion with two RMP's, *again*! They had been sitting in wait outside The Kelper Store in order to catch someone parking there. The last time in February, Taff had been reported for not having indicators, illegal parking and having three in the cab. It had gone no further than the SSM. This time it might go higher. "Don't you have anything better to do than book us for parking when there are no lines here on the road, in fact there is hardly any road"

"You know that there is no parking here, Cpl, we have told you before."

"Well where the hell, am I supposed to park? In the multi-story car park next to the West Stores I suppose." (There was obviously no such car park)

"Don't get funny with me Cpl, Give me your number, rank and name" this time it was a Sgt, and he was using the rank card to its limit. Taff gave the details again and Jock, again the peacemaker grabbed Taff's arm and pulled him away before it could escalate. We drove down the jetty, complaining all the way. Once was a laugh but twice was taking the piss. Jock, after tea, gathered all of his gear and got onto another ship that had entered the harbour. From there it was to visit all of the bays in The Falklands that the Squadron were working and he was to look at, and inspect the plant. We were going to lose him from our small room for a few weeks. The petrol that was covering the inner harbour earlier in the tour was discovered coming from a Dracone. Dracones were large condoms that were full of aviation fuel and floated in the harbour. It was discovered that two were beyond repair and were towed out to sea for the Harriers to use as target practice.

Wednesday 6th April

We took back all the kit to 15 Sqn. resources. The Geraint sailed to test her guns. Mike and Brian stayed on board to have a go. We had a puncture and I lost my wallet. I hope it is in the county or the Rover. 49 EOD found an 'Eric' today on Stanley common.

We are now entering the realms of second hand information. 49 EOD Squadron, Royal Engineers are all bomb disposal men. They had trained to do that silly task of walking up to an unexploded Second World War bomb, and saying, "It's still live, stay away, I'll defuse it". In real life there is no thrilling music in the background, there are no close-ups of the sweat pouring off his brow like a hose pipe. He either does it or he dies. They have a fatalistic view on life. If it goes off, you'll never know. I did the same in Kuwait, ten years after this story.

It is a good profession to have when you meet someone new in the pub. When they hit you with "Oh, yes, I'm a MD of a small electronics company" you hit them with "I'm a bomb disposal expert. I defuse bombs." They usually make their excuses and go off to find someone less interesting to try and impress.

In the Falklands their training in being media heroes was all in vain. There, they had line up in extended line and walk the entire Falkland Islands looking for pieces of ammunition that had not exploded. A very boring task! The only highlight of their task was finding a piece of ammo or a dead body. Some of the missiles that were about then had optical eyes on the front of the missile. The missile could be lying on the ground, you walk up to it and approach from the front, and it sees movement and blows up. That heightened ones senses. The other morbid fascination of peace time soldiers is dead bodies. They found one this day. Dead bodies were named by the first ones that they had ever found, and they were named by the name that was on the name tags of their uniforms. Those found lying down were named "Eric's" and those standing up "Johnny". They had even found some that were standing up but had died in a crumpled position. These had no name. Some had bullet holes in their feet where the Argie Officers had shot the conscripts in the feet in order to keep them in their trenches. This day they found an Eric. Wow, red letter day!

Not for us, Taff and I had to return all of the nice equipment from the minefield clearance to the Stores Squadron, 15 Field Support Squadron. The Geraint crew found out that we had a couple of soldiers that had fired a machine gun in Canada. They were ear marked to test their guns on the ship.

"Sir! Sir! There is a very slow plane coming in to attack us! Can I use the machine guns to shoot it down?"

"Have you successfully completed an All Arms Machine Gun Course (Grade 2) within the last six months?"

"Er... no Sir"

"Sorry, you're not allowed to fire it."

Loosing one's wallet is not such a unevent as it is in Civvy Street. In Civvy Street you cancel the credit cards, get more money out and buy a new wallet. Not so in the Army. I should expand on that, not so in the Army if your ID card is in your wallet. First charge was a £50 fine, then a £100 fine, then a court martial.

I had lost my ID card twice and was on my last chance. The first time I lost it was in Tidworth. I was a young Sapper and I shagged this woman in Andover. Unbeknownst to me she was a kleptomaniac (compulsive thief) and stole my wallet along with the ID card. She even helped me look for it that morning, back at camp all hell fell down on my head. I was up in front of the OC and he read me the riot act: "Do you know how you loosing your wallet, has breached security, Beirne?"

"No Sir"

"An IRA terrorist could find the ID card and posing as you, get into the camp and blow us all up, and all because you are too **incompetent,** (it was emphasised and had a pause) to keep control of your wallet"

Many questions leapt into my mind, all of which my common sense told me to keep to myself. Questions like "Well he would have to look like me wouldn't he Sir?" and "Wouldn't the guard notice the difference in the picture and the face, Sir?" but most importantly "Why doesn't the IRA terrorist just walk over the grass, past the NAAFI and blow us up that way instead of coming through the gate? Sir! You wanker you think the Irish play cricket?" The camps in the late 70's and early 80's were all open plan. No fences, no barbed wire. We'd been fighting the IRA for nearly seventy years and as yet had not taken them seriously enough to put up barbed wire. When I used to guard camps as a Sapper, we would have 7.62mm rifles with a magazine but no bullets! The bullets (ten of) were always kept in the safe in the guardroom. The only people who knew the combination were the Orderly Officer and the prisoners, because that was where their fags were kept. If we were attacked we were to phone the guard room, who would phone the Orderly Officer in the mess, who would run down to the guardroom and open the safe to allow us to get our ten rounds, so that we could fire back. Yeah… fucking stupid eh? I thought that at the time. So did Margaret Thatcher, then Prime Minister, (God bless the hallowed ground that she walks on). She visited a camp and on seeing the soldiers with their guns asked "Are they loaded?" meaning is a bullet up the spout! The answer was an "Oh no Marm, the bullets are kept in the guardroom" in a 'We aren't so stupid as to give these children bullets in their guns' type of voice. The Officer thought that Maggie was concerned for her own safety.

The reply was an angry "Well how the hell are they supposed to shoot back if they are attacked by the IRA? Get them bullets immediately!" Red faces all around and the start of a policy where the British Army, for the first time in my fourteen years, gave the guard, bullets in their guns."

The second time that I lost my ID card was in Germany. I lost the wallet and all. I was given the same talk by the OC almost word for word, and a £100 fine with a weeks' ROPS (Restriction of privileges) and a warning that the next time was a Court Martial where I would have my testicles removed with a blunt screwdriver. This 'Third Time' was today. I was kacking my pants with the though of going through that silly talk and the pointless punishment and walked the entire area that I had been that day. No joy, I was ID card less. The silliest part of the whole ID card saga is that they were just a piece of plastic with a number pressed into it. Well beyond the capabilities of the average terrorist with millions in the bank from American Noraid.

Thursday 7th April

Moved kit and dossed.

It was the end of Project Ironworks and soon I would have to start to work for real. I was making all possible use of the free time by doing nothing. I had to track the tractors down to the stores squadron, 15 Sqn, tomorrow I would have to track the Hymac's to the Coastell road. Not an enviable task. The old excavators had travel levers. One for each track. They were along side the seat. Push one forward and that track went forward, pull it back and it went in reverse. This was if the base of the machine was facing forward. As these things can turn through 360o there was always a good chance that you were facing backwards and didn't know it. Push the lever forward and you would shoot off backwards. The one advantage of these older type Hymac's is that the levers stayed forward. TC used to put it into travel and jump out of the machine and walk alongside it. On these new Hymac 590's the levers had to be held forward. Bloody tiring on the arms when travelling long distances. By long I mean two hundred metres. I had to track these excavators three miles! There were no low loaders on the island. I had already tracked them from the jetty in Stanley to the common, a piffling distance of only a mile or so. Tomorrow it would be three miles EACH! Taff had conveniently found something else that he had to do and I was to track both of them. Bugger!

Friday 8thApril

Dossed, moved Hymac's. I made the travel levers stay forward with string. I had a good argument with Andy. I was gonna take out a fence in my way by smashing it when George pulled out the pole. Taff went back to the site. I watched porn till 1 o'clock. Taff, TC, Spunky etc were on the piss in the bar. They fell asleep watching porn.

HAH! The one individualistic attribute that is encouraged in the Sappers is one of Improvisation. I found some string and tied it to the seat arm rests. Then putting a loop in the end of the string I could push both levers forward and loop the string over the levers keeping them forward. That left my hands free for reading a book. The excavators sped along at a maximum speed of one and a half miles an hour. Two, down hill with the wind behind it on a good day. Any hazard came up on the driver very very slowly. Steering usually entailed releasing the lever a little, this slowed down the respective track and the excavator turned. I couldn't do this, but the Engineers had trained me well. The hydraulic oil for the tracks first went through a spool valve. If I operated the bucket it would steal oil from the right track and slowly turn the excavator right. If I operated the dipper arm it would do the same to the left track and turn it left. Voila. In order to cut a half mile off the route I went cross country. I got to a fence and being too lazy to get out of the cab I was in the process of smashing the fence down. Hell there had just been a war on with tanks and everything. What was one more fence, but a conscientious field Sapper called George run up to the fence and pulled out a post and lowered the fence so that I could track over it. Damn! That was going to be my only bit of enjoyment on the route.

Later on that night the word went round that there was porn on in the bar. When I got there the bar was packed. We sat and watched the couples on the video and improved our German. "Oh, Oh, Fick mein arsch. Ja, ja, tiefer, das ist gut… etc." if ever we had he chance to appear in a porn film we knew the words off by heart. We even used them in everyday situations. "Beirne, go up to the workshops and pick up number 24 Muirhill"

"Ja, Untergefreiter, fick mein arsch"

"I'll fick your arsch if you don't get your arsch up to the workshops now"

"Ja, Ja tiefer tiefer, staff"

"We should never have let you boys watch that smut"

In Germany, or BAOR as it was called, we had our own language. I guess it could be called Germlish, a cross between German and English. We would use well known English phrases but in German. For example.

*****

"TC, what did you find?"

"Kein ein wurst" (not a sausage)

Reading squadron orders and finding that I am on duty "Jezus, I am on weekend duty again, bloody Deinst Zitreone" (bloody Duty Lemon)

"Hey, concentrate on the road; you're Alles uber der platz" (all over the place)

"Kein mehr bier fur der Bundesweir" (Bar's shut)

"Karton Kopf" (Boxhead, unfriendly term for a German citizen)

*****

Saturday 9th April

Spunky swamped his bed. So did someone else and he put his maggot into the tumble drier. People are ignoring Lumpy now. He is the one who is the pain at the site. Another day off for me. The lads were really envious. I did my washing today. SNCOs and Jnco's now have to do a duty on public jetty as MP's got beaten up and pushed into the sea.

The main jetty in Port Stanley was manned by RMP's. Their duty was to make our life a misery, a job which they did with great zeal. We were watched when we started and finished work and were scrutinised for our dress. Port Stanley garrison was in a period of 'normalisation'. In other words, the period during and after the war when soldiers could wear what they want was over. We had to abide to all normal UK or BAOR rules. No hands in pockets, no berets on back of heads and no drunkenness. That was us, the other Regiments and Corps still wore the Extra Cold Warfare deerstalker hats and parkas. The Redcaps or 'Monkeys' were the ones that pulled us for our dress code. At the end of the evening the little ten metre by thirty nine metre jetty was packed with soldiers. There was a small wooden hut that the Monkeys occupied and we had to book in and out from the hut. As the jetty was so full the Monkeys were unable to pick on individuals and so just threw out malicious comments. "Get your beret on properly" Ten hands would go up to their hats and put them on properly, TC was always one. At the start of the project he would wear it on the back of his head, later on he changed to wearing it backwards. He looked like a Frenchman but it suited him. "Stop pushing at the back; get your hands out your pockets you over there."

This day I was near the edge of the jetty, there were three rows between me and the sea. A couple of nights ago Benjamin Byrne had fallen into the sea when the crowd had surged and he had run out of jetty, he had lost his camera and a fishing reel. He had also sunk to the bottom of the Canache and had had to take off his combat jacket in order to float. It gave me an idea, I was standing next to Spunky and Jeeves, and the Redcaps had been herded to the edge of the jetty by the influx of three Bedfords at the same time. Shouts of "Stop pushing at the back" were having more and more urgency to them. It gave me an idea, an idea which I think everybody had at the same time. I noticed that the RMP Sgt was in direct line with Spunky and another two guys; we were all shoulder to shoulder. I nodded to Spunky and whispered "He's a bit close to the edge isn't he?" Spunky looked. As he looked a smile crept up on his face, and he took a half step backwards so that he was in line with the other two guys. When he was in line I grabbed the back of his combat jacket, Spunky looked at me and the understanding registered on his smile. Spunky elbowed the guy next to him who was from the RCT and nodded towards the Monkey. Spunky grabbed the mans combat jacket and nodded to his mate. The Driver looked at Spunky, me, my hand on Spunky's jacket, his mate and then the Monkey and smiled. Slowly he grabbed a handful of loose combat jacket of the third man's jacket. Before he had time to look back at me I turned to face Spunky and shouted "HEY, WATCH IT" and shoved Spunky sideward, he hit the next guy who in turn hit the other who unfortunately bumped into the RMP Sgt and knocked him ten metres into the sea. We all pulled on jackets and the third man was jerked a metre away from the edge and we bumped into the crowd. A huge cheer went up when the Monkey hit the water, the cheering shot through the crowd as soldiers realised what had happened. It was the perfect snooker shot. There was just enough backspin on the last guy to stop him going in.

The RMP Cpl, who was also on the edge of the jetty realised, that he was in trouble and started shouting "BACK! GET BACK NOW!! BACK! THAT IS AN ORDER!" I looked towards him through the jeering crowd and saw a pair of hands come from behind a parka and push the Cpl in with a "Fuck Off." A second and larger cheer went up and the whole congregation, as if on cue, shuffled away from the edge of the jetty. No one wanted to be the one who was standing next to the scene of the crime when the Monkeys got out. A SNCO from another unit broke out from the crowd as it was moving back and threw a life ring into the water for the Sgt. The atmosphere was like when a cinema crowd comes out of a funny movie. Everybody was laughing and chatting. The Monkeys got out using the CSB jetty which was at sea level and climbed the ladder and went into their hut. A couple of minutes later a LCT and a small Phut Phut came in together and the crowd surged forward and disappeared to their respective ships. The next day on Squadron orders it was announced that a SNCO and a JNCO from each unit would replace the RMP's on the jetty duty.

This wasn't the first time that someone put their pee saturated duck down filled sleeping bag into the tumble drier, again the deck stunk of rotten carrots. I had to use my party trick of breathing through my mouth and not my nose in order to get into the wash room and do my Dhobi.

Sunday 10th April

I had another day off today. It gets boring when you have too many days off. 1 is ok, 2 are not bad but slow, 3 are terrible. The Sir Tristram left for the outer harbour today. The quay looks bare without it.

For the last four months one of the landmarks in the harbour was HMS Sir Tristram. The Sir Tristram was hit by a bomb during the war. She was still afloat and was harboured up next to the public jetty in Port Stanley. It was being used as accommodation by one of the R.E. Squadrons. We didn't envy them at all. The ship looked like a gutted hull. She wasn't sea worthy so the RN sent up a recovery ship to scoop her up out of the water and give her a piggy back ride home. It was all very 'Thunderbirds' to us. The Dan Lifter was a huge ship that had the ability to sink its middle and let a ship sail over it. The middle would then be pumped free of water and it would rise and lift the broken ship out of the water. The Dan Lifter had arrived and was costing the British Government a pretty penny so there was no time wasting. A couple of our welders were sent out to the Dan Lifter to weld the Sir Tristram into the Dan Lifter. It was a 'good number' job as the civvies treated the soldiers better than the British Government did.

Monday 11th April

I had first hand experience of Bignose's ignorance today up the site as I joined the Coastell 2 road again. I went to my first CSE show. It was a good laugh; there was Bob Gelding with his dog called spit. He is off Tiswas and OTT. A nice girl singer and Janet Brown were the other stars with a never-heard-of 3 piece band. I had 30 p of chips from the van then we had better and more chips on the shore.

The OC would not have won any popularity contests. He was a hated man and not just by the Troops, the SNCOs and the Officers also had a reason to dislike him. For the 'dirty unwashed' (the Troops) it was a very basic, down to earth, reason. The man was a knobber. He shouldn't have been put in charge of a kiddie's roundabout let alone have the last decision over the lives of one hundred odd men. He would tell Cpls to stop bluffing, Sgts to shut up, and call Officers morons in front of the Troops. It was as if no one on this planet had any significance to him except him. He believed that the world revolved around him, not the other way round, but he was messing around with soldiers' lives, not namby pamby civvies that go home and take it out on their wives. Soldiers do something about it. And they did!

I was walking up the Coastell Road to where it joined the Port Stanley - Airport Road and I saw the OC's Mercedes parked on the verge. Standing next to the jeep was Cpl. Lowland. He was one of my training NCOs in Southwood camp, (Now a shopping centre in Farnborough) and I knew him well. He was one of the Cpls for 1

Troop. I ambled up to him for a chat, he saw me coming and I saw his lips move but he was too far away for me to hear what he was saying. When I got to him, I asked him if he was guarding the OC's Mercedes. "Am I fuck! I'm guarding Ginge." Ginge Tapper was another Cpl. in 1 Troop and the two were always together. They were catalysts for each other's humour. It was good enough to stand on the edge of a group with these two Cpl.'s in and enjoy the banter. To get too close was to get dragged in and become the object of the joke. I looked around and couldn't see Ginge anywhere. "Er... what have you been drinking, Kev?" Kev was at the rear of the jeep and I was at the front. Kev nodded at me to come round to the rear. As I rounded the rear corner I saw a pair of legs sticking out from under the jeep. "Oh! There he is" I laughed "is he repairing the OC's Merc?"

"Is he fuck" Kev whispered "he's cutting through the bastard's brake pipes." Realising the potential danger in this, I tried to dissuade them even though they both outranked me "Hey Ginge!" I bent down and shouted under the vehicle "it's the ten mm pipes you need to cut, mind the brake fluid when it comes out."

"I can't cut through them, they're too thick" came the strained reply

"What are you using?"

"Pliers"

"I'll get you a hacksaw!" I shouted to the pair of legs and I walked off laughing towards the D6, happy to help in the demise of the OC. As I started walking down the track I looked back and saw that SSgt Simpson had pulled up in his Rover and was walking towards Kev. I quickened my pace and walked right all the way down to the bottom of the road. Having been bust twice I didn't need the drop in pay yet another time. I put distance between the horrific act that I had nothing to do with, the totally innocent me.

Later Kev told me what happened; "I was watching you walk down the track and was laughing when Homer crept up on us, he asked me, in a quiet voice, what I was doing. I jumped out of my skin and said that that it had nothing to do with me and I legged it, when I got round to the front of the Merc, Homer shouted under the vehicle to Ginge and asked him what he was doing, all I heard was a large thud where Ginge jumped in fright and smashed his head on the rear axle. Ginge collected himself and shouted back that he had seen a loose wire under the Merc and was securing it. Homer told Ginge to leave it and he would book it into the workshop for a service. When I spoke to Ginge later he hadn't managed to cut through any of the pipes."

A couple of days later I was walking through the edge of Port Stanley when I saw Jeeves having a fag outside a small wooden shed. "Woto mate, what you doing here?" I asked.

"Hey Bernie, how's it going, I'm in the servicing bay" he took a long slow drag on his fag. He clearly had a lot of time to kill. I looked around and couldn't see the servicing bay anywhere. It was all houses, so I asked him "Where is this bay?" he nodded towards the small hut. "You're joking" I laughed. He wasn't and shook his head "Hey, come inside and look at this, we're servicing the OC's vehicle right now, he wants it back immediately."

"Is that why you're having a fag?"

"It's my third in half an hour" he laughed and pointed towards a large expanse of fag butts that were littering the floor. Clearly there was no rush here. He led me round to the rear of the hut, it was just large enough for a car and two people either side. It had a pit; on top of the pit was the OC's Merc. I went down in the pit with Jeeves and he showed me the underside of the Merc. Words were not needed. I burst out laughing when I saw that every cable, wire, pipe and tube had either been cut through or crimped. The brake pipes were crimped along the whole length, from the front to the rear. It was obvious that many more people other than Ginge and Kev had tried to cut his brake pipes. Port Stanley had a huge 1:6 hill that lead down to the sea. A loader lost its brakes down that hill and smashed into a house. I told Jeeves of Kev and Ginge's adventure and he told me that they weren't the first. He pointed to the brake pipes with his cigarette "See these pipes are nice and silver"

"Yes"

"Well they are three weeks old; we put them on three weeks ago because the old ones were cut through. Bignose sent his vehicle in because his brakes were 'Spongy'."

"Shame he didn't drive down the hill" I added sadly.

"E fucking did! E went down the fucking hill and along to Moody Brook with no brakes, drove back to the Squadron office and then gave the vehicle to Harry out of the office, and told him to get the brakes fixed. Harry shat himself when he tried to stop, had to use the handbrake. Luckily he was going up hill. Three weeks is all his brake pipes last, we've ordered another ten complete sets."

"Did you hear about Sandy on the Haulamatic?" He hadn't "Bignose forced him off the road, took three hours to pull him out. His Haulamatic was full of sand, sunk down into the peat on the verge, straight after the notice on orders about cars giving way to dumpers. Sandy was fuming. The Haulamatic drivers have a contract out on him, whoever manages to kill him or send him home gets a crate from other drivers. We've matched it and will also give the driver a crate. They aim for him now, but he always swerves at the last minute and they miss him."

"They don't miss him," Jeeves laughed "Follow me" we climbed out of the pit and Jeeves showed me a pile of Mercedes' wing mirrors "they hit his mirrors, he has gone through our entire supply, and look at the side of his rear bumper" it was scratched and had British Army green smeared on the Argie green. "Damn! They are close but not close enough"

"Someday" Jeeves mused "Someday."

Some bright spark had an idea to ship a mobile chip van to the Falklands. This arrived recently and we, (the British Forces on the Island) were supposed to flock to the van and make this man rich. His first problem was the cost of shipping the van eight thousand miles from the UK to the Falklands. This shipping cost went on to the price of the chips, second problem was that most of the servicemen were aboard ships and couldn't be arsed to go through a thirty minute, wet crossing to get a bag of chips, his third problem was that his chips were shite. White and floppy! Just like chips in the UK! There was a chippy on the Island whose chips were cheaper, browner and crispier. Hmmm tough choice! We went to the mobile chippy after the CSE show and met Janet Brown and Jim Davidson who was also in the show. We had a laugh and made our way back to our prison ship. Jim Davidson's routine was legendary around the Islands. There were Sappers who were working up on the tops of mountains who had seen his show along with the thirty other soldiers on the mountain top base. Word had got down to us that it was crude and hilarious. I went to the Port Stanley show and it was supposed to be for the service personnel only and definitely no children. We walked in and sat next to a Benny family who had brought their kids of around seven to ten years old. Jim Davidson walked onto stage, saw the kids and said "Well, there goes 90% of my material." The cleaned up version of his act was crude enough and as he got towards the end (he told us by the chippy) he thought 'fuckit' the servicemen are not going to get a cleaned up version just because a father ignored the requests for no children.

Tuesday 12th April

Countess came into the harbour this morning with all the relations of the dead. When it left, the RAF put on a fly past which was filmed from a sea king by ITN. It's the OC's birthday and he is throwing a party. 3 people have been knobbled for waiting. People have been collared for cleaning silver, loading their extra booze and no doubt cleaning up. I went into Jeeves' room and found that he has got Mabel Cowcorn as a pen friend.

I lay on my bunk and wrote to Sandra. It was not the perfect writing place but it was the only writing place. I was lying on my side, with the bluey resting on a book and scrawling on the thin blue paper with a biro. My writing resembles a spider that has walked through an inkwell at the best of times, writing under these conditions and I'm surprised that Sandra could read anything at all. I finished writing the day's exciting events and folded the bluey, addressed it and sealed it. It was seven o' clock and I was bored. I looked down to the floor and looked around the bunks. Jock was flat on his back with a pair of headphones over his ears. He, as always, had fallen asleep whilst listening to a taped story. He must hear all of the stories in his sub consciousness. I'm sure that when he comes to hear them and manage to stay awake he will suffer from continuous deja vue. Taff, Spunky and TC were out at the bar and that left Mac who was writing to his wife. I raced through the alternatives of what to do. None appealed to me. A thought hit me to go and visit the Knockers. I jumped down from my third floor bunk and walked down the corridor to the other cabins. We were in one of the smallest cabins, there only being twenty two bed spaces. The others were more crowded. I had my hands in my pockets and ambled into one of the larger cabins. I didn't have anyone in mind but didn't need to. I knew everyone intimately.

Tiny Black:

A tiny young soldier, from 3 Troop who went down town in Nunburg, and got shitfaced in a bar. He woke up, (on a work day) in a strange bed with a woman lying naked next to him. When he told us (he was late for parade and got two extras) we were all gobsmacked. (I can remember my mouth hanging open) He was eighteen but looked around twelve and here he was waking up next to a naked woman. "What did you do?" Stig asked. Tiny went bright red and told us that as he didn't know where he was, he sneaked out of the bed and got a taxi back to camp. This answer got him a smack around the head and everybody piled on top of him for being so stupid. He got horse bites and licked all over his face for his 'crime'. It was a gift from god and he had wasted it. He didn't even take a peek under the sheets and had no idea where the flat was and so couldn't go back.

Ray Parker:

The coolest guy in the squadron! Which wasn't hard for him, he was black and good looking. Always dressed in the most fashionable clothes and always had at least two girls down town.

Lofty Leblanc:

Basil Fawlty's double, in appearance and in humour as well. The tallest guy in the squadron!

Dave Randall:

He was getting out of the Army after this tour. He was also getting divorced. He was intending to get a job as a check out attendant, when the divorce goes through the court and when she is awarded half his salary, quitting and getting a job for a construction company.

They all had stories about them and were part of a large family. They still are. I ambled down the aisle of the cabin and nodded to anyone there. I came across Jeeves who, like me minutes before, was laying on his top bunk writing. "Hi Jeeves"

"Hello Bernie, alright?"

"Naw… bored stupid. Wotcha doing?" showing mild interest.

"Writing to a pen friend that I got from The Sun newspaper" The Sun newspaper had asked for, and got thousands of pen friends for the soldiers down South in the Falklands. There were so many that they had to be distributed by the bag load. First they were divided into Army, Navy and Airforce. Then into Regiments, Engineers, Signals, Guards, RCT etc. then in the Regiments the bags were split up for Squadrons, 75 Sqn, 51 Sqn, 16 Sqn. In the Squadron offices the mail clerks split the bags up into Troops. 1, 2, 3, Spt, MT and HQ. The Troops would divide the hundreds of letters between the Sections, to anyone who promised to write back to the girls. Jeeves had a few to write to. It was purely random. In the cabins were boards that held pictures of the girls (and women) some were pornographic, some were sickly sweet of girls in their Sunday best, but most were of girls down the pub with their mates. Jeeves held up a picture to me of the girl that he was writing to, "Not bad eh?" he boasted, it was pot luck whether you got a good looker or not, most didn't have photos in. I glanced at the photo and did a double take, I looked closer, Jeeves pulled the photo away, "No, you can't have her, she's mine" the good lookers were prized possessions and he only showed me the photo so that he could boast of his luck.

I decided to pop his balloon as harshly as I could "That's Mabel Cowcorn, give her my regards when you write to her."

There was a silence that I enjoyed while Jeeves intently scrutinised me. Suspicion was all over his face. He looked at the photograph as if the picture would jump out and talk to him, "Her name's not *Cowcorn*" he said with a sneer and a twist of his nose.

"Well it was when I went out with her. She lives in Burwell, Cambridgeshire, is around twenty three, has a snotty brother called Steven and lives with her mother, her dad is dead." I smiled the smile of the Triumphant! Boy was I glad I came into this cabin and not another, I was enjoying this immensely.

Jeeves looked at his letter, then at the photo, then at the letter from Mabel and his face fell "Fuckit!" he handed over the photo and letter to me "you might as well have her."

"I already have" I lied, I held out the photo to him as he had to me, I delivered the coup de grace "Fucks like a rabbit" he made a grab for the photo and I pulled it away "nope. Mine now, thanks" I smiled from ear to ear and turned and walked out of the cabin, as I did I talked to the photo loud enough so that Jeeves could hear "Aahhh, Mabel, was that horrible man bothering you, don't worry, nice Bernie will look after you." The guys in the bunks who had heard the whole thing laughed. "Fuck off!" Jeeves shouted. I let him have the last word. It was all light hearted and good humoured. I walked back to my pit, my head spinning at the chances of me getting that letter from Mabel. Anywhere down the line it could have gone elsewhere. I am a firm believer in fate and I believe that some things happen for a reason. I was meant to get that letter from Mabel. Something made me go into that cabin. I hadn't been into that room for months. I never went into it again during the tour, and yet something compelled me to go into there when Jeeves was writing to Mabel.

Think of the odds of that chain of events happening. I read the letter, she had son and was divorced from the husband. That surprised me; Mabel was such a sweet girl. But she was too sweet, always deferring to my way, "What do you fancy doing?"

"Whatever, you want to do." I wanted to shag her rotten but we were in the High Street.

"Do you fancy the pictures?"

"If you do"

"Oh" thinking that she didn't and that was her way of saying no "What about the pub?"

"If you want to"

"No, we always do what I want to do, let's do what you want to do?" Fairs fair after all.

"I want to do what you want to do" AAARGGG!

"Lets go into the middle of the road, strip off naked and I will shag you up the arse with a pineapple"

"Ok, if you want to"

Do you get the idea?

All that was forgotten, or at least been pushed to the back of my mind by the chance meeting. I wrote to her and told her what a fantastic coincidence it was that I had got her letter. Asked her how she was and after her family. Told her that I was married and living in Germany, told her about my time in the Army. All very nicey nicey stuff! Wow, was I in for a surprise. Read on dear readers. If you cannot wait for the reply like I had to, go to page???

Wednesday 13th April

San got a job today. Well, she got it on Monday but I got the letter today. It snowed today. I had to work on a Hymac with no cab, talk about cold!! A bloke came up to Taff said that the Hymacs are coming loaded with sand. He meant Haulamatics. OC calls everything a Hymac.

Today it snowed! The weather had been deteriorating day by day and it was cold enough today to snow. As The Falklands are on the other side of the world the weather pattern is upside-down. As the weather turned nice in Europe it turned nasty down South. To make matters worse I was given the broken down Hymac 580 Bt to work on. It had no cab and very little else. The bucket wobbled around on the dipper because the pin was too small for the dipper arm. It was part of the war stock, equipment, which is held in huge warehouses, for a war. It should be kept up to date but because of budget cuts, never is. We were to get the new armoured Hymac 590 CT's that Taff and I used on the minefield clearance. The diary comment about Hymacs and Haulamatics says more about my attitude at the time towards the Knockers than it does about the knowledge of the Knocker. I'm afraid that we had an elitist attitude towards them. But they had an elitist attitude towards us so it was fair game. They thought of us as lazy lever pullers, which was a description that we tried to live down to. If a Knocker dug a two man battle trench and I dug a fifty yard by two metre deep hole, he would have expended more energy than me. It was a very cushy job. (To save you looking at the front, a Hymac is a 360 degree, tracked digger with a one cubic metre bucket on the front. A Haulamatic is a six wheeled dump truck with a ten cubic metre skip on the back.)

We had all been banned from wearing the Extra Cold Weather gear by the SSM; he didn't want us looking like a bunch of untidy warm soldiers. He wanted us to look like smart cold soldiers. The Hamm roller has now become the machine to operate. Its diesel fuelled heater is the best on the Island. If we have nothing to do we sit in the Hamm. The missing windows are lined with polythene. The windscreen of one of the Muirhill A5000 wheeled tractors (diggers or JCB to you) has been missing since we got it. The heater only warms the legs and all of the heat then disappears out the window. Today we picked up a crate that had the windscreen in. Jock and I undid the thirty six wood screws with our jack knives, a pen knife that is given to all Sappers. Some still have the horses hoof spike on. It also has a short blade that can be used as a screwdriver. We unscrewed all thirty six one inch screws and removed the lid. Jock reached in and lifted out the windscreen which was wrapped in grey plastic and was full of dehumidifying silicone granules. "Why the hell have they put so much silicone in a windscreen? Are they afraid of the glass getting wet?" Jock laughed. He slit open the plastic and burst our laughing.

"What?" I asked looking into the open plastic bag which held the £800 windscreen that had been shipped eight thousand miles to us.

"The windscreen is broken. That isn't silicone granules in there, it's the windscreen."

"Fuck! Let's use the plastic for a windscreen"

"We can't! We have to be able see through it. You'll just have to get cold." Jock laughed at this also. He wasn't the one who had to sit in a machine with snow coming in through the window.

We sent the windscreen back and the stores blamed us for breaking it. I blame the manufacturer for putting it in a crate where it can break.

Thursday 14th April

I worked on the 590 all day ditching. Great fun, doing what I am paid for, not enough though! Taff is going on a swan tomorrow, so Lumpy told Jock to come down the site and smarten up the Groyne. Taff went mad and he told Lumpy so. The Oggie SNCOs are like fish out of water. Capt. Salter is the only guy that knows what he is talking about. St. Helena left today.

I got on the 590 today, what a difference. A full bomb proof cab, (personally tested ten years later in the minefields of Kuwait) fantastic heater and hydraulically operated levers. The 580 has massive two foot long levers that pushed levers under the cab. The 590 had short dumpy six inch levers that operated hydraulic valves in the arms of the chair. When you are a good operator with a 360 degree backactor it is like a part of your arm. You don't realise that you are pulling levers, all you see is the bucket and if the bucket comes up against some rock you find that you are pulling harder on the lever, not that it will make a ha'pence of difference.

When I was back in Germany I was sent on a CET course to Bovington. When I got back I was raring to go on a CET. The Squadron was in the middle of an exercise and I had to go out and join them. But horrors of horrors I had to join 1 Troop, Lumpy Gills troop, the SSgt from hell. There started the most depressing week of my entire Army career. (Apart from when I was in the regimental jail) SSgt Lumpy Phillips held no concern at all for his men. Only the task mattered. If they weren't fed, clothed or watered didn't matter, if their boots were dirty it did! I was told to find so and so's section and work with them. I wasn't part of their section and as an outsider didn't know the score. I had to sleep outside their lean to as there wasn't enough room for me, I wasn't fed as there wasn't enough food and was just another hand. Fuck that for a game of soldiers! I was never so glad to get back to Support Troop at the end of the exercise. Lumpy knew everything there was to know about combat engineering, but he was like a fish out of water as far as construction plant was concerned. I saw this when he asked me a question about plant.

He had just finished shouting to a Sapper to get a roll of cable when he turned to me and looking up at me in the cab of the 590 asked "How long it will it take to dig the ditch, LCpl Beirne?" He asked in a deadpan voice, a voice that I had never heard come from him before. I looked up and down the road and looked above his head whilst I did some calculations and replied "if I keep this 590 I should be able to do it in one week Staff," he nodded and started to turn but I stopped him "Staff, I'll be putting the fall from there to there" I pointed to parts of the road "and then out along there for when we construct the Coastell 3 Road, is that OK?" I asked him as a test to see if he would know what I was talking about. A plant SNCO would not have had a problem with that question. He would have taken it in his stride, but I saw an emotion in Lumpy that has stuck with me for the rest of my life.

Fear!!!

I saw fear, uncertainty and unease. At the age of twenty four I felt sorry for this monster of a man. I immediately regretted asking him and putting him on the spot. It was cruel. I saw inside his head and it surprised the hell out of me. It also changed the way that I look at and treat people. Lumpy was well out of his depth with something that I saw as simple. I had done the course and he hadn't. I had always thought that he was the master of everything but it was not so and that popped a bubble, destroyed a myth that had build up in my mind. Although I still went along with my peers on the condemnation of the Knockers and Lumpy, I never again looked up, *or down* to him or anyone else for that matter. He was my equal and I always kept him over informed on what I was doing for the rest of my time in 75 Sqn. He must have appreciated that because from that moment on he treated me different, whether it was because I was talking to him differently or whether he was afraid that I would ask him another question that he couldn't answer I don't know, what I do know is that at that very moment in my life I learned compassion for my fellow human being, whoever or whatever he or she was. A big moment in my life!

We were behind schedule with the Coastell Road and so had a night shift as well as a day shift. TC and Spunky were on the night shift. I was on the day shift with Taff. Spunky had realised that for each load of stone he had to drive the roller up and down four times and that was it. The rest of the time he could spend sleeping, so he took the roller. The Hamm roller was German and had the best heater on the entire Island. When we took it over it had three windows missing and the heater didn't work. I, using Sapper ingenuity, repaired the windows and more importantly the heater. It was a heater that used diesel fuel and would run independently from the main engine. It also turned the cab into a sauna. When the snow was outside you could run the Hamm with your top off. The reason it had windows missing was because a Sapper was rolling the runway just after the war (repairing the bomb holes that the Vulcan bombers made) whilst a Hercules C130 was lining up for take off. The Hercules revved up his four large propellers to take off thrust, and the windows of the Hamm were blown in knocking out the Sapper. He was discovered when the Hamm went on its own little way oblivious that the man controlling it was unconscious in the cab and it ran into a ditch. There were only two people who were qualified to drive the rollers and they were Spunky and me (the two full Cpls don't count) so Spunky was fast asleep in the Hamm, snow was steaming as soon as it made contact with the hot metal roof of the roller. TC was sitting in the Caterpillar D6d bulldozer with his feet up on the dashboard, selfish stereo earphones in his ears and his beret on the back of his head, fag in gob which wasn't allowed on plant and the heater was on full. I suppose you could say that he was dozing in the dozer. It was two am and he was waiting for a load of stone and sand to arrive so that he could push it out. Spunky would then roll it.

TC saw a person walking towards him. You can recognise who people are by the way that they walk. TC didn't recognise this person. "God, who's this" he muttered to him self. The person walked up to his dozer from the side, out of the beams of his front and rear spot lights. He reached up and opened the door and before TC could shout his customary "SHUT THE FUCKING DOOR," when he saw the red lapels on his combats. That meant that the person sat close to God at the dinner table. Major General Thorpe shouted up "Good Morning Sapper is it nice and warm in there?" and climbed into the dozer. TC pulled out the earphones, stubbed out his fag, straightened his beret and dropped his feet to the floor in one swift movement. It went unnoticed as the General was climbing in at the time. TC and the General had a long, friendly talk. The General was returning from a high echelon meeting at the airfield and stopped to talk to the Sappers who were on night shift. No ceremony, no fuss, no gaggle of Officers and Sergeant Majors listening to his every word and more importantly to your replies. That sat and chatted until the Haulamatic turned up with the stone. The General said his goodbyes and left TC bewildered at the high ranking Officer's visit. This is how you gain the respect of the soldiers. TC told us and we told everyone else. By the next day all the Engineers in Stanley knew, by the end of the week it was all of the Engineers on the Island and most of the other Troops. We admired the General for taking time out to see the men at the bottom. He was a man that we would have followed into battle because of small events like that. He met me once in the Officers' mess in Tidworth. I served him with a drink. I was Officers mess barman. He looked at me and asked "Didn't we meet in Cyprus? You were doing the UN track with 6 Squadron," I was so pleased and surprised that he had remembered little old me over all that time. I certainly remembered him. A real leader of men!

Friday 15th April

☻ the road is just about if not already finished. I went to sleep in the grader today; there was that much work on today. Lord Montgomery is back today. So is Andy Scott. (Montgomery killer). No mail.

The road stretched from the Stanley to Airfield Road down to the inner harbour or 'Canache' where the second Coastell was coming in. There was already a Coastell harboured up at the end of the runway. It was used by the RAF. An understandable choice as it was next to the airfield, RAF Port Stanley. Coastell 1 was a four storey square box sitting on a floating pontoon. The boxes were made up of smaller boxes. The smaller boxes were International Shipping Container size. Handy! They were the living accommodation for the oil rigs and Coastells 2 and 3 were being towed down to the Falklands, by the AA I presume.

*****

"Hello, is that the AA?"

"Yes Sir, where have you broken down?"

"Er… Newcastle Shipyard"

"OK and where are you going?"

"The Falkland Islands, South Atlantic"

"Right, yes… (sound of hitting computer keys) sorry Sir, but you do not have AA Relay, all we can do is to send a disinterested youth to you, to wiggle your dipstick in its holder"

*****

Strangely enough Coastell 3 was arriving before Coastell 2. So we were also building 3's walkways out from the road to the area where we were told that the doors should be. Pretty important if you didn't want to fall ten metres into the water every time you walked out the door. Unfortunately we didn't get the 'Groynes' in the right place. Read on.

'Lord Montgomery was a fresh faced youth who was also the Troop commander of 1 Troop, Lumpy Phillips' Troop. He was rumoured to be well connected. Either Daddy was a Brigadier or he was related to a Peer of the Realm. Whoever he was connected to he was very well educated, very intelligent, and very very naive. He had no concept on how to communicate to the lower classes and this occasionally led him into trouble. Trouble that shouldn't happen to a British Officer but in the case of Jeremy, did.

Andy Scott was out in Fox Bay working with 1 Troop. Lt. Montgomery proved to everyone that even the calmest of us have a breaking point, he found Andy's breaking point and went well past it, and the consequence was that Andy chased him across the site shouting that he wanted to kill him. Jeremy locked himself in a portacabin. A portacabin is no defence for a pissed off British Paratrooper. Andy started to punch his way into the cabin before he was pulled off.

The above was the story of Andy and Monty that I heard and kept with me for 29 years until I finally asked Andy what had happened. He told me that Monty had upset him and Andy had gone into a port cabin and punched the wall in anger, making a hole in it. He never chased Monty across the site and Monty never locked himself into a cabin for protection. This illustrates how stories get blown up in the army and considering that I was in the same Squadron and the same accommodation as Andy, it didn't have far to travel to get to me and yet when it did, it had changed beyond all recognition. Personally Andy, I prefer the first version.

In my diary I had started to put smilies when I received mail and saddies when I didn't. It was the highlight of my day. Other than that it was get up, go to work come back, sleep.

Saturday 16th April

☹ *No mail. The Geraint moved again to let a destroyer in. its like musical chairs, when the music stops last one to get a mooring goes to the outer harbour. 2 months and 23 days till we leave here, or only 8 metric weeks. They have 3 Mondays in. All plant work on site has finished except Spunky's ditch. My confidential was great. So fucking what! Recommended for promotion and section commanders course.*

It was too depressing to think of all of those days to do so we invented a metric week. It went Monday, Tuesday, Monday, Wednesday, Monday, Thursday, Friday, Saturday, and Sunday. Looking back on this week I now see that it was a mistake. We should have had three extra Saturdays in. Monday is the worst day of the week. It did mean that we only had eight weeks to do (metric). Looking back on the maths of it now, it is all to cock. I was going to correct it but no, dear reader. I am proud of the fact that I am so bad at maths that I did the 11 plus when I was ten. I get number blindness. Number dyslexia! Now that is a good new fashionable illness to have. When asked to do a long sum in your head you just have to say "Sorry old chap, but I suffer from number dyslexia." You can rip people off by short changing them and if they find out tell them about you're number dyslexic and short change them again" Nobody but an utter BASTARD takes the piss out of a dyslexic for not being able to read. Think about it, you are short changed by fifty pence and when you challenge the culprit s/he goes all embarrassed and stutters "oh… oh. Sorry but I er… I suffer from number dyslexia" and then s/he gives you a twenty piece bit. What are you going to do? Shout "You dyslexic twat, give me another thirty p.?" Who becomes the bastard then?

Sunday 17th April

Day off

Now I go into my date dyslexia period. I was so bored with life that I couldn't even be arsed to write my diary. I tried to catch up days later and by then I had lost a total day. Read on and try to keep track. I didn't. The crossing out is what I did in the diary when I wrote it. We were living to work. There was no social life at all except the bar and I didn't frequent that too often. I would try a write a letter home, write my diary and then train karate on the tank deck and shower and bed. We were in the middle of the tunnel. No light at either end.

Monday 18th April

Bogged the Hymac in well and good. The OC bollocked a group of soldiers for not saluting his car. There was a Staff Sergeant in it. When Bignose had finished the SSgt walked away and said so that all could hear "Fucking Burke." What a very astute observation.

Lord Montgomery- 0

Support Troop – 4

This was reference ditching which end to start.

I've lost the 19th of April. Anyone seen it?

High ranking staff cars had to be saluted. Bignose thought that his car was to be included in that list. The SSgt didn't.

Lord Montgomery thought that the ditch should be dug from the top down. We knew that if you did that then the ground water that was backed up in the ditch would flood the new section. He ordered us to dig it his way and then was bollocked for doing so. The reason being, that we were now trying to dig a three hundred metre ditch with a 1 in 80 slope when the ditch was full of water. We were pulling out buckets of water with soil in, god knows what the bottom of the ditch looked like. (Hey! It was important to us, then) Pinko, our leftist Sapper, had joined us and immediately been so upset of his treatment by the commanders of 1 Troop that he went on a 'Go Slow Strike". This entailed driving the bulldozer across the one mile long site in first gear on tickover. This would not even register on a policeman's radar gun. It was slower even than the Hymac excavator and that was only 1 ½ mph. The rest of us would drive the bulldozer in third gear reverse because it was faster than forward, around 13 mph.

One strange area of excitement was the compo processed cheese that we were given every lunch time. We had lunch delivered from our cooks who were at the Secretariat in Stanley, our HQ. When it was stew, Ugh! Usually it was some type of dead animal with chips in paper,, along with a few tins of processed cheese thrown in. This cheese was from the composition rations that soldiers took to war with them. It was designed by bastards to give you constipation for three weeks by which time you would probably be dead. It also was full of carbo-somethings which gave you the energy to fight. Trouble is most wars are full of hours of waiting around followed by a few minutes of shear fear in which your body is driven by adrenaline. The point of the cheese was that every tin was different. Some were crumbly like Cheshire cheese, some were like real processed cheese, but my favourite was the mouldy stuff which, if you screwed up your face you could fool your tongue that you were eating Danish Blue. It was a combination of the mould and the tin that had leeched into the cheese. Lovely! Opening the tin was always an occasion that the Troop would wait for everyone to be there. It was like opening Christmas presents or Liquorice Allsorts. Everybody had their favourites. We would pierce open the can with the brilliant can opener and pass round the can so that all could savour its 'nose' (the smell you ignoramus!) Guesses would be presented on its texture and then the can would be opened amidst cheers or boos depending on what it was.

Tuesday 19th April

20th?

Jock gave Bignose a shaped tube for a 27kva, to take round to the site on the chopper. Bignose grabbed the pipe, put it across his knee and said "does it bend any more?" meaning to bend it to put it in the mail bag! We were invited to an old ladies at the site for coffee & biccys. Mac's wife has had a kid today.

We had moved site. We were now carrying out the earthworks for a heliport at the top of Port Stanley. There was a house at the entrance to the site (the site being an open field) and in that house lived an old couple. The husband still worked but the lady was a house wife. Her son had left the Island many years ago for UK and the only person that she had to look after was her husband. Enter the scene twenty young soldiers and she was out at ten am with an offer of a cup of tea. We happily obliged and on entering, found a kitchen from the past. It had a large peat fired range (cooker / heater) on the left of the kitchen and a deep, old fashioned, Belfast kitchen sink, on the right. The taps were on the ends of long white painted pipes that were running down the outside of the wall. In UK and Germany they would have been hidden. The floor was tiled and the room was scorching hot. She had the range fired up and the smell of just-cooked biscuits assaulted our noses. The reason for the smell was sitting on the table. A clean white lace tablecloth, decorated the table and newly cooked biscuits decorated the tablecloth, but not for long.

"Help yourself to the biscuits, boys" the old lady said and we did. Within ten minutes they were reduced to crumbs, crumbs that we were picking up and eating like hungry pigeons. We chatted about life in general and she asked us to join her again the next day. We promised that we would. Her name was (and probably still is, Jane). Outside went back to work digging out the peat so that we could lay

concrete mats for the helicopters to land on. The weather has started
to turn, it is more common for it to be wet than dry. It isn't too bad
for me as I am usually working inside the Hymac 590 CT. It has a
lovely heater and a blast proof cab so no wind gets in. Mac
McGuire's wife had a kid today. He was told by the SSM who
apparently found out when the rear party phoned the news to him.
There is a Pissup in the bar tonight.

Wednesday 20th April

~~20~~ 21 th???

*I spent the day on the Hymac and showed some kids the controls.
Big news. The Groyne, containers and everything else is out
according to the CRE surveyors. Dave Randall is going to check it
all tomorrow. Jane the grandmother has said that we can go in her
house any time tomorrow for coffee and biccys. I met her husband
and nephew today. He is a nice kid. We found a bazooka today. Now
all I want is some ammo.*

As we are working at the top of Port Stanley, we always have a
gaggle of kids around us. We enjoy them being there as it reminds us
of being at home, of being humans. One of the kids was Jane's
nephew so I sat him in the cab of the Hymac and let him dig up
some peat. I sat on the seat and he sat between my legs. That way I
was able to grab the controls if he did something silly. The lads didn't
see it that way. I am now earmarked as being a child pervert. Every
little boy that we pass in the truck going to and fro work they ask if
he is pretty enough for me. I laugh along with them; I know that it is
only a joke. The surveyors surveyed the Coastell 2 site and it is all in
the wrong place. The Coastell 2 can only go in one place and
everything that services it, paths, anchors, Groynes must fit in with
this placement. Well it doesn't. It is shit-hitting the fan time. There
are a lot of worried faces on the SNCOs. Thank god, that I am only
LCpl.

This is all I can remember about the 18th and the 19th.

Thursday 21st April

I got lumbered with talking with the OC today cos everybody else was drinking coffee in Jane's.

Happy Birthday Queen

I went aboard the Irishman and got leaping! I didn't get back on the Geraint until 0400; I was to be up at 0545 but didn't get up until 0645. No more booze for me.

Everyone had piled into Jane's Coffee House for their NAAFI break and I was just finishing a dig. Along comes the OC when I am walking towards the house and I have to indulge in meaningless conversation with him:

Me: Hello Sir, (Saluting)

OC: Hello Lance Corporal Beirne, (Saluting back and looking round) Where is everyone?

(There is a half second of silence as I consider all the lies that I can tell him and the possibility of getting found out. I go for the truth as the house was only ten metres away)

Me: Having a cup of coffee around Jane's, Sir.

OC: Good, Good, (putting his hands behind his back and coming up onto his tiptoes.) How's it all going?

Me: Fine Sir, fine.

OC: Good…Good.(The OC now considers me a dummy and is desperately thinking of a way to politely detach himself from me) Machines all right?

Me: Yes Sir, Fine, just fine.

OC: Humph…(lost patience) tell Cpl Davies that I was here won't you Lance Corporal and without waiting for an answer turned and disappeared off in his Mercedes.

Back on the Geraint that evening I was practicing my karate when a man not from the Squadron started to walk past. He stopped and watched. My ego perked me up a bit and I tried to give him a demonstration of perfect Kata. A task in which I probably failed! When I'd finished he spoke. "What style is that?"

"Shotokhan" I replied.

He held out his hand "Baz, I'm from the Irishman."

"What's an Irishman?" I asked knowing that I was leaving myself open for abuse here.

"It's an ocean going tug. We're tied up alongside you right now. Mind if I practice with you?"

I didn't and he did. He practiced a different style that required a double movement. We taught each other our techniques. After we were knackered he asked me if I fancied a beer on their boat. The beer I didn't fancy but a look-see on somewhere no one else has been… yes! After a shower I went to the side where there was a commando-style rope ladder with dodgy moss-covered wooden rungs. He had told me to climb down and go into the bowels of the boat to look for the mess, or galley or poop deck or whatever sailors call their canteen. I found it and entered Utopia.

I had been on a diet of compo rations interspaced with mutton from the island. Two cans of piss, passed off as beer was our daily ration of alcohol. (No, not Fosters, worse piss) and here I was looking at five plates of half finished fry-ups with a tall beer sitting in front of each of the sailors. A thick cloud of tobacco smoke hovered at eye height like a miniature San Francisco Bay. But I had no eyes for the smoke or the beer. There on every plate was at least one half eaten, crispy brown sausage! There had to be three complete sausages looking up at me if you stitched them back together. Scattered around these round orbs of delight were a few chips and egg yoke, sausage, egg and chips. Oh heaven!

Introductions were done, and the cook seeing my gaze repeatedly return to the unwanted sausages asked me "Would you like some sausages?"

"No doesn't matter, I'll have these" I raced out in stentato and without waiting for an answer scooped up the bangers and thrust them into my mouth, tomato ketchup, old egg yoke and all.

As I did my hamster impression I noticed seven pairs of eyes on me, regarding me as you would examine a man from Mars.

"MWAT?" I mumbled smiling, I was in heaven, and the dark crispy skins of the sausages were making love to my taste buds. After such a long barren period of taste these were like a bright oil painting hung on a public toilet wall.

Richard the Skipper smiled through his ginger beard. He spoke slowly like he was talking to an idiot, or a crazy man. (With whom you have to tread carefully) "We have enough for you not to have to eat old ones. Would you like some new"?

My eyes must have doubled in size showing enough white to illuminate a coal bunker. He took that for a yes. "Make him a fry-up" he nodded to the cook.

If the bangers were an oil painting the fry-up was the art gallery. IT WAS BEAUTIFUL.

After the meal I was given an endless supply of cold beer, real beer. I kept on drinking, talking and being the life and soul of the party until they retired to their bunks. I was the performing monkey. I performed for beer and sausage egg and chips. (With Sarsons vinegar)

I then realised that I had to climb up that ladder again. It wasn't as easy as on the way down and after two nearly fatal slips I swung my legs over the handrail of the Geraint. I giggled at the feeling of being on (kind of) firm ground. Tottering to my cabin I climbed up to my pit at four am absolutely blottoed! I slept in and missed breakfast but with a fry-up inside me I didn't care. What a great evening! I had one more task from this day and that was to rub it in with my Troop. They wanted to know where I had been and when I told them they were insanely jealous. Great!

Friday 22nd April

The OC went down the Coastell 2 road, got put of his car, threw a G10 cable (a roll) at Lord Montgomery and said "Measure the fucking gap, it should have been done at 7 o clock this morning, you cretin" He He He. I felt rather sick this morning. I must get an early night.

The shit has definitely hit the proverbial fan. The Clerk of Works surveyor's report about the road being in the wrong place had filtered down to the OC. Unfortunately it was his entire fault. He had told Cpl Price not to bother with the theodolite surveyors' device. He had ordered him to use G10 electrical cable. So now not only was the road in the wrong place but so was the placement of the Groynes. The Groynes had to line up with the doors of the Coastell. If they didn't, the first step from the Coastell was going to be a bitch, ten metres into the sea! The O.C. was in one of his better management days. He raced down the stone built road and skidded to a halt by the young subaltern. There was a speed limit on the road as it was always full of pedestrian workers. This speeding Mercedes attracted everyone's attention, as it was the OC's Mercedes that got our full attention. He leaped out of the car and threw, yes threw, a thirty metre cable at 2nd Lieutenant Montgomery, obviously forgetting that his father was an influential Brigadier. His next comments were known around the Squadron within the next hour and by the whole Island by the end of the day.

"Measure the fucking gap, it should have been done at seven o'clock this morning, you cretin!"

2Lt Jeremy Montgomery was a young baby faced Officer who would blush red for the slightest reason and now he entered Full-Emergency-Crimson-Red mode. He muttered a positive response and the OC jumped back into his car and sped off, throwing stones from his spinning tyres in his angry exit.

Taff Davies, ever the politician walked over to the still blushing Jeremy and nonchalantly asked "Sir, What's a Cretin?" Nobody laughed out loud but sniggers were we were unable to hide.

That didn't help matters and Jeremy in true British Army management fashion then took out his anger on those who couldn't answer back, his Troop. He ordered the diver, LCpl Wes Hardy, to get into the water and measure the distance between the Groynes with the thirty metre tape.

"But the gap is around fifty metres Sir, the tape is too short. Why don't we get some string…?"

"DON'T ARGUE CORPRAL, JUST DO IT!" Jeremy was, I think the term is, 'Livid'. If it was at all possible, he had flushed even redder.

"OK Sir, but wouldn't it be easier to get some string…"

"I SAID DON'T ARGUE WITH ME. GET IN THERE WITH THE TAPE AND MEASURE THE GAP!"

"For Christ sake Wes," I muttered to Taff "measure the gap before his head explodes."

The divers had a friend in high places; the 2IC (Second in charge of the Squadron) was a diver. Captain Ball had heard the commotion and ambled across. He asked "Any problems Jeremy?"

"No. No, none at all, LCpl Hardy was just going to measure the gap between the Groynes"

"What, with that thirty metre tape? It is too short. Get some string Wes and measure the gap, bring the string to shore, half it, measure the half and double the measurement, OK"

"OK Sir" Wes smiled. 2Lt Montgomery stormed off in a huff. Taff followed him to press home his question about the definition of the word 'Cretin'. Jeremy was fun. He broke up the boredom by doing and asking stupid things. A great Officer! He would have made a great General in the First World War. He had all the right traits.

Saturday 23rd April

I nearly killed the OC because he walked into my slew arc. I chose to ignore him and slewed but missed him. Bignose threw a wobbler because the new road was higher than the old road. Taff sorted him out and had an argument over Bignose ordering sand when we needed stone. Lieutenant Sugar joined the site. Clocks went back one hour, TC ran the bar.

The left side of an excavator is a blind spot for the operator. There is a huge dipper arm in the way of the line of sight. Anyone with any common sense would stay out of the way of this large steel arm. Not Bignose, I am operating and out of the corner of my eye I notice that he is walking towards me from the blind side. Now bear in mind that the Squadron had a contract out to kill the OC. Anyone who achieved this would be rewarded with a crate of beer. A princely sum in the Falklands! When he entered the slew arc I swung the boom round to hit him but with agility that I didn't know forty year old men possessed, he leapt back. I had to look at him now and he waved his arm towards me. I motioned for him to approach which, unfortunately he did. He gave us a bollocking for the difference in heights of the new road compared to the existing one, it was water off a duck's back to me. Right now I couldn't give a shit if the road was painted pink and decorated every ten metres with a dead hamster on a skewer. I was just an automaton, on autopilot. Taff also had gone past the caring stage and told Bignose the reason for the difference. He then went on to chastise the OC for ordering sand when we needed stone. We all looked on in amusement, we knew the OC was still in the shit and we loved it.

Lt Sugar was one of those Officers, that although coming from a different class from the Troops, he was decent. He was the Troop commander of 3 Troop and everyone in the Squadron warmed to this young Officer. He had a way of talking to the men, which got the best out of them, he loved going to Jane's.. Even though I really needed sleep that night, TC stood in and ran the bar so I went to support him.

Sunday 24th April

Pete the pay is getting charged for smoking in the corridor. It's about time someone did. The squeaks got a compressor as the Hymac wouldn't cut through the stone. They hadn't a clue on how to work it and panicked when the pressure went over 80 P. S. I. Nights are spent either drinking or sleeping, I do neither, and everybody is so lethargic at night.

Working twelve to fourteen hours a day, every day is getting us down. We eat, work, eat, sleep and that is our day. The humour is leaving our day. We still have a laugh now and again but the monotony and lack of a social life is stripping us of our humour. Cracks are starting to show in friendships and our relationships are being put to the test. Old friends argue over anything. I threw a wobbly at Mac over his towel. Totally unreasonable I know but then it pissed me off so I spoke out.

Monday 25th April

An explosive device was found in a civvy car rigged up as a booby trap, they say that it wasn't anything to do with the Argies. I suppose it's one way to get rid of Smythe. I sparred with Baz and learned quite a lot. It seems that we have to fight the Bennies as well the Argies.

This incident never reached the National papers. Whether the bomb was aimed at the Army or it was a feud between two villagers we were never told. We were told to be aware of explosive devices on our plant. That is all we need to know.

Tuesday 26th April

People are just mindless working zombies living for a day 73 day's distance, me included. TC has gone to 52 and to the Coastell 1, he wasn't happy.

We are like a family. Taff and Jock were the two fathers and TC was one of the sons. When he was sent to another Squadron it was like being disowned. He was being taken away from those he associated with and thrust into a different social group to which he didn't belong. And not belonging was NOT part of culture. You needed to belong. You belonged to a Section, a Troop, a Squadron, a Regiment, a Corps and a Service and then right at the end there were servicemen and civvies. When TC came back that evening he recounted his day's work as we did to him, at least we would see each other every evening.

Wednesday 27th April

I sparred with Baz and gave him a magic round house (reverse) to the gob. Later we both tried to do front thrust kicks and he kicked me in the foot, ow! Apart from that sparring is great. The bazooka we found we gave to the Irishman. Baz's jaw was slightly dislocated, he he.

I took the Bazooka and wrapped it up in Netlon, the white fabric that we were using for the road, and carried it into the ship when we finished work. I ate the required compo/ fresh evening meal and went to practice some karate on the tank deck before having a shower. A little gym had been set up and I enjoyed using the punch bag. Baz as usual showed up and we taught each other a few different moves and then came the suggestion that we both loved, "Fancy a spar?" of course we did.

I am no Jet Li being long and gangly and my Sensei will be the first to tell you that my roundhouse kick is probably the worst in Karate history. So I was probably as surprised when my foot came up and round and smacked Baz full in the face. "How the hell did that get up there?" I wondered as I jumped across the mat to see if Baz was alright. He claimed he was and that it was his fault for not blocking. Nice eh? He tried to rearrange his jaw which at the time we didn't know was dislocated. Baz wanted to continue, as did I. I wasn't going to risk another high roundhouse. He'd be ready this time. A few useless punches, a couple of them funny double twisting kicks of Baz's style and I saw my opening. A front thrust kick would catch him right in the stomach. I went for the kick at exactly the same time as did Baz, my stomach being unguarded as well.

We kicked each other's toes and then hopped around holding our feet laughing and crying at the same time. That brought the practice to an end and I told Baz that I'd see him later as I had something for him, we both hobbled away.

After a shower I limped over to the starboard side of the Geraint where the ocean going tug had moored. There were two, The Irishman and The Yorkshireman. We had The Irishman tied alongside us. I went over to the railings and climbed down the ladder and went, unannounced into their mess room. I had been taken there before by Baz and had been received with a very warm welcome. This time was no different. "How's it going guys?" I asked as I peeped round the bulkhead door.

"Hey, Bernie, com'on in and have a sausage" the Skipper shouted across the small mess deck. The crew all laughed as I had eaten six sausages with piles of chips the last time that I had come aboard. They had also got me shitfaced. It was payback time.

"In a minute," I smiled "I've got something for you." I went back up the ladder to get the Bazooka. With great difficulty I climbed down the rope ladder with the Bazooka still wrapped up in the Netlon and when I was out of sight of prying eyes on the Geraint, I un-wrapped it and slung it on top of my shoulder. I tiptoed down the corridor and leaped into the mess deck with the Bazooka pointing at the skipper as if I was going to blow his brains, and half the ship, clean away.

"AAARRGGHHHH" I screamed in my best homicidal maniac voice.

There was a stunned silence except I noticed, for the cook who disappeared backwards into the galley eyes like saucers.

"JEZUS Fucking Christ! What you got there boy?" Richard the Skipper sighed when he saw the smile on my face.

"It's a souvenir for your mess deck, thought it would go well just here" I lifted it up to over the portholes as an example of a good position. Pleased? You have no idea. The tugs were very competitive with their sister ships. The Irishman crew now had a war souvenir. They would be able to invite The Yorkshireman's crew on board and show off their Bazooka. They showed me their gratitude by getting me shitfaced again, after, I must say, a very, very large fried meal.

Thursday 28th April

The Doc gave me three-day light duties, oh goody!! I had to hobble to the hospital and back, apart from that today was totally non-descript. The lads found a rifle grenade and some mortar bombs up the site.

I woke up at the prescribed time and pulled the towel back from across my bunk. I had to see who was up as there was an order to getting up. Mac's towel also came back and he looked up at me, "Morning Ugly"

"Mrng" I mumbled. I've never been a morning person. Mac, who was probably hyperactive when he was a kid, lit up a minute rollup and leaped out of bed to go for a wash. I slid my out over the edge of the bed and down onto the handrail of the bunk below and a pain shot up my leg. Its amazing how pain has an ability to bring back your memory. I hopped down on my good leg and examined my foot. It had swollen. I would not be going to work today. Great, time to milk this! Taff came in and I showed him my foot. "Get yerself along to the medical centre Bernie" he said.

"Where is it? I've never been"

"By the Secretariat." (Our Squadron office)

After a slow wash and an even slower, longer, larger, breakfast I watched the guys leave from the back ramp. The ship suddenly became very quiet. When I was on board, so were the rest of the

Squadron and there was always noise somewhere, now it was ghostly quiet. Like the stage of a Zombie movie. I half expected one to shamble out of the corridor.

*****

"LCpl Beirne!" The SSM would shout.

"Yessir?"

"What is that?"

"It's a zombie Sir"

"I know it's a fucking zombie, Beirne, what's it doing on my ship?" How does one answer questions like that? "Let me ask it Sir" will get you into trouble, as will "How the fuck should I know?" so you're left with a lame, "Dunno Sir" letting the SSM think that you are a moron.

"Well get rid of it, the OC is inspecting in thirty minutes" and that would be the end of a Zombie film in the British Army.

*****

I picked up my camera and sat on the rear ramp and watched a Chinaman from Hong Kong fish for tiddlers using a line and his fingers. We chatted for a while until joy of joy a CSB started approaching us.

In Germany I operated a CET, a Combat Engineer Tractor, a tank with an earthmoving bucket. The only piece of R.E. equipment more fun than a CET was a CSB. A Combat Support Boat and one, hopefully was going to take me to the jetty. These wonderful metal boats were powered by two Jaguar engines. All their power was put into two Dowety propulsion units, it was jet powered. A good operator could stand one on its nose. Literally I mean! He could stop it so quick that the nose would go under the water and the rear stand nearly vertical out of the water. They were fucking fast and anyone silly enough to sit rear of the front screen would always get soaked. Luckily for 75 Squadron, Royal Engineers the boats were operated by Titch Fuller and his lads. Of all the men in75 Squadron and it was Titch who was operating this one. I prepared my camera and as he hit a wave clicked a photo. We shared the Geraint with some Royal Signals and half our cabin was taken up with them. There was two waiting on the ramp with me. Titch pulled up to the ramp front on and when his bow touched he increased power to the powerful engines and held the boat fast.

"Hop on lads" he shouted. As the Sigs jumped aboard he handed them life jackets and directed them to sit down at the rear. As I passed him he handed me a jacket and winked, "Stand in here Bernie" indicating to the cockpit. He cut the power; put the drive into reverse and increasing the power moved away from the ramp. "Not working then?" he asked.

I told him about the karate and my need to report sick. And he told me that the water was "a little choppy" and nodded to the Sigs guys in the rear. "You may want to get that ready" he indicated to my camera and a huge smile stretched up on his face.

He opened up the throttles as fast as he could and I nearly fell backwards out of the boat, stopping only by grabbing his life jacket. "First time on one of these?" he asked. I shook my head, whilst trying to unclip the lens protector and hold on for dear life. The CSB 'fucked' its way through the waves. Speedboats are slick and slim and cut through waves, the CSB relied on power and any wave stupid enough to get in front of the bow was destroyed and 'fucked' off in to the back…right where the Sigs guys were sitting.

They were sitting hunched up with their backs to the cockpit and every wave that went over us landed squarely on their backs. We didn't even get our feet wet as the cockpit had duckboards. I was laughing so much I didn't manage to take a photo until we left the shite smelling Rangatira. Titch told me about an RAF Officer who pissed him off, after ordering him to take him to the Rangatira. Although out ranked, Titch told the Officer that Island regulations forbade non drivers from standing in the cockpit. The Officer sat in the back and Titch aimed for every big wave that he could find. We landed and I took a photo of Titch when he tied up next to the other three CSBs. They were harboured up behind the RFA Sir Tristram.

Another Sapper Squadron had the Sir Tristram as their accommodation, their only advantage was that it was tied up by B jetty and they could go ashore at any time if they wished. Not that there was anywhere to go! It still had the hole from the bomb that hit it, but by now it was just a piece of the landscape. I limped my way down the Coast road of Port Stanley and reported sick in the hospital. Eventually the doctor gave me three days Light Duties which meant no work for a Sapper. That was it, it is now official. It's milk the situation time. I ambled around Port Stanley taking photos of the NAAFI store which was in The Kelper Store and of a beautifully painted fire hydrant.

Friday 29th April

A nice easy day today, I spent most of it on the Irishman, I saw the Uganda been pushed out, how I wish I was on it. It's a pity my foot wasn't broke, I got a letter off San saying that she had a bad time in the Reeperbahn, I'm worried sick, she didn't tell me anything else, even Spunky said that I was in a bad mood when I read her letter, too right I was.

I suppose the good thing about being a Sapper on Ops on Light Duties is that unlike back at camp, there are no 'light duties' that I can do. As a Sapper all the duties are heavy so the powers that be just let me get on with getting better. Again, the easy breakfast and watching the guys go to work, I don't exactly stand on the rear ramp waving a white handkerchief. That would be sticking my head above the trench and it would surely get shot off, by the SSM. No I have breakfast and stay there until the ship goes quiet, then I come down to check. I left the writing of blueys until today. I could write in peace with the ship empty. It was my only contact with a person whose memory was growing more and more distant. I had one phone call during my seven month stay and it was over so quick I couldn't remember what was said five minutes after leaving the booth. I spent a happy day on the Irishman just swanning round the harbour. We pushed out the Uganda. It was full of very happy servicemen, all going home after their six month tour. That evening I got a bluey off Sandra. In it she described the Wives Club trip to the Reeperbahn, the notorious Red Light district of Hamburg. It was quite a long bluey and at the end she wrote that something bad happened and she would tell me the next day after getting some sleep. It sounded bad. She obviously didn't want to tell me until she had slept on it. Where there was a lack of information, my imagination filled in the gaps. I have a very good imagination, hence writing this book, and now my mind was full of terrible things that could have befallen them in the Reeperbahn. My mind was devoted entirely to this subject. I couldn't concentrate on anything else; it consumed my being and would do until I got the next letter.

Sunday 30th April

Another day of doing nowt, I went to bed at 4 o'clock, Taff and Jock went to the sundowners club and Jock was going to throw Lord Montgomery out of the window because he tried to grip Jock about a ramset bolt gun in a Pissup. Nearly everybody saw but said nothing, Montgomery ran out of the club, what a wimp. Taff stopped Jock. Got a letter off San, it was written before she went to Hamburg. I'm still very worried!

So dear reader, have you skipped from the front to here? If you skip to here you will not have the same surprise as I did when I discovered the real Jock, a guy that you really want on your side in a battle. I think the best way to write this, is as Jock told me the next day. So these will be his words. As for me, my day was spent idling round the ship. I did my laundry and when I walked into the laundry room my nose was overcome with the usual smell of rotting carrots. I grew up in the Fens, (East Anglia) and farmers would leave piles of carrots to rot. This is the overpowering smell that attacked me whenever I entered the small laundry room. For those of you, who don't know such a smell, think of the oldest male public toilet where the piss has been growing on the urinal like a urine stalactite. It is solid and yellow. Now, *that* is the smell I'm talking about. I breathed through my mouth, shutting off all air to the nose, and investigated, and there in the tumble dryer was a swamped sleeping bag drying. Some 'wag' had pissed his sleeping bag and thought he'd dry it in the tumble dryer when everybody was at work. That smell haunts me to this day!

I got another bluey off San but it didn't tell me what happened at Hamburg? I was still worried shitless. There were no phones, no Internet, no mobiles and no contact quicker than four weeks. I had to just wait, but I was so worried.

It was that evening when the Cpls came back from the Sundowners club. This was a soirée for Cpls and above, a little team building. The main drink was Pimms #1 cup. They were in very high spirits and slightly drunk. I was in bed and opened my curtain with all the other 'untermensch' to listen to the adventures of our Cpls, Taff and Jock. Jock told the story with Taff interjecting now and again.

Jock started; "Fucking Montgomery, Fuck… ing. Montgomery"

"What? What?" We all demanded. Jock now had our full attention. Even the Signallers at the far end of the bunk were looking. He continued "We were invited to the Sundowners club, Cpls and above. It's a little piss up where we can forget work and relax, have a few Pimms and get to know each other. Oh, but not that twat Montgomery. I had just come from site, remember that I had to use the Ramset bolt gun to fix those bolts into the concrete pad for tomorrow Bernie; well I did it before going to the party. I parked the Rover behind the cabin and went in, Taff was already there."

"I skipped work at five o'clock in order to go to the Squadron office and went to help set up the punch. I'd been drinking for two hours when Jock arrived. Ha ha ha." Taff added to the story. Jock laughed and continued "Yeah, I walked in and Taff was *well* oiled at this stage."

"I was, I tell you man" Taff revelled in the compliment.

"Yeah, Shuddup Taff, this is my story"

"Right you are man"

"Anyway, I walked in and Taff handed me a Pimms. It was a really good atmosphere in there, OK some people were talking shop but what else have we known for the last four months. It was relaxed, friendly and relaxed, d'ya know what I mean Bernie?"

I admitted that I did when in reality I didn't. Jock was a good story teller and was including the audience and extending the tension. He continued, "I was on my second or third Pimms." Taff interrupted "Ha ha ha, it was more than that! I brought you two and you went up for two yourself, then Homer brought you one across so did Ray."

Jock laughed at his miscount and continued, "Well I'd had a few when in walks Montgomery and comes straight for my table. He leans across my table and says 'You've left a loaded weapon in your vehicle.' Well at first I thought he was joking 'cos everyone was laughing and joking. It was a good atmosphere, no work, no serious topics and I'd had a few. So thinking he had cracked a joke I laughed at him. Well, let me tell you. He went bright red."

"Like a fucking Belisha beacon" Taff added.

"...and he said it again but more officious 'Cpl Henderix, you have left a loaded weapon in your Landrover, it should be in the armoury.' I realised then that he was serious. The entire Squadron's management was in that portacabin enjoying themselves. There was no rank in there, we were all having a good time and in walks this *WANKER* and starts burbling on about a loaded weapon. He must have been talking about my Ramset bolt gun which wasn't loaded. I know I was supposed to hand it in to the armoury, but the armourer was there, in the Sundowners club, pissed along with the rest of us, and just made sure the cartridges were in my combat smock pocket. I was lost for words, I was still not sure if he was joking and then he said it again, 'Cpl Henderix, you must put that weapon into the armoury right now'. Well I was on this side of a six foot table and he was on the other, I stood up and grabbed him by the lapels and pulled him across the table. I continued to smile in case anyone was looking they would have thought we were having a laugh, and through my smile said to him 'If … you … don't … fuck … off …

with… your … loaded … weapon … crap, I'll throw you through that fucking window behind you, now fuck and leave me alone you cunt.' That's when Taff tapped me on the shoulder and said 'Jock'. I said 'leave me alone Taff' and continued with Montgomery 'we are here having a good time and you come in here and ruin it all by talking about a fucking Ramset bolt gun. For your information the cartridges are in my fucking pocket so how the fuck is it a loaded weapon?' I had already devised my plan. I was going to continue smiling so nobody knew what was happening and throw him through the plate glass window behind him, but Taff touched me on the shoulder again and said 'Jock… look'." (Taff was laughing hysterically now) "I looked round still smiling with Montgomery's collars in my hands and saw that everybody had stopped talking and everybody was looking at me, the OC, 2IC, SSM and everybody else in the portacabin!"

We all burst out laughing at this scene. Taff added through his laughter "When he grabbed Monty by the collars the whole room went quiet. Everybody was looking; everybody knew what was happening except Jock"

Jock chuckled "I'd had a few and thought that by smiling I would fool everybody. When I saw everybody's eyes on me I let go of his combat jacket and he ran out of the cabin."

"What happened?" I asked incredulous. I knew that he was going to be charged and bust if everybody saw it.

"Nothing!" he laughed "Absolutely nothing. Everybody went back to drinking when he ran out, even the SSM. They must know what a twat he is."

What impressed me about the way that Jock explained this to us was the cold calculated way in which he was going to deal with Monty, the fact that he continued to smile whilst offering threats of extreme violence. He must have looked like Jack Nicholson in The Shining, totally deranged! I received another bluey off San. We numbered them as not only was there a four week delay but they didn't come in order. This was the case today and even before I opened it I realised that it was written before the Reeperbahn letter. I was still worried but realised that there was nothing I could do about it here. I just had to wait.

Notes

A nice fast month, due to working on the Hymac, I can see the light at the end the tunnel now; it's getting closer every day. One highlight was the whisper about civvy contracts, San getting a job was another, the seniors don't get on our tits so much as we are now building the Port Stanley heli-port road. The Coastell road is all out, 75 Squadrons fault. Not a day goes by without me thinking about getting home, I hope it isn't an anti-climax.

The OC called Monty a cretin this month. Stig called the OC an idiot on video and the OC called Stig a punk! A Hymac operator and A Harrier pilot had a rival competition in their machines, the Hymac won by tracking to the right, slewing left, and raising and lowering the boom.

The Squadron decided to make a video for the wives and to send it back so that they can see their men. An early version of MSN messenger or Skype. We all had a little say, everyone even the single soldiers. I was not on it as I was working. It was Stig and the OC who stole the show and whose comments would be burnt into my memory.

One of the Combat Engineers who was working with us on the Coastell Road was Stig. We nicknamed him Mongol from Blazing Saddles and he appeared very thick and slow. The truth was quite the opposite, he had more qualifications than the entire Plant Troop and for that he had our admiration, but he still seemed slow. It was Stig to whom we gave the brightest-of-bright day glow orange work gloves. And it was Stig who was walking up the Coastell Road wearing these gloves when a Chinook came in to drop stores. The pilot hovered ten metres behind and twenty metres above Stig, who was wearing his bright gloves. A Chinook hovering behind you is not the sort of thing you miss and Stig looked back and with both hands waved the pilot away getting a face full of rotor rash for his troubles. (That's the crap that the rotor(s) kick up hitting you square in the face). He started to walk quicker up the road and the pilot stayed on his tail. It hadn't occurred to Stig that you couldn't outrun a Chinook. Stig turned around again and frantically waved them away, still wearing his gloves. The pilot hogged his tail making stones and bits of debris hit Stig in the back as he tried to evade the Chinook and I've no doubt the massive downdraft or air was assisting him in walking forward. Eventually he gave up and took off his gloves and threw them into the peat bog. The Chinook sailed over his head and as they passed over me I could see the teeth whites of the pilot, co-pilot and loadmaster as they laughed themselves silly.

When they interviewed Stig on the Coastell Road he said that it was a good job and everyone was pulling their weight but the only thing that spoilt the tour was the OC as he didn't know what he was doing. The OC who was behind the camera stormed up to Stig and spluttering with rage called him a Punk! "Out of the mouths of babes… huh?"

> **Hymac 590 CT with armoured cab and swamp tracks**

Sunday 1st May 1983

Another boring day

Monday 2nd May

Brummie Cooper hit Rob Wong last night, don't know what is going to happen to him, who fucking cares? It seems that REME don't know how to fix machines, bastards! They left all my plates off and didn't even do the job!!!

Tuesday 3rd May

I got a letter of San today; it explained about Hamburg, my in mind is at rest now. Ginge "Rab" Watson is really mad that his wife went to Hamburg, I don't mind San going, it's her life, I was just worried for her safety, I really do love and want her so, I would hate myself if any thing happened whilst I was away.

This is Sandra's story; "The CO's wife had arranged a trip to the famous Reeperbahn of Hamburg, the infamous German Red Light district. The trip was only for the wives of 75 Sqn, and although most of the wives, had husbands in The Falklands there were a few wives from the Rear Party. The CO's wife was West German and the coach picked us up from Nunburg at eleven at night. It dropped us off down a side street and as twenty eight women got off the coach we noticed prostitutes around us. They had definitely noticed us and some went for us with lighted fags, they must have thought that we were coming to steal their business. Whatever the reason, they didn't like us being there. (This was the trouble that San had wrote about in the bluey and this was what had caused me so much distress over the last few days)

We left the area and split up into small groups. My group went into a sex shop and started to look and laugh at the toys on display. The shop manager didn't like us being in there and chased us out shouting "Raus, raus!"

We didn't feel safe on the streets so the CO's wife decided that we'd be better in a sex show. She chose one and haggled on the door for not only a discount but a free Asbach Uralt brandy and coke. When we walked in I was behind Sue Crane and as we walked into the darkened room she screeched "My God, look at that!" Lit up on a stage was a woman in the doggy position and a man was having sex with her. The woman was totally disinterested and was tapping her nails on the wooden table and occasionally when that didn't occupy her mind she would look at her nails whilst her partner shagged her. We stayed in there until five o'clock in the morning when we all went down to the fish market, looked around and caught the bus back to Nunburg. It was an experience but not what I'd expected."

Wednesday 4th May

A Knocker asked me today how many times the Hymac (excavator) can turn around. Does this man possess a brain?

For those that do not know, it is unlimited but his mates had told him that after fifteen times the top unscrews from the bottom and falls off. We POMS, he was told, had to keep count in our minds and when we got to fourteen we had to turn the top the other way and screw it back down onto the bottom half. I can't remember the exact answer but it was something like "ten times mate." He went away happy that the info that his mates had told him was incorrect and sure in his mind that when he corrected them, he would bask in their admiration. He was in for another one of life's great disappointments.

Thursday 5th May

At 5:30 I had to track the Hymac to the Coastell road, I didn't get on the boat until 9:35. I heard that our parcels that came down on the Uganda went back on the Uganda. There was nobody there to organise the unloading. TC is back so is Mac.

75 Squadron had spread over The Falkland Islands to carry out tasks in the different hamlets. The tasks had finished and the Troops were coming back which meant that our nice spacious cabin, started to loose its precious space. Every bunk was now taken again and getting up in a certain order was paramount. TC and Mac had to fit in and we had to give them space to fit in. That usually meant lying in your pit for a few minutes longer…. except for where TC was concerned as getting him out of bed was not only near impossible but dangerous.

At 1730 Taff told me to track the Hymac to the Coastell road as it would be needed the next day. It would take about an hour for the journey but what was worse was that I'd have to make my own way back. Walking and hitching to any vehicle that passed me I eventually got back on board at All-food-gone hour. The only advantage to this was a hot water for a shower and being able to raid the kitchen for anything edible.

Friday 6th May

I'm getting more and more tired, I can't be arsed to do any thing. When I get back on boat cold showers don't help at all. Tonight's food was crap!! Usual boring crap!

Saturday 7th May

I got 4 letters of Sandra and a letter of Nicole. My foot is still swollen, aches from karate a couple of weeks ago. I nicked a convection heater from the tank deck to heat my room, it did.

It was starting to get really cold 'Down South'. The weather pattern is the opposite to that of Europe and we were entering the period of horizontal snow. Heaters would start to play a major part in our comfort. This was a three kilowatt electric convection heater put onto a Zeppelin-sized tank deck in the hopeless uneducated attempt to counteract the cooling effects that a metal ship, sitting in the icy water of the South Atlantic, has on that open space. With great effort, I calculated that the heat was ineffective in that open-ended tank deck and sought a smaller space where the heat would be effective.

I found the perfectly sized space in my cabin.

Sunday 8th May

I got up at 0500 hrs to do my washing. It's the only time to get a washing machine, in the afternoon I noticed that the Irishman was aside so I went aboard. We went to the fort to collect water, I was on the bridge. It was great, I had the best meal of the tour, chips, sausages, mushrooms, liver, gravy, then trifle and real whipped cream. They really are a hospitable bunch on the Irishman. Baz, Chris, Richard (skipper), Tasker, Tony (cook), Trevor (poof), Ron (engineer), Alan (engineer).

This food stood out from the mutton-enhanced compo crap that we daily shoved down our throat like a brand new Bugatti stands out next to a 1973 Moscvich. If food would have been my sexual kink, I would have been masturbating like a safari chimp for the rest of the tour thinking about this.

I wonder if poof was Trevor's job description in his contract. I would have slept with him for the grub that they gave me. Obviously when I got back on board I told anyone that would listen to me, which wasn't many as Sunday was a day to get drunk.

Monday 9th May

We had a stupid parade for whole squadron; it was the OC's and the SSMs day. The divers got extras for turning up early; Sergeant Hislop got called a cunt on the parade. As usual support troop didn't get a mention. The OC has got a prestigious job of building a HGB. across the Canache. It will be given to the troop which reaches its task first. Maybe support troop will get the task. N.F.Way. I think my happy period started today.

The official text in the squadron newsletter is: On the 9th we even had a Squadron parade in Lookout camp with one hundred and thirty nine men on parade:

All you servicemen are wondering why the divers got extras (extra work, guard duty, kitchen GD work etc) for turning up early and not late. The thinking was that if they turned up early, then they must've skipped work. For that they got extras. This was the second time that Sgt Hislop got called a cunt by the OC. Sgt Hislop wasn't a cunt at all, in fact the opposite was true. He was one of the best SNCOs in the Squadron. It was absolutely verboten to curse out your SNCOs in front of the Troops. This is not Sandhurst training. Bignose did not allow hundreds of years of British Army experience to alter his mismanagement techniques. You can now understand why the OC's new brake pipes were cut through within a week of being fitted. There are some really steep hills in Port Stanley.

Bignose told us that he had volunteered the Squadron to build a Heavy Girder Bridge across a small inlet called the Canache. This is an extremely heavy bridge with heavy panels, heavy deck plates, heavy pins and it probably even had a heavy coat of paint. It was NOT something that Sappers wanted to build, but the OC thought that the visage of hugging round vertebrae crushing steel would motivate the Troops to finish their Troop tasks quicker. He congratulated all three Troops for their hard work but missed

Support Troop, MT troop and HQ Troop without who, the Field Troops would not have even got to their tasks let alone built anything.

Tuesday 10th May

Gaz Puttings was caught shaving his chest, hoping that it would make it grow more! Really tired tonight! Showers cold again. Gaz even cut his chest shaving it. Brought in the heater again. The SWO caught me and we had an argument. I bet his room is warm.

The new Coastell 3 arrived today as did the new RSM for 37 Engr. Regt.

Bugger! I was caught redirecting the heater by the Ship's Warrant Officer. Arguing with a WO would normally get you a handful of extras or worse jail. What could they do to me? Send me to The Falklands? I couldn't have been more pissed off. We, the Sappers, got a new RSM who brought with him all that home base discipline that we had been missing like you would miss a hole in your water bottle in the Sahara desert.

Wednesday 11th May

Coastell 3 came in today, so did TC. So much for R&R, they had to work humping bales of wool. They got one can of beer (small) for their work. Andy Scott tried to bump start a Muirhill. Benny bogged in the Hymac 580 B. T. on the side of the road. R&R consists of walking 34 miles across hills, living in a shed, sleeping on a concrete floor, and eating Compo. God knows what adventure training will be like!! Wives club video on tonight.

Around half way through our tour we were sent on R&R (Rest & Recuperation). I had a buggered foot so couldn't go. 'Ha ha ha' so it turns out. They were dropped off thirty-odd miles from a farm and had to stumble across the Elephant grass to get to their place of rest. These rest areas are more commonly known as farms, working farms. They had to help the local population with their sheep farming.

Loads of hard heavy work to help them rest from the hard heavy work and prepare them for another few months of hard heavy work. Pinko was extremely pissed off and vocal when he came back. Always vocal and complaining he took exception to having to work unpaid for the farmers who wouldn't even let them sleep inside their houses. They had to sleep in the barn outside and eat compo rations. They were actually glad to get back to work…. Hmmm, maybe not such a bad idea after all!

As for Andy trying to bump start a Muirhill it is a type of automatic and so cannot be bump started. It is worthy to note that I found his behaviour ridiculous at the time but a year later I tried the same thing with a CET which has the same style of transmission. I was also unsuccessful.

Thursday 12th May

Spunky's second dry night of the tour, might have something to do with the bar having no beer. I started digging the Coastells anchor holes. My eye is better than a level. We are spreading the rumour that support troop is building the HGB bridge. We rub it in to the squeaks that we ain't done any work since we have got here!

Squeak = Knocker = Oggie = Field Troop personnel.

I got the long awaited reply from Mabel Cowcorn today. She was the girl who I used to date when I was a teenager and whose bluey I stole from Jeeves.

You could have knocked me down with a feather! Rather than the friendly 'Wow, what a coincidence, how are you ' letter that I was expecting I got a 'I love you, I have always loved you and I want you to come and look after me and my kid as my husband has left me' letter.

I was actually a little bit angry at the reply. In no way did I lead her on and at this time in my life I was in a bluey love affair with my wife and not even Madonna could have persuaded me away from her let alone a clingy ex-teenage girlfriend from the village whose clutches I had escaped.

I showed it to TC and he took control of the situation in an effected barrister style tone; "As the manager of your emotional affairs it is my duty to take care of this trollop who has tried to steal you from your wife." The only thing that was missing from his performance was the white wig as he had his right hand clasping his non-existent gown collar and had his nose stuck up in the air.

I saw the chance for a bit of diversity to relieve the tedious boredom and responded "Ah, my advisor, yes please my man. I would appreciate your assistance in this delicate matter of the heart."

"Of course Mr Beirne, let us put pen to paper and transcribe a suitable response to the forthsaidwith Cowcorn, Mabel, to whit, the desecrator of my client's reputation."

Utter bollocks but it was fun and we sat down and wrote a reply that was set in a similar tone, advising the said Miss Cowcorn that her response was inappropriate and legal action for a restraining order would be sought in the case of any further likeforthsaidwith communications. By the end of the reply we and most of the room was howling with laugher including the sigs in the other half. With my sides aching I put the bluey mailbox.

To save dragging out this story we got one further reply around 4 weeks later.

To say that she was pissed off would be an understatement. Well what did she expect? Apparently now she never wanted to hear from me again which in reality put us back in the position that we were in before I got hold of her bluey. So nothing lost nothing gained then. Years later I did regret any suffering that she may have had due to our letter, but if she was desperate enough to throw herself at a teenage boyfriend without even meeting him, then perhaps that reply was just what she needed to get off her arse and get a grip of her life... or maybe not.

Friday 13th May

Mac got a parcel today. Taff got one yesterday, I sent a letter to myself again, I put the wrong BFPO No. on. Watched a porn video, how do them blokes do it? All them women doing all them nice things to them and they can't get hard, bloody Kermits. I discovered how food is rationed. It all goes to RHQ cookhouse, they take out the stuff that our stomachs couldn't digest, i.e. fresh veg, good cuts of meat, fresh bread, they then give the crap, rest to us, aren't they kind. RHIP pricks.

Friday 13th! Ooer. RHIP =Rank has its Privileges.

Saturday 14th May

Squadron had a day off. Except me and a few others, like support troop. The Yorkshireman pulled the anchor, everybody expected it to dig in. it moved about 1 m. I feel the same here hearing B. F. B. S. as I do in Germany hearing radio 1. It is a bit of home. The Norlan left today, lucky sods.

The anchor for the Coastell was a thirty foot shipping container stuck in a hole and filled with concrete. It was flown in by a Chinook, the same one that followed Stig with the Hi-vi gloves down the road. We had to pretension the anchor to take up any slack and for that we got the Yorkshireman Ocean going tug, The Irishman's sister ship, to give it a good pull.

BFBS is the British Forces Broadcasting Service. They had a radio station across all of BAOR (British Army on the Rhine) and it broadcast English pop and programs. On the Island they had FIBS or Falkland Islands Broadcasting Service.

You couldn't be in the British Armed forces without knowing a plethora of acronyms. PTI, NAAFI, RSM. I was in 75 Fd Sqn RE, Spt Tp, operating CETs, LWT and LMDs. We used OMD and OEPs. Fired SLRs and SMGs, cooked on BVs and Blueys. We filled out 1045s and 1033s, were charged on 252s under section 69. Our whole vocabulary was full off these and we were only beaten with the military speak by the Royal Navy who could talk to you for a whole hour without making sense to anyone except another Matlot. We did a car park project in HMS Collingwood. There we discovered 'heads' 'galley' and 'run ashore' which was strange as we were ten miles inland. We also didn't salute RN Officers as they didn't have any pips on their shoulders, and carried on walking when a horn went off in the evening, and everyone stopped and looked at a flag being pulled down a flagpole. That lasted one day before our SSM ripped us a new asshole whilst educating us about RN traditions.

Sunday 15th May

The day started off sunny but cold, then came the wind, then the snow, then the hail, then the wind rain snow and everything else it could manage. The hail is horizontal not vertical. I got caught in it without my waterproof on, we still aren't allowed to wear Parkas, and I am now building up courage to make a 100 m dash/stumble over to the bogs. Taff had to go and recover the Haulamatic.

We were working on the Lookout Camp which was a portacabin camp just west of the end of Stanley. We also still had work on the Coastell Groynes and the heliport. I had managed to get an Armstrong motorcycle from MT department and spent a lot of the day racing between jobs delivering parts and tools for the guys. They were 500cc single pot beasts. They had a decompression lever in order to kick it over (no electric start) and to start them was a knack that virtually nobody had. This ensured that only a few actually got to use them. Don't get me wrong, everyone tried to requisition one but after a few hours of trying to start it they would give up and go back to a Landrover. I got caught in a horizontal slush storm on the Armstrong without my waterproofs. It was pointless stopping as the wind was so strong it was driving the slush into my lightweights and combat top, so I pushed on to Lookout Camp and wrote, whilst drying out my clothes in what would be our cabin. We had stolen a paraffin heater to heat up our cabin as there was no electric. Lunch used to be served in the Squadron HQ or the Secretariat. Now it was being cooked in Lookout Camp on number one burners. It was like being on exercise again. Crap weather, running to the cook's tent to get a stew in wet gear and then running back to somewhere dry to eat it. Washing was done anywhere with running water.

Monday 16th May

Snow everywhere today, very pretty but cold! Taff borrowed a plate for tea, it was dirty and the cook said "Are you back for seconds? Whereupon Taff replied, "I'm not that stupid!"

There is no water at all in Lookout Camp as the pipes have frozen, so I had the semi wash in snow, it's rainy now, only 28 left, Lumpy is a moron, he talks down to anyone below Cpl. Shit.

We laid all the pipes above ground. Mr Ice came to The Falklands and immediately froze our water pipes, 'cos that's what he does. Amazing that our Officer Engineers didn't know that isn't it? We were sleeping in Lookout Camp now but had kit both in the camp and in the RFA Geraint. We weren't moving across officially until Sunday. Right now I'd be glad for a cold shower; it had to be better than washing in snow. But we didn't give up; we washed in snow, got dressed and went to work. Twenty nine years later I had a translator in my office at work who wouldn't screw together his new ergonomic chair. Either he believed it was 'below him' to do this or he really didn't know how. Hire a Sapper in your company and he'll do anything and *BE GOOD AT IT*. Jack-of-All-trades and Master of s*ome!*

Wednesday 18th May

We redesigned the counting system for the Chaff chart. There is only 49 days left of work before we get on the ship. That is fuck all. Weather was really bad today, snow, hail, wind. I packed to go to Lookout camp already, we are moving out on Sunday, thank god. It's bloody freezing on this ship.

We would do anything to make it seem closer to going home. First we used Metric weeks where every week had ten days, then we removed all the days off counting only working days and now we removed the last boarding day making it a day closer. We can see the end of the tunnel clearly now. Spirits are high. Taff will be leaving early as advance party lucky bugger. Also he will be going home on a Hercules C130 up to Ascension Islands and then by Tri-Star to Gutersloh. His chuff chart is very very low. We slept on the ship today and it was like a fridge. The little heaters that were put on the tank deck did little to compensate for the cold water. For us, moving to Lookout Camp was the start of the end and we couldn't wait for the end to start.

Thursday 19th May

We got the Smalley working. It's quite a good machine when you can get it to the place you want it. Dave Randall had a talk with a bloke from Fairclough. He gets £400 a week. He says that POMS won't come out here as it is to cold. I'll have to write them a letter tomorrow. I love Sandra. Only 48 days left. All we ever talk about is going home. I've been invited for tea round Herman's.

The Smalley was a tiny excavator, more like a kid's toy than a 'real' man's excavator. It was like a Punch and Judy booth with a digger arm sticking out. It had two trailer wheels and was towed into place, or in our case pulled by three Sappers. You then put down two stabilisers got out the crank handle, hand-started the engine and then dug holes, small holes. Slowly! It was still quicker than by shovel and was weather proof. So I liked it especially when watching Knockers working in the horizontal snow. Bugger that, the Smalley even had a heater. I was on £280 a week so to do the same job for double the money was an inviting offer.... Except that no one had offered!

Friday 20th May

I went and had tea round Herman's parents. It wasn't much but it was very nice. Nice company as well. What surprised me are the things that we take for granted that they don't have. I.e. TV, oranges or fresh fruit etc. it's weird. I'd hate to be born here. 47 days.

Herman was the young lad who came up to the heliport when we were building it. He was Jane's nephew and was the young lad who I sat on the seat and let him operate the excavator. I got a lot of stick for that. Kiddie fiddler etc. he had asked me to tea at his parents' house so graciously I accepted. He was around eight– ten years old. When I got there they showed me into their front room and the first thing that I noticed was that there was no telly, only a huge ham radio. Apparently nearly every Islander had one. I'd taken some fruit from the canteen as I had nothing else to give them, they were so excited to get the oranges. It was then that I realised that everything that they have, except sheep related products, has to come in on a ship and now it has to come from the UK. Trade with Argentina had dried up for some reason. It was also nice for me to be in a family situation. A mum, dad and son, dining room table, social graces, pleasant small talk, pictures on the mantle place, and the smell of peat roasting away in the fire place. The smell of burning peat always reminds me of The Falklands. I walked back to the jetty with a smile on my face which even the cold couldn't erase. I'd seen a bit of home life in advance, got a preview of family life again. I considered myself very lucky.

Saturday 21st May

46 days, three twroopie had his birthday today, we knocked off at three o'clock and had a beer made out of cinnamon, entirely I think, put it this way, the cook didn't have any. I am packing to move to Lookout camp. I'm looking forward to it. I didn't think that I would be. The change is as good as a rest, I hope they don't put me on R&R. Spunky went today.

Excerpt from the squadron's newsletter 'We had a Squadron dinner party today, to say goodbye to the RFA Sir Geraint and happy birthday to Lt Sugar, his 21st!'

Nobody was envious of Spunky going on R&R. It was, after the first reports got back, as sought after as a dose of the pox.

An instruction came out on Part One Orders today. It forbade the use of the term 'Benny' as it was derogatory. It is but that is just human nature, them and us, their tribe and ours. Armies had pet names for locals everywhere; Ragheads, Box heads, Nips, Argies, Eyeties, Gooks, Bennies. We called Americans 'Yanks' or 'Leathernecks' and they called us 'Limeys' or 'Bloke.' It wasn't just none-Brit, Jocks, Taff, Scouse, Paddy, and Brummie. Then we had names for Regiments and service personnel. Matlot, Blue job or Crabs (Borrowed that one from the Fleet Air Arm.) When aircraft land on an aircraft carrier the ship turns into the wind. You can't do that with an RAF runway so the aircraft has to 'crab' when it lands and straighten up at the last second. So the Navy pilots named the RAF pilots Crab Air. We had Planks (RA), Tankies (RAC) Monkeys or Redcaps (RMP) Spook (14 Int), Slopjockey (ACC), Sockstacker (RAOC) and the RE were Sappers, Ginger Beers (Rhymes with Royal Engineers) or just Queers. Navy called us Pongos and we called them Porthole benders, Merchant Navy was the Wavy Navy due to their wavy gold strips of rank.

So we stopped calling the Local inhabitants 'Bennies'… they are now called 'Stills', which stands for 'Still Bennies.'

Sunday 22nd May

We moved to Lookout camp amidst much waiting and humping of kit. At Lookout camp it is the pits. Quality of food has gone down, there is mud everywhere, and no electricity, no heating, and they haven't opened any wash rooms on our side so there is no hot water. The wash rooms are miles away, and to cap it all I have broken my razor mesh. I only hope West store has one. I can't charge it up anyway. 45 days.

Moving in the Army is not like in Civvy Street. In Civvy Street you get transit boxes, bubble wrap, porters to carry your stuff and organisation. In the Army, (and this will surprise civvies) it is every man for himself. It all gets stuffed into whatever you have, sausage bag, suitcase, bog roll carton, and then you drag it along the floor and throw it onto the rusty metal deck of a tank landing craft along with a hundred others. Your suitcase is packed to splitting which is exactly what it does when you throw it onto the back of the four ton Bedford along with ninety nine others as someone's always gets lost. It is then thrown off by two soldiers who would win a world wrestling competition with their eyebrows alone, into the mud. You then drag along your split suitcase and three compo cardboard boxes to an empty portacabin. Beds have not been reserved, your name is glaringly absent on any bedspace, it's first come first served and even then RHIP may unceremoniously kick you out of your hard earned bedspace.

But eventually you are there and after lying on your bedspace with your kit, defending it against all newcomers in the cabin by making sure that everyone has seen you and your kit on that bed, you can relax. Then comes the unpacking and that's when I discovered to my horror that the metal foil on my razor had split. No, I didn't have a spare. Have you EVER been able to buy a new foil for a razor three years after you got it as a Chrissy present? They don't sell them. What chance did I have on The Falklands where a toothbrush was a highly prized item in the shops? As I pointed out, there was no electricity, no water in the shitters opposite us, no lights, no heating…. Well, er… that's not strictly true. We

Mac trying to kill himself

stole a paraffin heater from the RFA Geraint as we left, along with the loaf of bread and butter with which we lightened the cook's supplies; we had butter on done over a paraffin heater. And you wonder why I eat stuff that's fallen on the floor. Outside was, a few inches deep in snow. There were toilets but it was a hundred metre dash / slip / slide to them. Mac braved it and had a nice warmish shower and then on his way back slipped and fell arse first into the mud. He entered the cabin with snowy mud all down his arse and legs. It was too much effort to go back so he let it dry in front of the paraffin heater whilst making toast for the guys. Mac became Head Toaster, a job which he did with pride, taking it even into the days of electric where he could be found sticking a metal coat hanger into the guts of an electric 3kw heater to make toast for the guys. After one piece of toast was ruined by the arching of the metal rod on the elements we persuaded Mac to give up the position of Head Toaster… against his wishes I might add.

Monday 23rd May

44 days. Spunky got back from R&R. He enjoyed it! Stig is being court- martialled for running over a cat. The gear cable broke on the roller whilst I was going full astern. Just thinking about Sandra makes me smile and laugh, she makes me so happy the even though she's 8000 miles away.

How could Spunky like R&R? He was too weird! For some reason he didn't get too much work and he got far more beer. Maybe he hit it off with a particularly good looking sheep?

Tuesday 24th May

Today I jumped of the D6d and sprained my ankle, badly. It got worse throughout the morning, until I had to go sick at dinner. They x-rayed it, it is a sprain, it is also swollen the like Hulk's and very painful, the lads from Mc plant hire are taking the piss. Porky Scratching told a squeak to operate the Hymac at The Kelper

Store site; he knocked down three power cables right after 75 squadron safety orders came out!

Once you sprain your ankle, you're buggered. You need to rest it for the next eight weeks. Stay away from the squash club, use a golf caddy to get around the course and only do nine holes not eighteen, get your chauffer to drive closer to the executive entrance and use the lift to your office etc. if however, you are currently working as a Sapper on The Falklands, you're buggered. You get three days light duties then back to work on a much weakened ankle which as soon as it *feels* ok, you use it for jumping off a dozer and it sprains again. The cycle starts once more. Bugger! Squadron Safety orders stated that only qualified operators were to operate equipment. We had set up a power generator right next to The Kelper Store. This provided power for most (all?) of the houses in Stanley. (It was a huge generator) Sgt Hislop, instructed a Squeak, Knocker, Oggie, non-qualified Sapper to operate the Hymac excavator… well what young lad could refuse an opportunity for a cabby? He hit the overhead cables and disconnected the town from the generators. Food in the shops freezers started to defrost, peoples dinners had to wait half cooked until Porky Scratchings got the cable reconnected. You couldn't hate the guy; he was just too loveable like your favourite childhood teddy bear. You just laughed.

Wednesday 25th May

41 days. I spent the day peeling potatoes. DRO's is good. I ate so much by dinner that I wasn't hungry. Hislop bogged in the Bomag twice, in the same place. I got a letter off San today saying she had a full-time job in the NAAFI. Great news, I bet she's pleased; I am, for her that is. I do so love her. Not long now my love until I will be the back where I belong.

A classic! Sitting in an Army cookhouse peeling potatoes! I was there; I've done that and talk about cushy! As much food as I could stuff into my gob…. And that was all I was going to write about this day until I really thought about it….

I had been peeling potatoes and I loved it. Even my wife thought that I would have hated it, but no. In all the films, peeling potatoes or DRO or Dining Room Orderly was the pits. The worst insult a soldier could get (apart from the Vietnam films where there was a worst duty), but we were Sappers. We milked every situation, good or bad, for everything that we could get out of it. Let me explain….

The room would get up at six thirty am, SSS, (shit, shower, shave) and then to the Slop house for brekky. Back to the room for a quick fag and then off to work around seven thirty. Meanwhile, Mr DRO is still sleeping or more than likely, swapping light-hearted insults with those going to work. You then slowly get out of bed and after a slow wash and half shave, shuffle over to the canteen using your best 'I'm wounded' whimper and limp. The Cookie asks you if you've eaten which you tell him you haven't so you have a HUGE plate with three eggs, six slices of perfectly cooked bacon, sausages, mushrooms and enough beans to re-float the Titanic with the resultant methane. Wash this down with two half pint mugs of tea and the really happy Cookie, sets you a task. Yes that's right, he's happy because you being there means that he doesn't have to peel potatoes, or wash the pans or mop the floor so you are his best friend and remain so for the rest of your time in the Regiment. Outside its minus one million and the snow is so horizontal it fills up one ear in seconds. The only way you can escape it is to turn one hundred and eighty degrees and fill up the other ear. Where I am, on the other hand, is so hot I strip down to my T-shirt, I eat anything I can see, and have so much hot sweet tea that I slosh as I walk. When my mates come into the canteen I take the piss out of them from behind the hotplate, and then give them extra food as 'they are my mates'. That raises my credo with them. By the end of the day I'm relaxed, in a good mood and stuffed whereas they are freezing, starving, and stressed tighter than a guitar string. I can't believe any serviceman would prefer hard work to that of a DRO. So next time you see a film with an unhappy soldier peeling potatoes and an unhappy cook shouting at him, say "That's Bollocks!" to whoever is within earshot. If they disagree with you, they're a film director!

Thursday 26th May

40 days. I spend all day relaxing on my bed, great. My foot is a bit better on the flat but the cross-country capability still leaves a lot to be desired. Pinko seems so good at bringing out the worst in me, if he can't win an argument he just clams up. He's a bit spoilt really, not in charge of his emotions; his emotions are in charge of him.

On the ship we weren't allowed to have alcohol apart from in the bar. In Lookout Camp we either didn't care any more or thought that we could hide it better so we bought some… loads actually. Problem was that The Kelper Store would not sell spirits to anyone under Sgt. So I got Benjamin Byrne, the Signals SSgt to buy a bottle of Southern Comfort for me. I figured it would warm me up after working out in the cold. When he delivered it I got Taff to photograph me glugging it down but I did it with the cap on. Even though we could see the end coming, we were still pissing each other off. Living so close with each other for so long has that effect. It happens in families, in marriage and it happens in the Forces. You cannot take my diary entry being the gospel truth. It isn't. What it does show is my state of mind at the time. Pinko was a very good friend. I only had to do DRO's for the morning and then the Cookie told me to leg it, so I spent the rest of the day dossing on my bed.

Friday 27th May

Another day dossing. We start operation slipknot at 7 o'clock tonight, night shift. I will have to take some Southern Comfort to comfort me down south tonight.

Didn't do much work tonight the time went quickly. Thirty nine days.

Operation Slipknot was to resurface B jetty with Class 60 track way. We spent the day kicking our heels as we had to work the night. As POMs we supported the Oggies, lots of grunting and smiles? It was wet o'clock at night, the guys had a thousand tons of steel to pull and they were smiling? The track ways are long sheets of metal designed to take a Class 60 vehicle. (60 tonnes). It is laid down and secured then another slice is slid down a grove into place... except you cannot just 'slide' it into place. You have to line up the first piece, connect a rope onto the end and with as many Sappers as you can fit onto the rope, and pull it along the grove. Mud in the grove doesn't help and the B jetty shore of The Canache in The Falklands is muddy. To help the guys we found a space on a rope as often as they would let us on.

Saturday 28th May

38 days. We went to bed at 8 o'clock. We woke up at 4 o'clock, the heater had run out and we were nearly all gassed. Not much to write as nothing happens.

We still had the paraffin heater and went to sleep in the morning after the night's work. The heater ran out of fuel but still had enough to pump out noxious fumes whilst we slept. We all woke up with headaches that wouldn't leave until later that night.

Sunday 29th May

We were woken up at 1500 hrs to be told that night shift was cancelled. We are to work down the b slip tomorrow so that Taff can have a day off. How self centred can one get? Still no electricity, the Uganda has broken down as well as the Norlan; we might be going back on the Rangatira. I don't care as long as we go back 37 days.

Monday 30th May

Everybody is so short tempered, we bite at anybody whose says something slightly disagreeable, I felt like hitting Mac but later this morning it was as if nowt has happened. Thirty six days left

Tuesday 31st May

I have to go round all the 'C' vehicles and fix all the 'A' jobs on them, for transport I will be using Chris Lucas's motorcycle, what fun! Thirty five days

OC is going in front of the CO for the state of 75 Squadrons documents.

We had to hand the plant over to the next Squadron, and in order to do that all of the operator jobs on it had to be done. I persuaded MT to give me their motorbike again and zoomed around Port Stanley in the pretence of repairing stuff. It's a great country for bondu bashing. Even the road was potholed and was a motorbike slalom. The Army like all Services is built on systems. We had a system for the documented the upkeep of the plant as well as everything else that one said, did or didn't do. When we got 'Down South' there were no such systems running. We were still on the war footing. In other words, just get it done and sort out the documentation later. Whilst we were there, the Army was trying to restore those systems that peacetime soldiers love. We were the buffer zone. We took over the plant in rag order but had to hand it over as per BAOR standards. So light bulbs that weren't working on the dashboard had to be replaced, an A type job, or Operator job. Things more serious like the brake system on the LWT Muirhill which didn't work (it had two brake systems) had to be replaced by a RE fitter or REME workshops. My task was to run around on this Army Armstrong motorbike in the snow. I would ride up to a piece of kit, a Caterpillar D6D bulldozer for example. Stop it working, carry out an inspection, then ride off into the snow to REME workshops to get the spares, return and fit the spares and move off onto the next piece of kit.

The reality was more like this; ride up to TC on the D6D, drink tea, give the Knockers a ride on the bike for two hours whilst chatting and laughing with the POMS. Drink more tea, go to lunch. Help shovel stone and sand for one hour, drink tea, ask TC what was wrong and try to write it down with my frozen biro, allow Pinko to warm up the pen with a lighter and laugh when he melts it, take a two minute pee on Ray Parker's frozen biro, laugh when writing with a hot pee soaked biro, look round the dozer with TC, drink even more tea, write more and laugh when Ray refuses to take his biro back. Wait for Taff to return with the bike whilst drinking tea whilst pissing and talking to the guys. Scoot off on the bike and stop halfway to the REME workshops for three minute pee, wave to the OC as he drives past one of his Cpls pissing on the side of the road, get to REME only to be told again that they have no spares, go to Razzit Ave which is where REME puts all their un-repairable equipment and with a six inch adjustable, take off anything that I can find that I need. I then ride to Lookout Camp as it is past knocking off time. I have a huge pee in the cold shower and after taking a huge slug of Southern Comfort (Thanks Benjamin) prepare for the evenings entertainment. Retire for the evening and next morning start again.

Notes

The last of the slow months. Tomorrow is Friday!!!

Everybody's tempers are getting short. Hurry up the sixth before I hit someone.

We redid the chuff chart some months ago to represent days. So the first month was Saturday and the penultimate month, June, would be Friday. Saturday was a non-work day. So when someone asked us how many days we had to do we would tell them three days which would pee on their parade.

Although I hadn't been on R&R I had had many days where I was on light duties and spent my time ambling round Port Stanley. Even with this I was still short tempered as was everyone. I hoped that this last month would be different. Although we were quick to loose it, we were also quick to forget and would be laughing about something a minuscule later.

Our Portacabin in the snow

Wednesday 1st June 1983

I went up 15 Squadron on the motorcycle and was biking around Stanley all day. I've just found out that whilst it has been freezing in our portacabin, the portacabin next door has got two heaters in it. The portacabin next door is empty!! Supposedly a drying room!!! People still short tempered.

Thirty-five days to do

Lord Montgomery fell head first in the Canache today, a pity I didn't see it. TC did.

Thursday 2nd June

We got electricity today that means 24-hour heating and percolated coffee. We are all so touchy, I must have argued with everybody today, I was working with the motorbike again today, its great fun but it does tire me out. 34 days to do. I was to go on R&R tomorrow but as I have got seven days light duties I couldn't go so Pinko went instead. Ha ha ha.

We were all sitting on the bench seats in the canteen after our evening meal. There being nothing else to rush off for we were telling stories and passing time in that way that soldiers do all over the world. On the table next to us were some guys from 1 Troop, one of them being a very young Dave Christian. Dave was small, thin and with a nice new face that would red up at the slightest embarrassment and didn't need shaving. He could be called 'sweet' by women and was fairly innocent of the nasty things of life. He was new in the Squadron. We on the other hand, weren't any of the above. Spunky laughed at something behind me and pointed to the next table, "ha ha ha, look at that lads"

We turned round and only saw the backs of some 1Troop guys, "What Spunky"?

"Dave Christian bum. It's shaped like a woman's." We all looked down and sure enough Dave Christian's arse, sitting on the bench had that pear shape that should only be seen on a woman. At hearing his name Dave and his mates turned round. The shape disappeared and we all complained loudly.

"Turn back"

"Noooo, lost it now turn back round Christian"

"What are you looking at?" Dave asked sheepishly.

"Your arse! It is shaped like a woman's and is beautiful. Turn back round you fucker 'cos I want to have a wank" Spunky bellowed. We all laughed as did Dave's friends. Dave turned instant scarlet, quicker than a frog in a blender. That was all the prompting that we needed to make light of a boring evening meal. Dave was speechless and turned round as ordered by these rough dirty old sweats and the ribbing continued. The tips of his ears were glowing like a toaster element, his mates were laughing and we were making rude comments about the shape of his arse. Later when we met him and made a comment about his arse he had a cheerful retort. He had grown a little bit wiser and had taken one step closer to becoming an old sweat himself. It was all in good humour and this is how boys are made into men, how childish traits are unknowingly eliminated and why British Army soldiers make excellent citizens. Their egos, vanity

and other bad human traits were deleted from their makeup years
ago.

Friday 3rd June

*TC is moping right now because when he usually comes in from
Lumpy site he moans when we speak to him, so today we didn't
speak to him, he didn't speak to us and hasn't spoke since. No
great loss. We have got two heaters in the room now and it is like a
sauna, it is great.*

Saturday 4th June

*Flat back Jock came back today with stories of the seven seas, I
was motorcycling again today. The weather was lousy. John Cowan
lost an assault boat, he reckons the rope snapped, Jock reckons it
was more like cut. Everybody went on the piss last night, I didn't,
I got two aerogrammes and a 15 page letter off Sandra. The letter
was the best that I ever received. I felt joyous all night and still
do. How I love her.*

Sunday 5th June

*Yesterday me and Spunky caught Jock with the light. It was a
day off, how boring, nowt to do but think about home and wank. We
had brunch.*

We were all in the portacabin passing time. It was Sunday and after
the working day which is clearly planned out the Sunday was without
structure. Just doss and chill out! I was leaning back on a chair
against the wall and could feel the light switch in my back. Spunky
was on a bed and Jock sat on a table in the middle. We were doing
what soldiers do all around the world to pass the time, we were
telling stories to each other. Jock was kicking his leg under the table
and the other was just on the floor. He was a short-arse after all. He
looked up at the light and clapped his hands at it as if it was sound
operated. He probably had a joke lined up for when the light stayed

on. Without missing a beat I leaned back and pressed against the light switch. It went off. Jock's jaw dropped open and he roared out with laughter. Spunky smiled and stared at him, "Betcha can't do that again." He smirked.

Jock looked up at the light again and clapped his hands. I leaned back and the light came on again. Jock's roar was now uncontrollable and Spunky's eyebrows were touching his fringe in amazement. He glanced at me and I nodded behind me, he immediately caught on and started to laugh which got me laughing. "It must be a faulty wire Jock" I said between guffaws. Jock looked at me but didn't see the switch, "D'ya reckon it'll work again?" he asked.

"Worth a try" Spunky chuckled. Jock clapped at the light and I switched it off again. Jock went into a full belly laugh but this time Spunky and I were laughing *at* him not with him. He looked at us and thought that we were as amazed as him and laughed with us, which made us laugh more and more at him. This escalated like a tornado picking up speed and Mac came in with us in hysterics, the light going on and off to Jock's claps and tears rolling down our eyes but for different reasons. Mac immediately saw what was happening with the switch and killed it all with "It's Bernie's back, Jock, it's on the switch!"

Jock, still laughing looked at me and I leaned forward revealing the switch. He roared out again as we did but this time we were all laughing for a different reason. Never in the field of human boredom has so few people had so much fun with a light switch.

Monday 6th June

Blizzard, snow, hail, etc. etc. the lads of 3 Troop were given the day off as the weather was too bad. Lumpy's and Homer's troops just stayed there and froze. The tracks of TC's D6d (10) broke just near 15 Squadron, the weld broke, what a heap, no mail as the weather was too bad. Taff and Pinko got pulled out because Les Oldcorn had bogged in the Hymac.

I learnt a lot about man management through the mismanagement of the Army. The weather today was terrible. A total whiteout, horizontal snow, frozen hail and strong wind to force the bone numbing snow through your clothes. Bearing in mind that we were not allowed to, wear our Winter Warfare kit so the cold weather really affected those who had to work outside. The 3 Tp SSgt saw that nothing could be or would be done in this weather and so told his Troop to stay in Lookout Camp. The other two Troop Staffy's didn't have the courage to do anything that the OC would see as 'against his wishes' and so sent their Troops out into the blizzard without the gear to keep themselves warm. So did they work their little socks off? Did they fuck! They spent the entire day finding ways to keep warm, the same as Hitler's and Napoleon's armies did when attacking Russia. 'Look after your men and they will look after you' is the Army adage. To be fair to the Troop commanders, if the OC gave them the piece of mind by supporting their decisions they would probably also have kept their men inside on this fearsome day.

We in Support Troop had machines with heaters and metal cabs to protect us. Not that they were any use when the tracks of your D6d bulldozer broke.

We discovered in the Kuwaiti minefields that the tracks of bulldozers were so tough, designed for longevity, that one could drive over lines of anti-personnel mines and 'pop' them with your tracks with no more than slight discolouration. Even a 2.2 kg high-tech anti-tank mine would only colour it black. Most anti-tank mines are designed to break the tracks of a tank, thus immobilising it, not blow the tank to pieces. (The British Bar mine is an exception) Tank tracks are built for speed. Dozer tracks are built to last so when a track falls to pieces whilst just driving in a straight line, it is truly worn to the thickness of a razor blade. At this time in The Falklands we didn't have the stores to replace parts and bulldozer tracks are bulky and heavy to ship. This is an indication of the poor condition of the equipment at that time. One of our excavators, a Hymac 580 BT, was such a piece of shit that no POM wanted to operate it so we let the Field Troops use it. Les Oldcorn loved it, much more fun than a shovel, even though there was no window and the heater was knackered. Trouble was that he didn't have the knowledge that we had gained over the last five months about the peat and he was always bogging it in. An excavator can usually pull itself out but only if you know how. Les didn't so whenever he bogged it in, someone had to go out and get the 580 out. Even this imbuggerance was preferable to operating that piece of shit.

Tuesday 7th June

Snow and blizzard again, a Chinook landed on a Lynx pad. I went downtown to buy some paper for docs. The wind makes the snow horizontal, on the icy road it is near impossible to walk; all heavy wagons are banned from using the hills. Pinko is being Mr perfect again

No motor biking today. I must have fallen over ten times on the way to the shop. Going down the steep (and I mean STEEP) hill in Stanley reminded me of when at Chepstow's Apprentice's College I had a girlfriend from Abertillery. The fashion at the time was to have as many segs in your shoes as you could fit in. I had *loads*! The down side was that I couldn't walk up the side of the valley. My girlfriend had to pull me up as I had no traction in my shoes. That was what the hill was like in Stanley today. You went down holding onto fences and lamp posts. Before you let go you looked for what would stop you next.

Wednesday 8th June

2°C. What a wind, it is so cold the pipes froze again. Hot water came in a dribble. The lads went on a ming last night, they were legless, and they still were in the morning. It snows, hails and rains one after the other, and horizontal not vertical. Spunky fell into my bed last night.

You may note that it was 2°C. Plain and simple! Nowadays we use complex formula to make it sound colder. "It's minus 30°C today" and then in a quiet whimper, "wind-chill factor."

Thursday 9th June

Minus one degree C today but no wind so it was warmer today than yesterday, we've got running hot water at last. Fairclough, across the road hasn't got any water, he he. Bignose is back, what a pity, it was great without him, work got done. Mail came and Phantom's went out. I saw one nearly crash as its re-heat cut-out too early. I thought it had had it.

One of the joys of being in the services is that you can get close to macho things that civvies can only dream about. (Or play on a computer game)

One pastime was to watch the RAF's F4 Phantoms of the take off over our heads from the end of the runway, or as my photos on the web site show, from twenty metres from the runway. This time I was at the end and sat and watched and felt the raw power of the twin afterburners thunder through my entire body. They would vibrate the very marrow in your bones. It was awesome to feel. The pilots would keep the afterburners on until they reached the end of the inner harbour, a distance of nine km. (Thanks to Google Earth for measurements). They would then switch the burners off and continue off into the distance at the front of a long black line of smoke.

This time the Phantom only managed afterburner for around one hundred and fifty metres from the end of the runway when there was a loud 'Pop' and the beautiful cutting-torch blue ten metre flames from the engines disappeared. The F4 dropped twenty of its precious hundred metres (Towards ME!) and then before I could react it was over my head, the Peri Road at the end being only two hundred metres from the runway. It spluttered and popped its way to the end of the inner harbour climbing like a geriatric with a walking stick. If the pilot ever reads this I'd like to thank him for not 'punching out' as I would have had no time to react and you wouldn't be reading this book. I never sat at the end when aircraft were taking off after that.

Friday 10th June

We are doing nowt to the moments just bumming around. 75 Squadron held a quiz in the bar tonight, I managed to stay for support troop's first team then the smoke got the best of me. We have done our portacabin out with balloons, paper chains and "Support troop is One Step Beyond." It looks all Christmassy, with the snow, it is quite good. In the quiz one question was "What do you associate with an Axminster" then "What do you associated with a red Setter?" Taff piped up "a fucked up Axminster."

Today you can read this book in a smoke free environment if you are in a public building. Not so back then. As it was so cold every window was shut, and every smoker was puffing away on his and everyone else's smoke. My eyes stung like someone had squirted lemon juice in them. We had decided to throw a party. Taff and Mac were going home early on the advanced party and they were over the moon, so for no other reason we started to use our initiative. A trait that is ingrained into the British Sapper. By the time we had finished the portacabin was decorated like Santa's grotto. We had sat for a few days and made paper chains like my mother had shown me, we made posters and bought balloons from The Kelper Store. We nicked six forty five gallon plastic drums that were used to store cement. We washed them out and filled them up with layers of snow, beer and more snow. During the days of preparation a few SNCOs and Lt Sugar came in on business. When they saw the room their eyes popped out of their heads. On a vow of silence they were invited to the party, as was a Fairclough 9 Para friend of Jock's, a Sigs guy we knew and quite a few laid back Sappers from the Troops. A good time was expected as long as we could keep it from the OC and his followers.

Saturday 11th June

The OC banned us from saying "days to do" yesterday. That just made everybody say it more. The OC had four requests on the radio yesterday. The party went hell of a well. By this morning we had 4 blue barrels of beer and ice left, so we are drinking it now. The ice keeps it cold. Salter, Sugar and boozy Lathem are with us. The radio requests say "days to do are getting a few; he is a poem from me to you." He threw a wobbler last night in the bar, the Squadron is like a wound up spring, soon it is going to spring back!. I only hope I don't unwind. I don't half miss Sandra.

There was a custom in the Falklands. Those Troops leaving would tell those not leaving that they have 'Days to do', that they will soon be on the Gozome boat. (That would be the boat that 'Goes home') and that the 'days to do are getting few'. One could also throw in a 'Stag on you turkeys' into the melee. It was a huge pressure relief after the months of monotonous work. You had it done to you when you got there and you anticipated the time when you could do it to others. It meant the beginning of the end of your tour Down South. Bignose in yet another brilliant stroke of mismanagement banned us from saying any of those sayings. In one stroke he cancelled Christmas, our birthdays and loosing our virginity all at once. We had dreamed of this time, of the pleasure of gloating to our friends in other Squadrons and he had taken this away from us… obviously we didn't pay his order an ounce of attention except when he was in earshot…except… on the FIBS, the Falkland Island Broadcasting Service, the radio that transmitted and was listened to by all the Troops on the Island and probably all ranks. On this we submitted numerous dedications to Major Smythe, to OC 75 Fld Sqn and to Bignose. They all had one distinguishing feature and that was the 'days to do are getting few' in the dedication. We submitted one, MT the other and two others from the Troops. We heard them all. Bignose had instructed us that we would be fined if we uttered the illegal sentence. Ten pence an utterance! Ten whole pence! My god, my world is over.

The party started this evening. It was wild. I can't remember much, just blurred images, Spunky sucking the teat on the end of a balloon whilst fantasising about a young Japanese girl. TC putting a pair of NI gloves on his feet and doing an impression of an owl, me throwing out empty barrels and dragging in full ones from the snow outside. Loads of smoke, loads of laughter, SSgt Benjamin Byrne came as did Lt Sugar and Lt Salter. He was unexpected, as he always seemed to be a bit of a square but he opened out and was a great laugh. It was a huge turning point in the tour, the start to the end. From this point onwards we were finishing and from this point on our attitudes changed.

Sunday 12th June

We started boozing almost as soon as we got up, Salter, Sugar and Benjamin Byrne came up. Taff slagged the OC down in the cookhouse singing "going home, going home, going home", so Bignose came across and said "that will be 30 p Cpl Davies" Taff died laughing and asked him if he wanted cheque, then Bignose came back, blubbering with rage and stated "in advance!." Thirty pence!! What a knobber. The lads in the bar last night were bottling each other and dancing naked on the roof, whilst swimming in beer.

It was Sunday, a no work day and we had four forty five gallon barrels of beer and slushy icy water to get through. As soon as I awoke it was 'Have a beer Bernie' and a cold can of beer came flying towards my head. It was only natural reflexes that stopped it from hitting my head. I opened the can and the beer escaped like an angry swarm of wasps and coated the roof and some of Pinko. He didn't notice being fast asleep so I took a slug. My bladder which was now the size of a small Zeppelin complained of this new fluid entering the body and forced me out for that first pee of the day. The ground outside was still covered with old hard snow, there had been no new snow during the night, and I skipped across the path to the shower portacabin that was now next to us and took a pee in a sink. The toilets were too far away when you were in your shreddies and flip flops in the snow. When I re-entered the portacabin I noticed the state of the place, something that I hadn't noticed on the way out, hit me. What brought it to my attention was the old bar smell of beer and stale cigarette smoke. I stood inside the door and looked around for the source of the stink. Beer cans ripped in half and with their sharp edges bent down were spilling over with fag butts. There were enough butts in this one room to keep a bum in fags for a month. The fags weren't just confined to the 'ashtrays', they had spread over the 'Table, , Wooden, Six foot, with Folding legs' and to the 'Floor, Lino, the portacabin was covered with beer and piss' or water or melted snow, I wasn't quite sure what was on the floor but only knew that it was liquid. Note to self; wet floor and flip flops means total loss of flip flop traction. Caution is needed in walking; End note.

Either in my short absence or I hadn't noticed them on the way out, sitting at the table was Benjamin Byrne, Ginge the Barman, the 9 Para mate from Fairclough from whom we had purchased the Carlsberg, (We were still only allowed two cans a night.) a bloke from the Sigs and Taff Davies, drinking! There were empty cartons of Carlsberg on the spare bed and cans crushed, full of fags and some half full of flat beer everywhere. Spunky was asleep in his pit as were Jock and TC and Pinko. "When did you guys get here?" I asked.

"They've been here an hour boy" Taff laughed. Through the thuggish veil in my brain a light came on and I woke up, "Ah well, I might as well join you then, didn't I have a beer somewhere, where's my camera?" I dug out my camera and took a shot of the morning-after scene and picking up what I believed was my new can, joined in the new party. A short while later, Lieutenants (how the hell do we get 'Left-tenant from that word?) Salter and Sugar bimbled in and grabbed a beer making it an official All-ranks party. I did notice when they came in that they were 'respectful' of us? Like they were gate crashing, but they were Officers and we wouldn't and couldn't refuse them, but that was why we liked them and that was why they were there and that was why we would have gone to combat with them.

Now Lt Slovey was a different kettle of fish as we would find out the next day.

By dinner that evening we were all pissed, SNCOs and Officers alike and we shambled off to the large portacabin dining hall. The SNCOs and Officers (the adults) were on a large island of tables. The children, (us) sat in rows like Hogwarts only in a different pattern.

Taff was on our table of six or so, he started singing which wasn't too much of a problem, except for the words that he chose. He sung "Going Home, Going Home, Going Hooooome," and laughed out loud. The OC jumped up from his table and stormed across to our table "That'll be thirty pence Cpl Davies." He shouted and went back to his table. Taff wouldn't let it drop, he was past caring. He burst out laughing and swayed as he shouted "Thirty pee? Thirty Pee, hahahahaha. Does he know I'm a T class Cpl? (the highest paid in the Army) thirty pee?" ha ha ha, ho ho ho, he he he, Does he want a cheque? Ha ha ha, ho ho ho, he he he thirty pee, hey guys" he looked at us through drunken glazed eyes "he wants me to pay thirty pee, can you lend me some money?" ha ha ha, ho ho ho, he he he, "Thirty pee" etc etc….. We were all laughing quietly and as I looked around I noticed that everyone in the cookhouse was laughing… except the top table. The OC jumped up and stomped over to our table again and hit Taff with the worst thing that he could. He shouted "IN ADVANCE!"

I don't know what effect he thought that this statement would have, but it just tipped Taff over the top into a blubbering, laughing drunken Welshman. The OC seeing that he couldn't win here went back to his top table where he continued to eat. When I looked around the top table, every single SNCO and Officer was eating his meal looking down at their plate. No one made eye contact with the OC or us. It was as funny as Taff. It also set the scene for a mutinous assembly with the Troops. In the large portacabin bar they had also obtained more than their ration of beer and sensing the end to the tour, which may or may not have been started by our party and Taff's outburst in the cookhouse, they let loose the spring which had been coiling tighter and tighter for the last six months. They went wild!

The same had happened on the Countess as I had heard on the way down and now in 75 Sqn it was happening in the bar in Lookout Camp.

Monday 13th June

Slovey blames us for the riot in the bar, Taff has to go in front of the old man, I really enjoyed this weekend. We've still got one barrel, come dustbin, of beer left. Taff got a lecture on how brilliant support troop have worked and then the OC gave him five extras. The video with Sandra on is on tomorrow and we are getting on the ship on the 5th, it will only take eight days. Happiness is all around me but especially in me. TC got the "Dear John" letter from Ami that he was expecting.

Apparently we, Support Troop, are the devil incarnate if Lt Slovey is to be believed. The brainless Field Troops would not have 'let their hair down' had it not been for Support Troop having a little soiree. Bollox Slovey.

If they hadn't run riot in the bar, it would have happened elsewhere at another time. Now we are all defused and calmer than a hippy hermit on hashish. I feel great. I am smiling for the first time in months as is everyone around me. Even when TC got the 'Dear John' letter from his girlfriend he didn't seem too upset. Maybe he was but with sympathy being in the soldiers' dictionary between shit and syphilis we don't give out too much of the stuff. Can you imagine the scenario; "Oh dear, you poor lad, have you got a splinter in your finger from that nasty handle on that stick grenade? Here, don't throw it, put it down and go get it seen to. Nursey will get it out."

Tuesday 14th June

21 days to do, video on tonight, beer is banned from rooms and spot checks from the all the orderly sergeants. I am really feeling great. It will take a lot to kill my spirit. TC is back to his normal self.

TC was devastated over the 'Dear John' letter. It took him all of one day to get over it!

Wednesday 15th June

I got the IH 630W excavator today. I made sure that 15 the Squadron did all the 'A' jobs on it, then at 17:30 I started to drive it back and got it bogged in just outside the airfield, shit!

The International Harvester 630 W was a wheeled excavator and great fun to operate. It could drive along the road at a giddy 20 mph… but didn't have the off road capability of the tracked Hymacs. Especially the 590s with the swamp tracks. They had less ground bearing pressure than a gnat's foot. Whether I had forgotten that or grown used to tracking across the peat with impunity when I tried it in the wheeled excavator I bogged it down to the axles. Things like that always happen at knocking off time and so again Port Stanley saw me hitching a lift along the Stanley – airport road. Again I cursed at the trucks that passed me, did they think I was going to mug them?

Thursday 16th June

We went and saw Jim Davidson on the CSE show, he was magic. Rogers got the 630 W out of the mud but it had water in the fuel system from standing with a half empty tank of fuel on the plant park for too long. I can't wait to get back to Sandra, I really do want her. I realised long ago on this tour that she is a most important thing in my life. Everything, money, clothes, cars, possessions takes a second place to her. Not so with Pinko.

We had heard about Jim Davidson's performance when he played in the outlaying regions. Today he was in Port Stanley and as I didn't have too long to go before getting the Gozome boat I went. After the show TC, Jock and I ambled down to the jetty to the chippy van. We got a bag of chips and some sausages and up ambled up to Jim

Davidson, Bob Carolgees minus his puppet dog called Spit and a woman singer who made such an impact on me I cannot remember her name. We chatted for a bit and remarked on the price of the chips and went our separate ways. No great memorable experience there. No invites back to the hotel for drinks and story telling and no invite for them back to our cabin either. We had nothing in common except a bag of chips.

Friday 17th June

Well if today is Germany's longest day, it wasn't here! It is only 18 days until THE day but the end is still so far away. The time is going quickly but not quick enough. The 630W broke down again today. Water in the fuel system. 15 Squadron wankers. I don't give of fuck any more! D.T.D.N.F.I. (days to do not fucking interested) so stick it up your arse Bignose. We were discussing more ways in which to kill him today, what a laugh!!!

Note to 15 Squadron Royal Engineers; Diesel engines run better on diesel than they do on water. Just thought you'd like to know that!

The discussion to kill the OC had months ago turned from hypothetical to practice.

The Squadron had unanimously agreed that who ever got him sent home, whether in a wooden box or not, would be bought enough beer to keep them drunk until they left The Falklands.

The Haulamatic drivers, who had priority on the roads, would aim for his distinctive car. Bignose wouldn't budge from the road and the driver always chickened out and ended up bogged in on the side of the road in the peat. Many people had attempted to cut through his brake pipes, new cables lasted not a week on his vehicle and I had tried to hit him with the excavator bucket. We had all failed. This man had more lives than a lucky cat.

Saturday 18th June

Mac got promoted to lance corporal today, all the Para's went to an airborne Pissup. They then came back in here at 1 o'clock in the morning. The queer captain came in and was trying to make a pass at a civvy. I just don't want to get up for work any more; I have got no incentive left! NFI! Life is just a big bore. Even operating doesn't raise any interest in me. Spunky is a wanking his life away.

I assume that today was Airborne Forces Day. I can't think of any other reason why all the Paras in the Squadron would burst into my portacabin at one o clock in the morning and wake me up to tell me that I was a 'Craphat.' One of the Para Captains was 'gay' as we say nowadays. It was more than his career was worth to try it on with a soldier, but a civvie was fair game. I have no problem with that. Rather him than me.

Spunky started wanking again in the portacabin and we had to read books, go for a walk or whatever in order to avoid hearing, seeing or being involved with his, what should be covert but was now totally overt habit. We only have one goal in life now, and that is to get on the boat. Everything else that we do is just to pass the time until then.

Sunday 19th June

We had to work today. No sweat, the time goes quicker, still no incentive, only 15 days, it is still seems years away, Taff leaves tomorrow, and he has been celebrating for 2 days. I can't even be arsed to write in this diary or to home. I can't and haven't had a good night's sleep for ages, I always awake with my sheets everywhere but where they should be! Taff got told to shut up by the QM when in 32's bar.

Monday 20th June

I got a load of bumf from Hymac today, and a letter from San saying she has bought a bike. Trouble is I know that we will be fighting over it. I'll have to buy another one. Taff got on the ship today. Without him and Pinko it is really quiet, not long now, I know that it won't take long; it just seems so far away. Did my washing at last, they are all Hotpoint washing machines, they remind me of Sandra. How I miss her!

Tuesday 21st June

Well, Tuesday has finished its Wednesday already. Soon we'll be in single figures.

Just cruisin' along man.

Wednesday 22nd June

Rumours that we are still going to finish with building the bridge! SSM has said that we start to hand back the plant on the first, not the 28th. It is finally sinking in that we haven't got long to do now, only 12 and a greasy egg today. Soon we will be in single figures; life is still the same, no preparing for handing back! It's wank! I want the going home atmosphere.

Thursday 23rd June

I went on the Coastell three today. It is beautiful, I didn't want to go back to Lookout camp, we made the tape to Sandra, and I didn't get any mail, very depressed, even though we only have 12 days until we should mount ship. The Coastell 3 should make life a little easier. I wish it would hurry up and come, any letter I write now, Sandra won't be able to reply to.

The Coastell 3 was the reason for all the road and anchor building. It was a floating hotel most commonly used in the oil industry and it was luxury! We had to put on little blue booties over our muddy boots to protect the carpet and then we had a good nosey, wall to wall carpet, lifts, a huge sports hall, squash courts and two to a room, sheer luxury! Piped music, beautiful canteen, heated showers in the cabins, curtains and a receptionist. We had hated living on the ships but to the people before us, who had bunked down on the floors of houses, the ships were luxury. We then moved to the portacabin camp of Lookout Camp which was a step up for us but the pit to those who joined us there and we will now be moving to the Coastell. Once we get there, it'll be time to totally switch off!

Friday 24th June

Snow is melting today, we are moving onto the Coastell 3, Safe Esperia tomorrow, Sunday off, people are quite happy. The atmosphere is slowly started to build up, I have packed to move. JC and Spunky got pissed on night nurse. Spunky pissed over the floor, we're sent him to Coventry. Jock caught his Dong in his sleeping bag and then earned his name "Donkey Dong" by showing us his knob!

Alcohol was banned since the weekend of debauchery. Spunky and JC, a Cpl from the Troops, bought some night nurse and sat drinking it like a couple of winos. By the end of the bottle they were pissed without any symptoms of a cold and without any idea of where the toilets were. Spunky swamping our cabin was going too far and we sent him to Coventry, which means not talking to him. Nobody wants to walk through someone else's piss.

Jock catching his knob in his sleeping bag was not an extraordinary occurrence. Jock, never shy to show the lads what his tiny wife has to put up with, made it so. After his shriek he walked around the cabin showing any who couldn't turn his head away quick enough, the small nick in his knob. It was hard to see any damage to his member because any glance just made us feel inadequate. He had given up his morning cock show parade after we left the boat but now he made up for it. As did we, insults were flying at him from all corners of the room but they were complimentary insults. "Where the fuck did you get that monster from Jock?" and "Is there an unhappy donkey somewhere in Keith pining for his lost knob?" Jock lapped it up and what well hung red blooded man wouldn't? finished his show by standing in the middle of the portacabin, family sized Salami hanging by his knees with a huge smile on his face whilst we continued to insult him; "Did the doctor pull you out of your mother by your knob?". "No, no, he found a witch doctor on his last tour and paid him a hundred dollars for a two handed trouser snake" Etc.

We packed up the room today. All the posters, the wall candy we left. All that I took were the photos, the chuff chart and the underwear. It really felt good packing up again. We were slowly moving back to civilisation, from the ship to Lookout Camp to the Coastell. Taff and Pinko had already left and now we were packing for the final 'stint' in luxury. Next time that we pack will be for the Gozome boat. Spirits were high.

Saturday 25th June

Benny Christmas. I went onto the Coastell 3, Safe Esperia today. It is only spoiled by the JRC and officers mess signs in Royal Engineer colours on the doors. Even though the Safe Esperia is here for us the lift is out of bounds all military personnel!!!! I don't really blame them with these stupid knockers spoiling everything. Went to the gym to limber up with karate. Now happy that we have got hot water I have a cold shower.

At nine am we threw our sausage bags over our shoulders and picked up our suitcases and walked out the door. The Bedford was waiting for us and we threw our baggage onto the truck which co-incidentally is exactly how it came off.

When we got to the Safe Esperia our kit bags and suitcases were lying in a large pile, two metres high. We were desperate to get inside in case there was a 'good bed' and a 'bad bed' to be had. We need not have worried. They were all 'good beds!' We were greeted at reception by a 'woman'. Hadn't seen many of those for the last five months! We were prompted to put on little blue plastic boot covers to protect the carpet. Later on coming back down to reception the carpet was covered in mud from the Knocker's boots and it went to the lift so they didn't pay much attention to the directions of the 'woman' either. Wait till they get home!

Sunday 26th June

What is a great night sleep! We are really winding down on his Coastell. I woke up the happiest that I have done for the whole tour, everybody is having hundreds of showers, Spunky spussed in his hand then licked it off Yeuck! Flat back Jock has been renamed Donkey Dong Jock! What a chopper! He wants us to tell all the pads wives!

The cabin is a two bunk self contained cabin. It has an en suite shower and toilet, double glazing windows, heater, blankets, sheets and a tannoy that blazed out the Royal Engineers march first thing in the morning. The trip to the canteen was all inside, no snow or slush to run through, the water in the showers was hot and piped music came through the tannoy at the twist of a switch. Now *this* was R&R!

I'm sharing the bunk with TC. I could be sharing with Bignose for all I care. I have switched off.

Monday 27th June

What a terrible day today, the sleet and snow was horizontal and not vertical. We (Jock and me) washed down the All-drive and got soaked, so we spent the afternoon throwing ether cartridges and bullets onto a fire. A rotten day until quite unexpectedly I got 4 lovely letters off Sandra; they not only made me feel very happy but also very horny.

When we woke up and looked out the window, the sleet and snow was rushing past the window. It had somewhere to get to and it had to get there fast. During the day it would try to get through my head by going in one ear and out the next.

Tuesday 28th June

Mac dug up some cables again cutting off F. I. B. S.(Falkland Island Broadcasting Service), all telecommunications to UK and the water pipes into Stanley, Icy, cold and lethal to walk, but I am still very happy, I can not only see the end is tunnel but can now see outside, it looks good! Letters from San are looking good, reading good and feeling good.

This was the second time that Mac had cut the cables in Stanley. I can't blame him as our 'Engineers' (officers) should have first marked out the cables and services from the drawings.

Wednesday 29th June

*Got drunk tonight on cider. Dave **"nice bum"** Christian puked over his and Yan Kitts's beds. £140, poor sod! Geordie Slailes went up to Danny Brown and asked him "Have you got any Wednesday's in your store?" Danny said "what do you mean." Geordie replied "75 Squadron haven't got any Wednesday's left." We had a talking by the RSM.*

Dave Christian really was steaming towards being an old sweat. Puking over your bed got you a reputation, puking over someone else's as well made you immortal. The charge was £70 a mattress. At this time I was on £12,000 a year. That equates down to around £46 a day and I was a top paid Cpl. Dave would have been on around £30 a day before tax! So £140 was a week's wages.

Thursday 30th June

33 Muirhill was handed in today; I thought we would never get that one in. We are still worried about if we are going to get all the plant handed in by Wednesday. Who cares? Nobody gives a fuck nowadays. I went and played squash and swam today, very nice.

We've just had a stupid fire practice, stood out in a 60 MPH+ wet wind for 30 minutes, then sang "going home" whilst going to go back in. Pits. Six days left.

33 Muirhill was a LWT or a little JCB for you not in the trade. It was the worst of all of them. Only one braking system, gauges not working, handbrake knackered, but we somehow got it handed in. One machine plus a lot of paperwork proving that we had ordered important parts like a 24 v brake light bulb.

Notes

Well this penultimate month went very fast. We saw single days and the last week. We moved onto the Coastell and that changed our whole outlook on life, we've changed from being impatient to being happy. On the Coastell we can really unwind. Better than the Lookout camp with its cold water and blizzards to face to get to the showers and dinner. July is the last month and we thought that we wouldn't care about any thing when it came. We don't, but our Squadron haven't started to finish and wind up, if any thing they are working harder! Stupid sods. We aren't, OC is still being an obnoxious bastard as ever. We can see outside the tunnel now and soon we will be outside.

FIBS

"Going home, Going home, Going home"

♫ ♪ ♫

Friday 1st July 1983

July at last!!! On Monday people start getting on the ship. We, supposedly on Wednesday, I'll believe that when it happens, BFT tomorrow. (Basic Fitness Test) We are just waiting for 'THE' day. 15 Squadron have been told by their OC to lay back and relax. Bignose wants us to work until the last day to try and finish the jobs, then he has a training programme for us on the ship. Roll on a normal life!

Get on the ship on Monday? Did I just write that? Can it really be that close? Friday, Saturday, Sunday and then Get-on-the-ship-Monday! After what seems like a life time we are outside the tunnel and basking in the glaring sunshine…. Except that Bignose is goading us to push on and finish the tasks. Fuck the tasks; we've been doing 'the tasks' for the last six months. We have four days left and should be relaxing and tying up loose ends. Not us. Shiny Seven has to work to the last day. The packing can be done in our own time. To get us back into BAOR life we will be doing a BFT tomorrow down the road to Moody Brook. Not looking forward to that after six months of no running. Why couldn't I be in 15 Squadron?

Saturday 2nd July

Well we have run out of Saturday's now! Plant is slowly being handing backed. Still having trouble with Lumpy with "his" plant. The ship should be coming in this weekend; it is supposed to be 24 hours late. Days to do! I got Sandra's penultimate letter today, she has promised me all sorts of naughty things, and I get hard just reading her letters. Fancy been a singly and going back to wank. BFT today.

Nearly the entire Squadron failed the BFT. We have to take it again tomorrow and continue to take it until we pass. That road to Moody Brook was sooooo long and straight. It was like we weren't moving. The end never got any closer, no matter how far you ran, I was absolutely knackered. When I was in Chepstow, the Army Apprentices College I was hopeless at running. I was the fat kid at the back gasping for breath. Then during our classes on the Otto cycle (internal combustion engine) I realised that our bodies were just organic engines. Food is the fuel that we burn. We need oxygen just like an engine and to increase power we need to add more fuel and more oxygen. Fuel is in our muscles and cannot be instantly increased but oxygen can. So to run better I first increased my breathing and suddenly I was a good runner. I had four breathing speeds that coincided with my running pace. Four steps – breathe in four steps - breathe out, then three steps in and one step out finishing in one step, in and one step, out. That was my 'top' gear and was reserved for when the end of the BFT was in sight. I became a 'runner' and ran for my Squadron and Regiment in cross country races. I completed a BFT once in nine minutes twenty two seconds. Today I didn't finish in time at all. Neither did most of the Squadron.

Sunday 3rd July

Well our Chuff chart has finally reached '1-day' tonight. I am Chuffed!! I spent today tightening Hymac track bolts, we are at last on the final week, just wait to the Norlan comes in! People are waiting to mount ship, it is 24 hours late. Dinner at Look-out and the Heliport tasted like sick, everybody failed the BFT again. It is only 2.2 miles long. Jock stood on a bloke's epiglottis on a pool table down Brewsters!

Jock and the entire Ex 9 Sqn Paras (Andy, Gus and Gobby Wally) went down to Brewsters bar for another 'Airborne Forces' Day. Jock had a fight with a bloke and recounted it to us like this:

"I was having a laugh with Andy, Gus and Stumpy Wayne the ex-9 Para guy who works with Brewsters when this civvy tried to throw us out. We had been celebrating on our own and minding our own business. It wasn't as if we were being rowdy or anything we were just telling stories and laughing, a lot. Lots of laughing in fact! Loads and loads of the laughing, the bar was packed with Brewsters and there we were in the middle having a great time. We had been drinking for about three hours by then. Well anyway, this civvy walked right up into the middle of us, looked me in the eye and said "Why don't you lot fuck off out of our bar, you ain't Brewsters, and you fucking squaddies shouldn't even be in here?" Well it killed the conversation dead, we all just looked at each other in surprise, I couldn't believe what he had just said. You could have knocked me down with a feather; we were invited there by Stumpy Wayne. Andy had had an argument with the barman earlier because we were there, maybe this was the company 'Hardman' who was going to throw us out. Whatever I was so gobsmacked that I asked him to repeat what he had just said, more in amazement than in anything else, I think I said something like "Sorry? What did you say" whilst still smiling. It was dawning on me what he had meant but I needed time to consider what to do, When he started to mouth off back to me I made my plan, I didn't want to hit him when his head was in the air as the force of my punch would be lost so I looked for something to put his head up against so that he would receive the full power of the punch. I saw the pool table behind him, not a full sized table but one of these little ones around six foot long, it would serve my purpose, while he was still gobbing off to me and building up his courage I dropped my pint and pushed him onto the table. I intended to hold his head on the table with my left hand and punch him with my right. When I threw him on the table the legs gave way and the table collapsed with him on top of it. This really fucked up my plans because he was now too low to punch so I stepped forward to his side and stomped my foot down on to his throat, he stopped gobbing off then for some reason, I was gonna stomp on him again but Stumpy dragged me off him, I looked around and the whole bar had erupted into a fight, so we exited the stage and legged it. We were on the Moody Brook Road and started to walk back towards Lookout. A Landrover came past and we thumbed a lift. I got into the front and Andy, Gus and Stumpy got into the back. God knows where Gobby had got to, we had ditched him earlier. As we were coming into Stanley I saw what looked like a shell on the side of the road so I stopped the driver and got out to have a look. It was an unexploded 105mm artillery shell, still fused. Well we couldn't just leave it there so I picked it up and walked round to the back of the Rover, I then dumped it on the floor and said "look after this lads, make sure it don't explode" and then got back in the front." Jock was laughing furiously by now.

"We bumped and rattled our way to Lookout with this shell in the back, every time it rolled, it hit the side and we laughed, it could have gone off at anytime and we found it hilarious, I'm not sure if the driver did, I was laughing too much to see him,"

"Where is the shell now Jock?" Spunky asked.

"I put it outside Bignose's cabin so that if it does go off at least it will kill him"

That bit we all found funny.

That is how Jock got the nickname "The Epiglottis Stomper."

Monday 4th July

We finally managed to do all the " A" jobs on the plant, Jock gave Bignose a hard time over the time that we had been given to hand over the plant! MV Norlan sailed into the inner harbour this afternoon. I sat and watched her, what a beautiful sight! It is all coming to an end and yet I still cannot believe that are ever gonna leave this island!

I'll never forget the sight of the Gozome boat slowly sailing into the inner harbour. What a beautiful sight. I sat on a cold stone, on a cold winter's day with a cold wind blowing through my ears but didn't feel a thing. I had a stupid smile on my face; there in front of me was my salvation and my vehicle back to civilisation, back to Sandra, the woman who I loved and the woman who I now felt was like a stranger. We had communicated so much over the last six months but had not spoken a word. No SMS, no emails and no phone calls apart from the one mid-tour which passed in a daze. When I thought of meeting her I was filled with nervousness, like a school kid on his first date. What would I say? What did she look like? Should I grab her and give her a snog or be restrained. Whenever the subject came up in my mind I got the collywobbles. It was still hard to realise that we were going, but there in front of me, sailing majestically into my life was the MV Norlan. Twenty four sodding hours late!

Tuesday 5th July

Were handing back the plant today, I finished by about 10 o'clock; everybody else didn't finish until tonight. We have finally finished! That is it!!

We got a brief from SSM. Tomorrow is off, and we get on, on Thursday! I can't believe it is happening. Big Pissup in the bar tonight. Beer cans went everywhere.

15 Squadron lined up in one rank and their OC walked down the rank, shook the hands of the entire squadron and thanked each and every one of them. Our OC? Well after fining Taff Davies 30p for singing 'Going home, Going home Going home' he was person non gratis. I doubt if the thought even entered his head.

I am finished. All the plant that was my responsibility I handed over by ten am. It wasn't because I was better than anyone else but because the plant that was used with the Troops was still working until yesterday. The feeling of overwhelming relief was indescribable, but I'll try any way. In my mind I was now sunbathing in the light outside the tunnel. I could still see into the depths of the despair in the tunnel… but didn't want to. It was far nicer to look forward to a nice cruise home, a short flight and then to be with my Sandra. There was nothing that Bignose could do to ruin that. Even if we trained all the way back, I'd only be there in body. The difference between the OC of 15 Squadron and ours was the difference between chalk and cheese, Night and Day, Crap and Good.

Wednesday 6th July

Supposedly mount ship today. But we didn't, tomorrow we mount ship, went down town for the last time! Bignose got Mac showing the 25 Sqn. operators how to build a road. It has been a good day today everybody is happy, we have been telling everybody that we go home tomorrow. I am on an all time high, it's great, like being eternally happy, I'm gonna see my San again.

Yet another delay to board ship but it didn't matter to us. We were going to board it very soon and we could wait. We had no work to do and so spent the day doing whatever took our fancy. I went to Port Stanley for the last time to get a few last minute photos. I had lost a lot when the NAAFI lost my film so had a few to retake. I ambled past The Kelper Store where we had been booked for illegal parking and for not having indicators, looked at the generator and the place where 75 Squadron had been responsible for cutting the town's power, twice, walked up to the house where I had had supper with Jane's grandson. Down to The West Store where I remembered when I was made to feel unwelcome by the locals then along to the post office where I bought Falkland stamps for my mother and then back to the jetty along the coast road past the church with the whale bones in front to the shop where I bought two Falkland crowns which I still have today. They're still worth bugger all! Going back to the ,Coastell, after hitching a ride in an RAF Landrover, the Blue Job started to regret his kindness when the conversation went "So how many days you got left mate?"

The atmosphere in the Coastell was buzzing. Sappers were drunk, somehow singing was coming from nearly every cabin. I went along to my cabin but was dragged into Mac and Jocks. TC was in there as well JW or Johnny Walker, a few cans of weak beer and the remains of a bottle of Southern Comfort, currently my favourite. I joined them and entered the high spirits; we were all on a high. I ascertained through the conversation that we all had packed leaving out only our wash gear and clothes for tomorrow. We didn't even have a day left, just a 'wakeup'. Cut three sheets to the wind, I much later staggered back to my cabin and tried to get to sleep, sleep that wouldn't come until many hours later.

Thursday 7th July

When I heard that stupid music over the Tannoy at six o'clock this morning, it was the sweetest music that I have ever heard. Although I was extremely high, everybody else was just the same. (Bored) we finally get to the Secretariat after a one hour wait on the Groyne. We paraded and watched Harry and Sgt Austin fumble the flag down, we then marched to the public jetty, Scouse Barley swam! We were giggling all the way, Jock was saying "fucking Muppets." We got on the CSB and got on the ship. Spunky thought he had lost his key. TC had it in his pocket. CO says that we are the best, it looked like cattle moved out of our accommodation last night, no showers, no tea, no luxury.

The Royal Engineers march blared over the tannoy shaking me out of my slumber. I couldn't sleep last night tossing and turning up to the wee hours thinking about the trip home. The consequence of this was that I was sound asleep when the tannoy blared out 'Wings'. Within a split second I realised that today was the last day of the monotony known as 'The Falklands and I was up and out of bed and shaking a snoring TC with gay abandon. I didn't care if he swung at me, it was GOZOME DAY! The day we go 'ome! TC also jumped out of bed and within ten minutes we had both shaved, washed and were on our way to the canteen. The party mood was still evident at breakfast. When we walked in Jock and Mac gave us a cheer, "Finally managed to get up then, don't you know we're going home today?" Jock laughed.

"What today?" TC shouted so that everyone could here. The whole canteen smiled and thirty people shouted at the same time "YES TODAY!"

"Hey Ray" TC shouted "is it today we go home?"

"Yeah mate" he laughed "Today, it is today isn't it Pete?"

"Er... yeah, I think so, George, is it today or tomorrow we go 'ome?"

We managed to make this last for the whole of breakfast much to the pretended disgust of the other Troops using the canteen. Although some rolled their eyes they also chuckled with laughter with us. It would, after all, be their turn soon enough and they shared our happiness.

"Hey TC" I shouted even though he was sitting next to me "Can I sit next to you in here at breakfast tomorrow... because I love you."

"No Bernie you can't."

"Why?"

"Because, I'm going home, and so, my dear lurrrrver... are you!"

"Me?"

"Yes you!"

Etc. etc. for thirty minutes ad nauseam.

A short while later saw us with our suitcase, and kit bag, standing outside the Coastell in a gaggle. The rooms had to be handed over and accepted by the management of the Coastell and we had to wait until they were accepted. Spunky had lost his key and was frantically searching his baggage as he was going to get billed for it. TC showed us the contents of his pocket, the key was there. He let Spunky suffer for a bit with us laughing before owning up. After an hour we got the order to load the trucks. When it came not a second was lost and our baggage and us were on the trucks. We bumped and swerved our way along the pot holed Stanley to Airport Road for the last time. We knew the road's landscape like we knew our own faces; we'd been on it that many times, not only driving but walking and tracking excavators down it at 1.5mph. But something was wrong, we weren't going to the jetty, we drove straight past it and onto the Squadron office, the Secretariat. We disembarked the wagons and were paraded in front of the flag pole and we started the OC's 'Freedom of the City parade'.

Whilst the OC and SSM saluted the flag Sgt Austin slowly, and with as much ceremony as he could produce in this unreal situation lowered the Squadron flag. It was then folded up for transit to Germany and the SSM faced us, "Squadron will move to the left in threes, lefffffffffffffffff, TURN!"

We turned left with as much style as a bunch of boy scouts. "By the right, quick march" and we set off for Germany. I would have marched the whole way there! We marched along the Coast Road past Falkland Islanders popping into the West Store for a bag of sugar and twenty fags. They looked at us with a "What the fuck….?" look. No one had mentioned a Victory Parade, were they missing something? All these fine smart soldiers all in step!

"GET YOUR ARMS SHOULDER HIGH!" The SSM shouted. We were parade marching, he wanted to set the best possible image for the Islanders. Then it all went to rat-shit (similar to mouse-shit only bigger)

Anyone who was actually on The Falkland Islands around 1983 will know that all the roads were more pot holes than they were asphalt. The transit of Argentina's mechanised infantry on them did nothing to improve the condition.

We hit the potholes.

Or more correctly someone in the front rank marched into a pothole and disappeared with a splash and "Fuck" followed by laughter from those around him until the one behind him hit the same hole and splash "Shit… ha ha ha." This went down the line like a big surfer's wave approaching, you could see it coming but couldn't get out of the way and then it was your turn. Scouse Barley who is probably taller than me, was besides me and he dropped so his head was level with my shoulders with a large splash. He was giggling and trying to mimic a straight face like a good comedian. "Shuddup, this is serious" he giggled as with arms slightly higher than his shoulder he dropped down and stepped back up the other side of the hole. It was hilarious. Jock who is a short arse at the best of times and was in front of me dropped down to a grunt of "Fucking Muppets" splash and then it was my turn, I caught my foot on the edge of the pothole on the way out and hit Jock on the back with my arm to steady myself as I fell. We must have looked like that game where you have to hit the groundhogs as they pop out of the ground. We were certainly leaving an impression on the locals.

Eventually thank Christ, we were at the jetty and were halted and fell out to wait for transport to the MV Norlan.

We, having Titch Fuller in the Squadron, had the full fleet of CSBs to take us to the ship baggage as well. My last journey in these beautifully powerful boats!

We arrived at the ship and mounted grabbing a cabin between two, I got one with TC. Stow (Navy speak) our kit and have a look round. That was my last day the Falkland Islands. Now for a nice relaxing cruise home. Boy was I in for a shock.

Friday 8th July

SAIL TODAY. And it did! We had a talk by the CRE and the C B F. I took too many seasick pills and feel very drowsy, it was a beautiful moment when we turned around and sailed out of Stanley harbour, not one person was unhappy to see it go! The ship's horn blew, we sang and shouted; the CSB's with Titch Fuller escorted us out and a Sea King helicopter flew past us low. We are on our way at last!! Home here we come. I burned our Chuff chart and watched Stanley disappear out of my life!

The pleasure that I am experiencing in reaching this part of the book bears no resemblance to the emotional high that I and everyone else was on when the Norlan started her engines. The ship vibrated into life, started to take on her identity. An identity that would be our friend for the next two weeks, would sing us to sleep with her reassuring rumble and would although loud, eventually disappear into the background. Right now, it was music to my ears. The throb of the massive engines, the rumble of the shafts on their bearings and the rhythmic beating of the prop blades pushing us, metre by metre closer to home. It was a party atmosphere on the decks as we waved to anyone we saw, Titch had brought the CSB crew and all the boats to escort us out and they raced around us like speed boats round a visiting cruise ship. Ships in the inner and outer harbour blew their horns when we passed and we replied with our horn. We passed The Irishman tug and I waved frantically from the back, the crew waved back and before we rounded the corner to the outer harbour I saw Baz from the Irishman holding the bazooka above his head and wave it to me. "What's that he's waving?" TC asked.

"My meal ticket for the last four months!" I replied

We stood on the rear blunt end of the ship with all the frothy white water coming out of it and watched The Falkland Islands get larger and larger as the rest of the Islands started to pan out either side of us and then recede and shrink as it sunk into the horizon.

"Thank Christ that is over" Scouse Barley lamented.

"You'll be recalling all the good times at NAAFI break once we get back." I told him.

"Never... that shit hole? What good time? I hated every minute of it." and with that he turned and went to explore the ship. TC and I followed a few minutes later, after a while one piece of sea looks just like another. The Falklands had gone and only sea was left where there was once land, a land where we had spent the last six months of our lives.

Scouse did recount stories of great fun of the Falklands months later. We all did to those of the rear party. We had all been part of something big and those back home had missed out...but thank Christ that it is over I also thought to myself.

Saturday 9th July

Longitude 7'. 40 S, latitude 50'.14 W. 364 miles from Stanley. 3023 to Ascension. 18.29 knots, I wish he would put it in second gear! The boredom is killing me, I'm looking forward to the training for something to do, and the water is cold. I'm on guard tonight. What an easy guard, sleep in the room and do only two hours walking around. Everybody is a bit bored but we can hack it as it is a Gozome boat, 18 knots in the right direction➔.

Each day, over the tannoy one of the Officers of the ship would tell us the ship's position. I would copy it directly into my diary believing what they told us landlubbers. The first position is in the middle of the Brazilian rain forest! The Army doesn't run on common sense. It just does it because it always did before. So we, as we did on the way down, had to post guard on ship. We weren't told what we were guarding against, more untoward bubbles perhaps, a periscope, or deserters diving overboard intending to swim the seven hundred and fifty miles to Argentina. I ambled around the ship for a couple of hours whilst all but the duty sailors slept. We were having a period of 'rest' and so sleep didn't come easy. We did sod all during the day and so weren't tired during the night. I saw a couple of card schools during my stint at two am, at least there was someone to talk to. I walk into one to find some guys from 3 Troop and Scouse.

"Hello Bernie, couldn't sleep either? Wanna game?" Scouse asked.

"No mate, I'm on guard."

Scouse laughed, he was back on form. He had been so depressed at the end of the tour, but then we all had, "What the fuck are you guarding? Are they 'fraid someone might steal the water?"

"Well no one's gonna steal your hand Scouse, its crap" I nodded towards his exposed hand of cards.

The guys laughed but Scouse was a Scouse and it was hard to get one over on a Liverpudlian "I'm leading them into a false sense of security before I pounce."

"What are you playing for?"

"Boilies" (meaning compo boiled sweets)

"Look out Las Vegas" and I walked on to see if any one else was awake.

Sunday 10th July

420 miles since yesterday at a speed of 18.29 knots, we are 794 miles from Stanley and 2594 miles from Ascension. I've just detected that all they are doing is taking the jobbies out and re-directing the piss straight through to our taps, I gave Scouse two seasick pills, and yes, they made him seasick.

I photographed TC playing 'tents' this morning. We have a sink; washing / pissing for the use of; in the cabin but the water is brown and stinks. If you wash in it, the dirt goes from the water, to you instead of the other way round. Tomorrow we start training, I didn't think I'd be glad but I am. There's only so much sea that one can look at, we needed something to do. Scouse was feeling seasick so I gave him two of my pills. I'd been taking them since we started sailing and had felt no effects from the motion of the ship. Whether it was the pills or it was going to happen anyway, Scouse threw up over the side dumping my two pills into a few trillion tons of water. I made a note not to waste any more on him. Walking round the cabins I found many lying on their beds suffering from motion sickness. Some like Spunky were green, Mac and Jock were both unaffected and I would see them in the canteen for breakfast. We would take our time and talk about nothing and everything. We were all glad to get back to our BAOR role of guarding the West against the marauding Soviet hordes.

Monday 11th July

Longitude 37.04 S. latitude 38.01 W. We have travelled 420 miles since yesterday at an average speed of 17.87 knots. We are 1714 miles from Stanley and 2173 to Ascension which makes an average speed of 18.15 knots overall. These figures are all to cock! We had a talk from Bignose this morning about NATO, then we had map reading in the afternoon, they insulted our intelligence by teaching us four and six figure map references. Couldn't sleep tonight! Weather is slightly hotter.

This had to be the first time that Bignose had spoken to use all together since he first told us in Nunburg that we were going. It was a rare occurrence! He taught us about NATO and its role in world, no one really cared, but it was better than mooching around. I was taught four and six figure map references when I was twelve in the Army cadets. Now here I was, a professional soldier, going back to the 'front line' against the Soviets and my betters decided that we had probably forgotten this valuable information. It was a start I suppose, we went on from there to relearn mines, bridging and other special info that the front line Sapper needed.

Tuesday 12th July

Longitude 31.32 S. latitude 32.01 W. We sailed 415 miles yesterday at an average speed of 17.6 knots. We are 1629 miles from Stanley and 1700 miles from Ascension, nearly halfway, we should past the Uganda soon. PT this morning, then a boiling hot shower. It is definitely hotter today, shirt sleeved order

We're slowing down, we must be going uphill!

Wednesday 13th July

Longitude 25.42 S., latitude 28.09 W. We travelled 434.5 miles at 18.5 knots making the distance of 2063.5 miles from Stanley and 1324 miles to Ascension. The air temperature is 22.3 degrees Centigrade and sea temperature is 22.7 degrees Centigrade. Getting better! We tried to sunbathe when we had finished our lecture but the sun was to cold. It's still don't seem as if we are a week from home! We got our flight details today at last. I wish I flew now. I can't wait to see Sandra. I can't sleep due to thinking about her; I haven't slept since I got on this boat.

I feel like a kid the week leading up to Christmas or a spotty youngster waiting for his first date. I feel like I don't know my wife. I have no idea what to say to her when I meet her in my flat. I know the men that I have lived with for the last half year inside out, but my wife is an unknown quantity to me. I get the collywobbles every time I think about meeting her. I know we won't be throwing ourselves into bed the instant we meet. It's going to be awkward. We've had no contact at all. No telephone calls apart from that one brief nervous call, no emails no video phones and no SMS texts, just bluey letters. You can say what you want in a letter but face to face is a different matter. God I'm nervous.

Thursday 14th July

Longitude 24.15, latitude 20.48, 365 miles, 15.53 knots. Stanley 2428.5. Ascension 959. Everybody except 75 Squadron was sunbathing on this first really good day, we got ours in but it had to be in between lessons. I should get back Wednesday morning. I even felt a little bit of excitement when I was told. Saw a killer whale in a near perfect sea.

Our day was filled with military and engineer training, revising on all that we may have forgotten. I'm sure that if we had a MGB bridge on the ship we would have practiced building it. 15 Sqn seemed to be spending all their time sunbathing. They were going back to Ripon to 'Strat Reserve' as we called it, or Strategic Reserve the full name. We were going back to the 'front line' to deter the Soviets from crossing the border and fucking up the rest of Europe.

"Vladimir, we only have one week left to invade Europe before 75 Sqn comes back."

"Ah sit down Yuri and have another pint of vodka, the potato crop is in and we have two whole potatoes each."

"Two! Ha… ha, I'll get fat. Let them keep Europe."

Friday 15th July

339.5 miles today at 14.44 knots. It is only 625 miles to Ascension. Everybody is walking around sunburnt, like glowing red beacons sticking out of their shirts. It is not only funny but pathetic, they don't realise that they are in The Tropical zone. I wish we were going home on Monday, it wouldn't feel so long. A bit windy today, I miss writing to Sandra, when I wrote she was with me, now she's gone, hurry up Tuesday! Sleep takes a long time to come. Putting the clocks forward half an hour each day doesn't help either.

Why is it that 'Whitey from Blighty', on the first sign of a sun warmer than a 60w bulb, must lay in it for eight hours? Although we didn't have the propaganda about skin cancer back then, we all knew that we had to ease into the sunbathing. Sunburn was supposedly treated as self inflicted wounds and you could be charged with getting it, but I never heard of a single case. Although we had no electronic contact with our loved ones, when you write a letter it is like you are talking to her… without her talking back which is the best part about a letter. It made you feel close, and now that I am closer both in time and distance, I feel further away than during the whole tour. I really miss the closeness of writing those letters. Whenever I think about getting home I get collywobbles in my stomach.

Saturday 16th July

332 miles since yesterday, a speed of 14.13 knots. We've travelled 3100 miles from Stanley and its only 291 miles to Ascension Islands!! We should get there by 0900 hrs thank God! Went to bed even earlier at quarter past nine. I can't wait to see Ascension Islands tomorrow. It should be here by the time we get up. From there the next stop is home. Still don't feel like I am going home. But I am, by Wednesday night. I don't know what, by Wednesday night. I wanna see my baby again.

Strange how even though I was travelling toward Ascension, I wrote that it was coming towards me. I wanted to see it outside the porthole, all I could see now was sea and the odd killer whale. (Like this wasn't a momentous occasion itself)

Sunday 17th July

Quite a good day, saw Ascension creep over the horizon and we are now sitting at the end of the runway, people are fishing and sunbathing, it is good but I'd rather be home. I ain't getting sunburnt like so many others; I want to feel Sandra touch my body, not shout because it hurts my sunburn. We go in two days. The Squadron put on a stupid knocker quiz for us; we lost so we went and watched Super Bowl. Went night fishing and hooked 2 goldfishes and a seven foot shark, as soon as it was hooked I thrust the rod at Mac and said "ere have this!"

News came round that the Monkeys were coming on board to do an arms and ammo check of all our baggage. Nothing is being allowed back in the country. I didn't have anything but I kept hearing the odd 'splosh' as a Falkland souvenir hit the water to be forever lost in Davey Jones's locker.

That evening I wandered up to the deck. All the fishermen were wiggling rods again. Mac saw me and thrust his at me, "Want a go?" he asked.

"OK, but I have never done it before."

"No probs, all you've got to do is to get the bait past the Triggerfish, and then drop the line to the bottom. You might catch a nice Angel fish."

I took the rod from Mac and made him put on the piece of Triggerfish, he revelled in the dismembering of the fish. Even today I still gag when I think of how he used to slash his knife around the fish. He loaded the hook and threw some fish into the water away from the boat. The Triggerfish went wild over the feast of their mate. I dropped the hook into the water and let the line freewheel until it hit the bottom. "Now what?" I asked,

"Move the bait around a bit" he suggested. This I did. I jiggled, I wobbled, and I reeled in. What are those fish Mac? I asked pointing to large blue spinning dolphin like fish that were approaching the lights of the boat. "Wow, they are Dolphin Sharks!" (I apologise to any fishermen if I get the name of the fish wrong) "See how they spin when they swim, they grow to around eight feet in length"

I found this mildly interesting, what I found fascinating was the fact that Mac's large sea fishing rod had just bent double. The bend hadn't gone unnoticed on Mac either "You got one! It's huge, pull it in Bernie, and gently pull it in."

"Fuck that!" I shouted "YOU pull it in." and I shoved the bent rod into his hands. He didn't need to be told twice, he grabbed the rod and started working. It was Mac's rod and he *enjoyed* this kind of thing. He would have been happy to watch me land the fish but that was not the way of the Troop. I wanted Mac to enjoy it, we were a team and *very good friends*. I was not a fisherman but was a good friend to my pals, therefore I instantly gave the largest catch of the ship to Mac. He would get the credit and credo for landing it. That made me happy! Mac spent twenty minutes pulling the fish to the surface. By the finish, the whole of the dirty unwashed was watching. Every porthole on that side of the ship had a head stuck out of it. Offers to pull the fish in through a porthole were many. When Mac finally got it to the surface one of the heads in the porthole that was next to the waterline shouted that it was a Dolphin Shark. "We'll never land it" Mac commented, sweat pouring off his brow. "Why's that?"

"The line won't take his weight, as soon as he reaches the surface, it will break" and break it did, but not before we all got a glimpse of a large blue Dolphin Shark. Mac was the hero of the night. No one caught anything even close to his catch. The first time that he recounted the event he mentioned that I was fishing and passed the rod over to him. As he did he looked at me and I shook my head. Later stories didn't include me and that was fine by me.

Monday 18th July

Got my sheaf knife out of military office. Another dossy day. I watched 15 Squadron leave and fly out, it'll be our flight tomorrow. Night fishing again tonight, it'll pass the time and helps me sleep, as I can't think of anything else right now except Sandra, it really IS the last day. Tomorrow will last until Wednesday, as we will be flying all night. Soon it will dawn on me that I will be home in a couple of days.

I had to hand in my sheaf knife when I boarded ship. Apparently I was not to be trusted with a four inch blade in a confined space like a ship. Maybe they were afraid that I'd rupture the ship.

We were told that the Norlan was a flattish bottomed ferry. Not built for long terms at sea. We had been anchored up a few thousand feet from the end of the runway and we were chasing the anchor chain around as the tide went this way and that. It meant that at certain times of the day we would be side on to the wind or waves or both. I can't give you a technical explanation, for that ask a Matlot, but for long periods the boat would rock ten degrees to each side. It wasn't a problem for us Pongos with our (calm) sea legs. We would compensate and were able to carry our food trays, laden with brekky and a full pint of tea across the galley to place it pinpoint on the tables with the lips to stop things falling off.

The new Squadron that was airlifted in to replace 15 Squadron was a different matter. They provided a whole new avenue of entertainment. They would come bouncing down the corridor walls and would shoot into the canteen as the bow dipped only to stop on a sixpence when their body suddenly doubled in weight and their legs refused to work. They would see us laughing at them and would make a superhuman effort to move forward at exactly the same time as the stern would come up again halving their weight. The double muscle power combined with half body weight would send them catapulting into the breakfast queue sending Sappers, trays and plates of sausage and bacon flying. It would then be their turn to hang on to the hotplate as the cook filled their plate with food and their comrades were head butting their spines. We were laughing so much there were tears coming down our cheeks. Our sides ached like after an arduous route march from the effort of laughing. Then one eager Sapper crashed into the queue and in his haste to back off stood on a fried egg on the floor and his foot shot up in the air and kicked a tray out of his mate's hands. Another guy tried to grab him and only succeeded in being pulled over with him as the tray hit him on the back of the neck, spilling scrambled eggs down his back.

This all happened within a second but the canteen erupted in a roar, even the cook lost control and his head disappeared down behind the hotplate as hands on his hips, spatula in his hand he doubled up with laughter. I had laughter cramp all down my sides. I was howling with laughter and crying with the pain of the cramp. The fallen men composed themselves and picking up their plates apologised to the cook (they still wanted breakfast). The cook couldn't speak, he just shovelled more food onto fresh plates whilst his shoulders jumped with laughter, his eyes were red and puffy and the fried egg vibrated off his spatula and onto the plate with his chuckling.

The fallen man stood with his tray and looked for a table. The closest was only three paces away. He stood and calculated the journey. His brain calculated the distance and height of the table. 'Two paces forward,' it told him 'then on the third pace start to lower the tray for six inches then when contact with table is made let go with fingers and sit down'. Calculations made and convinced that he could make it he headed for the table, as he started to lower the tray the table disappeared to the left as his body shot to the right. The tray was now lower than the table height, which was unfortunate as the next table came up and hit his tray side on spilling all onto the floor. The room erupted with renewed howling and the Sapper had had enough, he stood up and with a loud "Fuck it, I don't want any fucking breakfast" he headed out leaving the tray and food on the floor. That made us laugh even louder and I cast a glance at the cook at his reaction of the food and tray left on the floor. I needn't have worried. His eyes were slits and he was laughing loudly and banging the spatula repeatedly off the hotplate in a 'no no no, stop it, stop it' manner. After fifteen minutes we had calmed down and were doing the 'ahhs' and 'gods' and 'I hurt' bits which would bring on more laughter. I was wiping my eyes and holding my sides and head, which made Jock and TC laugh, which made me laugh, which made me hurt, which made them laugh more. I best heard this condition described on a Brit sitcom called Coupling. It's called a Giggaloop. It's a loop of laughter which creates more laughter. A loop which you cannot get out of! It's even more dangerous somewhere where you shouldn't laugh, like at a funeral. Your mate snorts a laugh and swallows it as it is a funeral, his discomfort makes you laugh which you suppress which makes him suppress laugh more which makes you…etc… until one of you loose it and laugh out loud. We were in a Giggaloop. The fun went on for the rest of the day with Sappers bouncing down the corridor like a ball in a pin ball machine but there were no more hilarious incidents like that one at breakfast. It was what we all needed to take our minds off home.

The journey home was subdivided into seven little adventures. From the Coastell to the ship, ship to Ascension, Ascension to aircraft, Aircraft to Gutersloh, Gutersloh to Nunburg by bus, then Camp to home. My heart is fluttering just thinking about that final journey and I write this, twenty nine years later. As we complete each trip, we cross that off in our heads. We now wait for the helicopter flight to the airfield doing anything to pass the time. Although we were here months ago, it is a very different attitude that we have now.

Tuesday 19th July

Flight 2800 at 0200 hrs to arrive at Gutersloh 0750 hrs on the 20th. Plan 2, both flights, today 1700 hrs and 2000 hrs. Flight went according to plan. Stopped at Dakar for 2 hrs and sat and watched Polish and Russian planes fly in, then we were off, I couldn't sleep, no way! I ended up drinking warm coffee. We flew over Cornwall and Clacton and then down to Gutersloh. I washed on the plane; come 4 o'clock people were coming alive! When we got to Gutersloh the countryside looked beautiful, all green and civilised. Waiting at the airport was the CO, the CCRE, the RSM and half the RE Band!

As usual in the Army , the plan changes. We mounted our helicopter on the rear of the ship and had a delightful hop to the airfield. All around the cabin I saw friends with large smiles. The door of the Westland Wessex (http://en.wikipedia.org/wiki/Image:Wessex_1982.JPG) was open and we watched the land appear underneath us, the camp housing flow under and then the edge of the runway, a smooth running landing and we had completed another part. We were ushered into a large hanger where we logged our baggage and after a short wait where no one was allowed to smoke we were pointed in the direction of the Vickers VC10. Without any fuss we boarded and selected a backward facing seat. The classic jetliner accelerated down the runway and into the air. We had finished another part of the journey.

The last of the exotic part, next would be Germany, home for us. I've never been able to sleep on flights. I just can't. The only flight that I have successfully slept on was a military one to Canada. I had unrolled my sleeping bag by the emergency exit, got in and slept until a military steward woke me up. Best air journey ever. But sleep was not to come on this flight. Apart from the cramped conditions I was far too excited and probably spent the whole time thinking about sex. I had abstained from visiting Mrs Palm and her five lovely daughters for a week or so and was having problems trying to think of anything other than sex with my wife. In an Army Bedford it is called 'Convoy Cock'. I must be having 'Jet Cock'. No, doesn't have the same ring to it does it? For Christ's sake, lets just get home, this is dragging on. No flight entertainment, no music. Just reading a book and thinking about home with a massive (honest) stiffy that won't go away. I was sitting by the window and had to climb over Jock to get to the loo. I really only wanted something to do, peeing would pass a minute or two. The cabin was dark and everyone was asleep. Everybody apart from me! I didn't see anyone else awake. I resisted the temptation to relieve myself and walked up and down the cabin a few times. That passed another two minutes. Bugger! Why can't I sleep on flights? I went to the galley and looked around and helped myself to a coffee. It was lukewarm. I finished that and made my way back to my seat. Eventually I was able to watch the sun come up over the wing and then watch England drift under the wing. England left and after a brief period of sea the continent dragged itself under my window. I took that cue to get washed, that taking up at least twenty minutes. When I got out there was a queue outside. "You been tossing in there Bernie?" The guy said with a laugh.

"Yeah, and it's up to you to discover where I left my deposit". He laughed as he walked in but I did see him carefully look round before he closed the door. Then came the sound that I had been waiting for "Please fasten your seat belts, we will be coming in to land soon."

Looking out the window West Germany looked a lovely dark green. UK was a lighter colour and The Falklands was more heather than grass. Apart from that bloody Elephant stuff by the penguin colony.

We bumped to the ground and on leaving the plane, were serenaded by half the RE band. It was a lovely touch. Even the Yanks didn't get that on their return from Vietnam. The top brass smiled and greeted us like heroes. I had no idea why. We went during a ceasefire and nothing happened of any military significance that I knew of. Still, Bernie, milk the situation. It was midsummer and we walked across the hardstand in twilight, as I walked past the CRE he shook the hand of a man in front of me and then mine, "Well done Son." He shook my hand with enthusiasm and I believe that he meant it. We headed in for our baggage.

Wednesday 20th July

Arrive Gutersloh 0436 hours. We queued up for our baggage and then went outside, the first thing I noticed was the smell. Germany smells like no other country, it was beautiful. After a three-hour ride by coach we got to camp, I waited for our baggage to come in and grabbed it and put it in my clean car. What a pleasure that was to drive. Everything I do is a pleasure, from driving my car to taking in the washing and of course I am at last as one, Sandra, me and our red house! Life has started again!

END EX. [A British Army saying that denotes the end of a military exercise. The END EX. is the finish]

The baggage was simply put into a room and we queued in line to take our turn to select our bags. Bear in mind that every bag is the same colour. Some clever wags had put tape or some identifying feature on their bags and suitcases. I wasn't that thoughtful and with three others searched all the bags. When I read out a tag of someone I knew I knew all our Squadron I shouted out their name and that name would be repeated down the line until he came forward and grabbed the bag that the men at the front were pointing to. It is that kind of team work that I miss in Civvy Street. One of the guys with me shouted "Yours is here Bernie." I thanked him and grabbed my bag and suitcase and walked toward the exit. Another Sapper took my position and continued in the same way.

When I walked out of the door the smell smacked me full in the face. Never before had I attributed a smell to a country, but sure enough every country has 'a smell'. West Germany had a smell of a billion pine trees sprinkled with a million Schnell Imbiss. I swear that I could smell the Schnell Imbiss, the pine trees, no problem. It was then that I realised that The Ascension Island smelt of sulphur and volcanic rock. The Falklands had smelt of burning peat, the same as the Isle of Islay and of Carrigaline in Cork. I stood outside the door and breathed in the succulent smell of pine trees and golden sap.

"Doesn't that smell beautiful TC" I said as he came out.

"Wot, you farted?"

"No you ignoramus. *That* smell." And I breathed deeply in. TC stood and snorted in.

"I can't smell anything, I reckon your nose is too close to your arse" and he walked off laughing.

The air left a chill on my skin, not as cold as The Falklands but nice and early-morning fresh and I revelled in it, as with Johan Strauss in my mind I walked towards the green Army bus.

I managed to nod off on the bus and miss most of the trip to Nunburg and was woken as we reached the outskirts. As we drove in past the road to the Wesserplatz it was like watching an old movie again. I recognised all the houses, the tyre place, the Lotto sign and then the camp gates. The guard waved to us as we entered. We were the 'guys' who went to The Falklands. Small heroes, but not for long as soon everyone would do at least one tour. My brother in law did two poor sod.

Our baggage was a short distance behind in a Bedford. Whilst I was waiting I got the keys for my VW Golf GTI from the Orderly Dog (Cpl) and opening the car reconnected the battery. Sitting in the car it was like washing off the last six months. The car was so quiet and familiar, it had been sitting there waiting for me. Not thinking, not changing, and just being. I turned the key and all the lights came on, after a short period to familiarise myself with the lights again, I turned the key again and the engine purred into life. I watched the oil pressure build up and the ammeter surge then slowly lower. A big smile joined my two ears into a line. Beautiful! Just beautiful! I saw the Bedford pass by in front of me and killing the engine jumped out and ran to the Bedford as did everyone else.

Two guys were on the back by the time I got there and they were passing the baggage down to us below, we would grab a bag and walk to the path whilst reading the tag. We would then shout out the name and return for another. Shortly I had both mine and I stood and watched TC and Mac get theirs. I wanted to leave but didn't. My stomach was in my throat. I had the collywobbles at the thought of seeing Sandra again. They both got their bags then they stood looking at me.

"Well this is it then," Mac said "End Ex!"

"End Ex" I repeated.

"End fucking Ex" TC laughed, "You two have got wives to go home to, all I have is Spunky and his Scalectrix."

That thought brought me round. Poor singlies, they had no woman to greet them home. I did and that's where I should be.

"Go visit the Eros Centre, I'm off home. See you all tomorrow."

"What at six o clock in the morning?" he laughed "Give Sandra one for me."

"Will do" I had no more time for small talk and was heading for the car.

The four km drive home was peaceful and as I passed all the landmarks that you register when you drive it was like they were welcoming me home. The HauptBahnoff, the Treffpunkt where the singlies will be tonight, Kaune the VW garage, Dave and Brenda's house then the turning towards Schwalbenweg in Ericshargen. My heart was doing 140 bpm the car 50 kph. I parked up in a space by my block of flats and stepping out smelt the pine trees and Imbiss again. It was summer and the morning was warming up. Grabbing my bags I locked the car and walked towards the main door. The light was on in our ground floor flat, Sandra was up and waiting. I was shitting bricks! She told me later that so was she except that she had nothing to keep her occupied. I pressed the buzzer and our door opened and the outside door buzzed. I opened the door and there, at the top of five steps was Sandra waiting for me.

It is always more romantic in the movies, with the perfect dialogue and sweet music. For us it was awkward. At the top of the stairs I dropped the bags and hugged her and she me. I could feel tears coming and to hide them I hugged even harder and for longer. This time there would be no Spunky to break the embrace.

"I love you" she said. I could hear that she was also close to tears.

"I love you too" and continued to hug.

"Do you want a coffee?" she asked breaking away and turning towards the kitchen. I noticed that she wiped her eyes as she walked into the kitchen.

"Yes please" God! It felt like I was at my Grandmothers, I was being so polite. This is so awkward.

She had the coffee stuff ready in the wall mounted Braun percolator. She pressed the 'on' tit and as she turned back towards me we hugged again. I had had dreams for the last six months of throwing her onto the bed and shagging for the rest of the day but dear fellows, it never happened that way. It never does, does it? Slowly we got to know each other again and we didn't go to bed until some time later. We had a lot of catching up to do, lots of gossip from me and even more from her. After a few coffees and a lovely English breakfast we went to bed, made love like it was the first time and slept entwined in each other's arms like new lovers. The rest of the day was spent touching each other and visiting our new neighbours and Nunburg. Everything put a smile on my face, from microwaving water for coffee to hammering down route six in my little VW racer but most of all Sandra put a smile on my face. I was back with the woman who is the other half of me.

End Ex. Fucking great!

Kelper store - NAAFI

Epilogue

Thursday 21st of July

Parade at 0830 hrs, breakfast is great; waking up with Sandra is great, life is great. Work was just cleaning weapons and handing back totally unused ECW. Kit, 16,000 miles that has travelled for nowt. I spent most of the day driving around sorting things out, I can get my Goodyear NCT tyres, 205 /70 S. and not /50, I don't want to have to buy new wheels. Got a 2000 Deutschemark loan today.

It was like being in your very own movie with you as the star. Waking up and becoming aware that you are lying next to the woman that you have been thinking about for the last seven months. That was brilliant, have her make me a full English fry up for breakfast was brilliant, getting into my car and dropping her off to work at the NAFFI was brilliant and handing back twenty kilos of Extra Cold Warfare kit that we were not allowed to wear but had to carry for sixteen thousand miles was also brilliant, just a different kind of brilliant. I had planned on upgrading my car with some tyres and I got a loan from Volksbank for the purpose. I couldn't quite afford new wheels as well. We all have two weeks leave starting AD today. (After Duties) All the singlies are going home or somewhere nice. The weather is great so I'm staying here, besides Sandra is working, so I intend to just chill in Western Germany.

Friday 22nd July

WE GET BACK TO NIENBURG TODAY, YE HA![written previously] No we don't, I've been back for three days now, and I did nowt but run around and buy hamsters and coffee tables. Herman the German hamster. San don't like it. I'm, training it to kill her. It'll be an S.A.S. hamster. 75 Squadron laid on a 'do' tonight, made it compulsory! Most singlies went home, not too bad except for the 40 Squadron group.

This was the original day that we were to return and I am already on leave. The 75 Sqn 'welcome home' function wasn't too bad. Good to socialise with all the men and wives again. You get very close and the pads all know each other because of these dos. 40 Sqn tried to gate crash the function and we had to throw them out. It got a bit nasty but 75 Sqn was a team. We had just spent the last seven months together. They couldn't compete with that.

Saturday 23rd July

Got my tyres today, what beauties, they hold the road like glue, must try and make them last. Herman has learned how to move his tread wheel, tomorrow I'll teach him unarmed combat. A lovely hot day, went to Mac's party tonight, it weren't very good.

Herman the German hamster kept us up all night with his running in the wheel... well, it kept Sandra up apparently. I slept the sleep of the dead, but one has to use the Royal WE doesn't one. I oiled his wheel in the morning more to keep 'her' quiet than the wheel.

Sunday 24 July

We slept in this morning then went to the gravel pits, there we met Mac and TC, it was crowded so we went to Steinhundermere, by the time we got there it had clouded over, still better than being in the Falklands.

Tuesday 26th July

33 degrees Centigrade according to weather report. I recorded 40 degrees Centigrade in the sun and 35 in the shade at 10 o'clock! We went swimming, lovely day. We went to Stolaznau but it was shut so we ended up at the barge locks, quite interesting.

Notes

I knew that this was going to be the best month of the tour. Already the Falkland Islands is just like a bad dream, and I must be forgetting things already! It feels like I've been home for ever and yet things are still new.

Monday 22nd August 1983

Started back at work! I've finally found out what turns Sandra on, it's not physical things like what turns me on but something completely different, all this time it has been under my nose and I've never even noticed, it's love what turns her on and my nagging what turns her off, plus my moods. It fits the equation and everything slots into place, why has it taken me three years to discover this and how could I have been so blind! I love Sandra so, and that's all there is.

Not the End but The Beginning of the rest of my life.

*****

Glossary

1 BR Corps
1 British Corps

APC/432
Armoured Personnel Carrier. A tank without a gun. Used for carrying Troops into battle or as target practice for the enemy's tanks.
A.C.C./Slop Jockeys or Sloppy(s)

Army Catering Corps. The people who you look after bar none. These heroes are the people who feed you day in and day out and can turn 14 days of Ration pack 'D' into something different every day.

AAC Chepstow
The Army Apprentices College in Chepstow. Join straight from school and learn how to be a bully.

Aquamatic
A Haulamatic that fell into the sea. [See Haulamatic]

B.A.O.R.
British Army On the Rhine. Probably now the **BAOH** or British army on the Helmond

Bedford
The British Army truck. Now some foreign rubbish owned by an Ex-soviet oligarch.

BFT
Basic Fitness Test 1.5 mile run

Blue jobs
RAF or Crabair.

Boffin
Army name for a Scientist

Bumf
Official paperwork

Bump start
How to start a motorbike or car with a flat battery. Doesn't work on automatics.

Civvies
Civilian population. Anyone not military or ex-military.

CO
Commanding Officer of a Regiment.

Combat Engineer / Knocker / Oggie / Squeek
All Sappers have two trades. The artisan trade and the combat trades. Those that practice the combat trades are known as Knockers or Oggies or Squeaks.

CRE
Commander Royal Engineers. A Brigadier or other such god.

CSB
Combat Support Boat. A mean bad assed speed boat that stops so fast it stands on its nose. For those not friends with the operator can be an unwanted sea-water shower.

Dhobi
See below

Dhobi Dust
No, lower than this.

Doing your Dhobi
Doing your laundry. From a region in South Mumbai called Dhobitalao, used to be a lake(now filled in) where British soldiers had their uniforms washed about 120 years ago. All laundry people in India are called Dhobi. Word left over from British Raj.

Dumping stores /Ground dump /Having a dump / Shovel recce
Going to the toilet. Comes from taking a shit on exercise where you dig a hole, and dump your stores in the hole and then backfill the hole.

End Ex
At the end of the exercise a shout would go up "End Ex" meaning that was the end of the exercise.

Gat
Gun. Action-men used to pick me up for calling it a gun. "Arty use guns, you have a rifle!" so my SMG should have been designated a SMR?

Haulamatic
A 10 ton dump truck that replaced the wonderfully British Aveling Barford. Picture me on the two lane A43 with a Haulamatic and tilt trailer loaded with a Muirhill LWT doing 5 mph whilst jugganaughts were approaching me from behind at a speed difference of 65 mph! Scary stuff.

Head Shed
Head Quarters

Hymac
Hymac 360 degree excavator ranging from the knackerd 580 BT to the modern [then] 590CT with armoured cab and swamp tracks.

NAAFI
Naval Army Airforce Families Institute. Women who worked

behind the counter were called NAAFI Tarts although not to their faces, unless you married one.... which I did.

Maggot
Sleeping bag

Muirhill LWT
A5000 Light Wheeled Tractor. A digger [JCB] The only other place I've seen these is the now defunct National Coal Board. A really solid bit of kit that was squaddie proof. The replacement for this stops working when the ashtray is full.
http://www.muir-hill.co.uk/Gallery%20A5000%20MOD%20page.htm

NAAFI Break
Tea break

OC
Officer Commanding a squadron

Provost Sgt or Provo
Man in charge of guardroom. Bad assed man with a red sash and a stick.

PTI
Physical Training Instructor. Usually a super fit guy who leaves your Troop and goes on a PTI's course. When he returns you find that he has been trained to be a bastard. S/He has magical qualities. The only people alive that could make my legs stay in the air for a count of one hundred.

Q
The name given to a Warrant Officer 2 in the Royal Engineers who was not a Sergeant Major but was practising an Artisan trade. Q Stores, Q Mines, Q Bridging for example. A most unfortunate custom for SSgt Cumber when he was promoted to WOII as an Artisan. For some reason he always answered the phone "WO2 Cumber". Sergeant Majors' names were "SIR"

RAOC
Royal Army Ordnance Corps now part of RLC

RE
Royal Engineers. A Sapper. Hopefully you knew this before buying this book.

REMF
Rear Echelon Muther Fucker (an Americanism)

RHIP
Rank Has Its Privileges

Rotor rash or jet rash
The name given to the injury caused by small stones being thrown up by helicopter blades and Harrier jets into your face.

Rover
Landrover

Sapper
A Private in the Royal Engineers.

Sassman /SSM
The SSM or Sergeant Major

SIB
Special Investigation Branch. The Sweeney of the Royal Military Police. They would not bother investigating a Senior NCO or Officer if they could prosecute a Sapper

SMG
Stirling 9mm Sub Machine Gun. A relic from the Second World War. During 20 years with the British army I never 'officially' fired this on automatic, always single shot.

SNCO
Senior Non Commissioned Officer

SQMS
Sergeant Quarter Master Stores. Or "Squisims"

SSgt/Staffy
Staff Sergeant or colour sergeant in other regiments

The pits
Something that is not good

WRAC
Woman's Royal Army Corps. Or something that you screwed into the wall.

WO
Warrant Officer

*****

Acknowledgements

I'd like to thank my wife Sandra for doing all the line editing and name changing and sticking by me all these years. I do love you so.

I'd like to thank Mark and Andy for giving me a boost a couple of years ago and providing me with the enthusiasm to continue.

And I'd like to thank Dan from Monday books for putting me onto Lulu.com and taking the time to send a *real* reply.

Other books of this genre that you may like.
Picking up the brass – Eddie Nugent
www.mondaybooks.com
Our Lad Ricky – Michael Ruston
www.amazon.co.uk

Future books from Julian Beirne
The Money Road to Baghdad by Andy Mount
The Human CPU
Sappers
The Water Thieves
Lenny the Leprechaun
The boy who couldn't touch the ground
Reboot
The Dead Spies

*****